ABOVE AND BEYOND

MY LIFE GIVING THE WORLD A LIFT

HANS BURKHART

as told to Pete Bansen

Printed in Korea

ISBN: 979-8-9867674-0-6

Cover and interior design: Ponderosa Pine Design
Cover composite by Pixel and Ink – Reno, Nevada
Edited by Laura Read - ReadWriteShoot
Photos by Hans Burkhart unless otherwise credited

12-25-22

Merry Christmas,

*A wonderful life of
a wonderful man!*

*Love,
Uncle Patrick*

"On the other hand, if you get into something that you like, then you don't know when you're working and when you're not working. That's what the lift business became to me."

Hans Burkhart

Dedicated to my grandfather, Anton Haag, my role model as a child and throughout life. He showed me the pleasure and satisfaction of doing good work.

Foreword

When my daughters came up with the idea that I should write down my life's story, I was undecided about the request, because I had no clue what is involved in writing a book. I stared at 8 large file boxes and 42 albums of photographs and all I could think was my great friend Hardy Herger's favorite expression, "Oh boy, oh boy...."

Since I never give up on anything, I decided I could tell at least part of my life, if I could find a person who was willing and able to put it on paper. The response from experienced authors was, "Too complicated, too technical and, mostly, too personal", but my motto is "Tell the way it was and the way it is".

I mentioned my unusual endeavor to my friend Pete Bansen and, to my surprise, Pete offered to give it a try. The result of Pete (and Cindy's) hard work took thousands of hours and over two years.

My daughters and I can only say thank you, thank you! We appreciate your major effort and hope to find a way to express our gratitude for your excellent work!

Hans Burkhart

Throughout this book we refer to a certain ski resort as "Squaw Valley." That was its correct name during all the events described within this writing and the use of what is now an obsolete name should not be construed as lacking in respect for the Native Americans who were the original inhabitants of the place or some sort of poke at political correctness—we intend neither. Although a name change would never have happened during Alex Cushing's lifetime, and although we both feel that Palisades-Tahoe is a rather dumb name, we recognize that the name change by the current owners came from considered respect for a people who have too frequently been cast aside and disrespected. We believe, however, that historical accuracy is best served using the name in use at the time of the events described.

It is pretty rare that we recall exactly when we become aware of someone, but I remember exactly when I first heard of Hans Burkhart. In June of 1978, fresh from college, I arrived in Olympic Valley less than two months after the Tram accident. Although it would have been hard to get anyone to say so, the community was still in shock. The green cabin—Cabin

1—stuck forlornly in the span below Tower 1 was a constant reminder of the accident and it cast a pall over the Valley.

But suddenly one morning in August, it was gone. It was quite a shock—you looked up to the spot where it had been and did a double take, thinking, "I must be looking in the wrong place", but no, it was no longer there – something was going on.

In mid-morning, the pink cabin—Cabin 2—very slowly appeared at Tower 1 and even more slowly crept over the tower heading for the bottom. A crowd gathered behind the Chamois; people had binoculars and a feeling of expectancy. I was looking up at the car moving ever so slowly down the line in the clear morning air and was amazed to see a figure standing on top of the carriage. I turned someone a few feet away who was watching through binoculars and said: "Who is the guy standing on top?"

"Hans Burkhart" was the reply.

I didn't meet Hans until a year or so later, after he had rebuilt the Tram and restored confidence in it with his day to day, hands-on involvement in the project. Had Alex Cushing called a news conference and declared that the Tram was open and safe to ride, most locals would have rolled their eyes and gotten in the line for the gondola but knowing that it was Hans's project was good enough for them. Old-timers recalled that Hans had battled with Alex over lift safety and finally quit over an unsafe repair of the Emigrant lift after a serious accident in 1971.

Hans and I both left and returned to Squaw Valley a couple of times through the 80's and 90's and were lucky enough to work with some of the very best people in the ski industry at Squaw and elsewhere. I left the company in 1993 to become Olympic Valley's fire chief, a job that I held until I retired in 2017, so in 2019, when Hans called out of the blue and invited me to lunch, I was delighted to have the opportunity to get caught up. Hans said that his daughters—after decades of hearing his hair-raising stories of near misses—had suggested that he write a book: Did I know anyone who could help him write it? We talked through the local writers who knew about skiing and lifts, but he had already exhausted the possibilities. I told him that I had no idea how to write a book, but that I was willing to try to tell his stories. That modest recounting of experiences that nearly killed him morphed over thirty months of Thursday coffees and a worldwide pandemic into a big project that we both found absorbing.

The creation of this book was a priceless opportunity to spend time with an old friend and to help others appreciate the details of his remarkable life. I am honored and grateful to have been given that chance—thank you, Hans.

Pete Bansen
Reno, Nevada - 2022

Contents

1   Oberammergau 9
    Near-Death Experience # 1: The Farm 15
    Near-Death Experience #2: Avalanche in Innsbruck 18

2   Aerial Lifts and How They Work 22

3   Laber-Bergbahn 28
    Near-Death Experience #3: Laber-Bergbahn 31

4   How Lifts Are Built 32

5   Canada 41
    Near-Death Experience #4: The Oldsmobile 47

6   Stein 48

7   Lake Tahoe 53
    Near Death Experience #5: Head-on collision in the Volkswagen Bug ... 55
    Near Death Experience #6: Alpine Meadows 56

8   Alex Cushing and the 1960 Olympic Games 61

9   Squaw Valley in the 1960s 69

10 Building the Squaw Valley Tram 80
    Near Death Experience #7: Squaw Valley Tram 86

11 Hardy Herger 94
    Adventures in Consulting: Maui 100

12 "I Need One of These" 102

13 Who was Dick Bass? 107

14 Bad Blood at Squaw Valley 109

15 Snowbird Tram 115
    Near Death Experience #8: Snowbird Helicopter 120
    Near-Death Experience #9: Snowbird Dozer 124
    Adventures in Consulting: Joe Zoline 128

16 Grouse Mountain, Vancouver, B.C. 133

17 Pacific Crest Trail—Ebbetts Pass, California 137

18 Smithers, British Columbia 140

19 1970s Squaw Valley 143

20 The Squaw Valley Tram Accident 149

21 Squaw Valley: 1979 to 1983 159
    Adventures in Consulting: San Francisco Cable Cars 166

22   1980s Mountaineering and Competition 168

23   Blyth Arena 175

24   First Look at Mt. Bachelor, Oregon 180

25   Janek Kunczynski 184

26   Mt. Bachelor—Bend, Oregon 188

27   Two Gondolas in Three Years 202

28   Late '80s 209

29   Alex and Nancy 212

30   Juniper Ridge 229

31   Rock and Roll in Squaw Valley 232

32   Single Dad 237

33   The '97 Flood 239

34   The Funitel 243
      Near-Death Experience #10: Verdi Culvert 248
      Near-Death Experience #11: Counterweight Pit Collapse 258

35   Ski Patrol Unionization 266

36   Janek Kunczynski, Part 2 268

37   Squaw Valley, the End 271

38   Golden Sage 280

39   Home Building 287

40   Jackson Hole Tram 296

41   Troy Caldwell and White Wolf 304

42   United States Citizenship 306

43   Las Vegas Zip line 309
      Near-Death Experience #12: Tree Trimming 310

44   Aftermath 313

45   Now What? 316

Appendix 319

About the Co-Author 326

Acknowledgments 327

Endnotes 328

Oberammergau looking toward the prominent rock outcropping, the Kofel.

Oberammergau

I was born in 1935 in Oberammergau, Germany in the mountains of southern Bavaria close to Austria, only about six miles from the border. A small town, it was home to about five thousand people in 1935, and the population has only increased by about ten percent since then.

Oberammergau is famous for the Passion Play, a dramatic depiction of the life and crucifixion of Jesus based on manuscripts written in the fifteenth and sixteenth centuries. The Passion Play is presented in Oberammergau every ten years, and the production goes on for months to accommodate the tens of thousands of tourists from all over the world who come to the village to see it. The tradition dates to 1633, when bubonic plague was ravaging Europe: the residents of Oberammergau vowed that if their village were spared, they would produce a play every ten years, forever. Shortly after they made this promise to God, the rate of infection in the town dropped dramatically, and the next year—1634— the villagers delivered on their promise and presented the first Passion Play. Following that inaugural performance, the play was performed every decade, always in years ending in zero. There was an exception the year before I was born when the community celebrated the three hundredth anniversary of the first performance —a special Passion Play was presented in 1934 to commemorate that momentous anniversary. No one knew it then, but it would be the last performance for many years.

The early Passion Plays were performed on a small, temporary platform with three walls to create a stage.

Wearing an outfit entirely hand-knit by my grandmother.

Then and now, the production involves the entire community. The play was originally performed in the graveyard of the parish church, in front of the graves of those who had died of seventeenth-century plague. In 1830, the community constructed a stage there to give the play a permanent home. Today, the theater on that same site accommodates more than four thousand seven hundred people. The Passion Play is no casual production: In the 1930s, the play ran some seven hours, starting at 8 a.m. and continuing to 5 p.m. with a lunch break in the middle. That timeframe has been scaled back somewhat, and in 2010, it ran a mere five hours, from 2:30 to 10 p.m. daily with a dinner break. The 2010 production offered one hundred and two performances between May and October featuring two thousand performers, musicians, and technicians.

Although the Passion Play was a community-wide endeavor and a big part of the cultural identity of the town of Oberammergau—not to mention a huge source of revenue—the play was not performed between 1934 and 1950 due to World War II. When performances resumed in 1950, my siblings and I were all old enough to perform and we all had roles that year—I played Tobias. In 2020, the global coronavirus pandemic forced another interruption, postponing production for two years until 2022.

My mother, Blanda Haag, was from Oberammergau—her father was a storekeeper and farmer—and my father, Johann Burkhart, came from a tiny farming village a considerable distance away. He was a policeman, and had come to Oberammergau because the town needed additional police officers to handle the influx of tourists during the 1930 Passion Play. The two were married in 1932 when my dad was thirty-three and Mother was twenty-one, and their first child, my sister Hertha, was born in 1933. I had four younger siblings: my brother Toni was born in 1938, my sister Marita in 1939, brother Norbert in 1941, and our youngest sister, Blanda, in 1944.

Oberammergau's location in the foothills north of the Alps created a fertile valley for farming surrounded by mountains. A small river—the Ammer—flows through the valley. The town is at about 2,700 feet in elevation (850 meters), and the surrounding peaks top out at a little over 5,700 feet (1,750 meters). Farther south toward Garmisch-Partenkirchen and the Alps, the height of the mountain peaks increases dramatically, and in Austria they surpass 12,000 feet elevation.

My mother's family had lived in Oberammergau since the early 1800s. My great-great grandfather built a store in the town in 1861 and my great-grandfather, Andreas Haag, took it over in 1882. My grandfather, Anton, married the butcher's daughter, Maria, and assumed operation of the store after returning from military service in 1917. My grandfather was an entrepreneur: In addition to the store, he had a farm and managed forest land owned by several hundred landowners in the area. In that capacity, he was their forester, harvesting trees off their land for use as lumber, firewood, and materials for the large wood-carving industry in town. I spent a lot of time working with my grandfather from the time I was old enough to tag along with him—working on the farm, doing little jobs around the store, helping him fall timber then skid the trees down the mountainside to the wood yard behind his team of draft horses—whatever needed to be done. My grandmother ran the store, my mother filled in there when extra help was needed, and my dad did, too. Although my father and the other police officers in Oberammergau protected the town and some of the surrounding villages, they were paid very poorly. Nevertheless, my father stayed with the department and eventually became chief of police. He came from very humble circumstances— his family members were rural farmers and he had eleven brothers and sisters. My dad had the unfortunate distinction of having been drafted into the German Army in 1915 to fight in World War I. He was seriously wounded in action, and then drafted *again* in World War II, where he spent several years in the Netherlands as a military policeman.

My siblings and I posing in our Passion Play costumes for the 1950 production. I played Tobias.

My mother, Blanda Haag Burkhart.

My Grandfather giving the family a ride in his ox cart.

When I was quite young—probably about six—my sister Hertha and I spent a summer with my father's parents on their farm in the village of Buch in western Bavaria. They had cows and horses and chickens, and we could do whatever we liked—play in the mud, get dirty, walk across the fields. It was quite different than Oberammergau, where we lived right in the village with buildings, streets, and people all around us. My grandparents had a little wash house with a tub in it, but no shower in the house. All the cooking was done on a big cast-iron stove in the kitchen, and there was a vent in the ceiling they could open to send heat upstairs to the bedrooms. They were simple country people—there was not even a radio in the house. My uncles and aunts mostly stayed in Buch and had businesses there—one was a baker and another had a store. That is about all there was in town: a bakery, a store, a church, and a lot of farmers. You could walk across the farm fields from Buch to Illertissen, where one uncle owned a repair garage. His business became a Volkswagen dealership that is still in the family today—Autohaus Burkhart. Those rural towns made little Oberammergau look like a big city.

As World War II raged elsewhere in Europe, the effects in Oberammergau were mixed. As I mentioned, the 1940 Passion Play was cancelled, which was a huge hardship for Oberammergau, because the Passion Play and the influx of tourists and visitors flocking to the town for the play represented a major economic boost to every part of the local economy. There was rationing of food and fuel—my mother could buy only two loaves of bread a week, hardly enough for our large family. Flour and other staples were rationed—each family was given a certain number of stamps with which to buy them. My grandfather had chickens and two cows, so we had eggs and milk and could make our own butter. He stored a supply of dried peas and beans in metal containers under the floor of his barn. My mother managed to make them edible by cooking them for the better part of a day. As kids, we were used to handing down our clothing and shoes to our younger siblings, but my grandfather was heartbroken when he had to hand over his prized draft horses to the army, never to be seen again. There was no television yet, but we had a radio that broadcast daily reports about the war. The news, however, was more intended to misinform the German people than to enlighten us: There was a great deal of propaganda.

Hertha and me in front of my uncle's repair garage in Illertissen about 1939 or 1940.

In April of 1944, we heard on the radio that Munich had been heavily bombed and was burning, so that night, my brother Toni and I hiked up to the top of the nearby mountain and could see the orange glow in the sky from the fires from about forty miles away. One day, an American bomber was forced to crash land in Oberammergau. We saw it coming into the valley—it was very low and on fire— smoke poured from the plane as the crew bailed out and floated to the ground under their parachutes. The plane ended up crashing in a marshy area and sank out of sight and the flight crew were captured by some German soldiers. Toni was about six and as the truck drove through town with the captured crew in the back he commented that the smoke in the plane must have really been bad, "because it turned that guy Black!"—we had never seen a Black man before.

Fortunately, by the time the American army moved into Southern Bavaria, it was clear to everyone that the war was over. We had no idea what to expect from the Americans, and my grandfather quickly cleared out most of the inventory in his store, thinking it was probably going to be looted by the Americans when they came to town. He hid a lot of it in a barn and even buried some. He sent all the women in the family to a cabin up in the mountains so they would be safe if any fighting took place—and would be well away from the American invaders, in any case. My brother and I were sitting in the window of the store when the American army drove into town. There was no fighting. There were

Standing in front of my mother's house in Oberammergau about 1946.

dozens and dozens of tanks and trucks and jeeps and a lot of dirty, grinning soldiers waving to us. The little boys in town followed the parade of military vehicles out of town a short distance to a farmer's field where they set up camp. We spoke virtually no English, and they spoke virtually no German (at least not anything we understood), but they gave us Butterfinger candy bars and Coca-Cola—the best things we had ever tasted.

The Americans sent out patrols to look for any German Army units that might be hiding in the mountains, and they found the little cabin full of women, surprising everyone. It soon became clear that neither group posed any risk to the other, and the soldiers seemed quite awkward and embarrassed at having discovered the women there.

While Oberammergau was a small, otherwise rural town, the influence of the Passion Play gave it a sense of being cosmopolitan. Every ten years, with the thousands of people in town to see the play, my storekeeper grandfather saw the need to have someone in the store who could speak English with customers who did not speak German, so when my mother was a teenager, he sent her to work for a family in England to learn the language.

Every Sunday, my grandmother's brothers—all butchers—would come over and sit with my grandfather on a bench outside the kitchen and visit. Toni and I would be sent a couple of doors up the street to a little restaurant, taking beer steins with us that the man at the restaurant would fill. We would carry them back very carefully to my grandfather and our great uncles, who would spend the afternoon discussing village gossip and politics on the bench.

I became an avid skier as a teenager, and chairlift construction and wire rope transportation later became my greatest passions and my life's work. But I did not always like skiing. My mother said when she put me on skis for the first time when I was three or four, I would topple over and just lie on my side in the snow. "I hate skiing," I told her. Before long, though, I found that I really liked skiing, and it became a big part of my life in the winter. Money for lift tickets was scarce—and the closest lift-served skiing was twenty kilometers away in Garmisch-Partenkirchen—so we would spend all morning on the west side of Oberammergau, hiking to the mountain top on wooden skis to which we attached strips of sealskin with a directional nap that provided enough friction against the snow

NEAR-DEATH EXPERIENCE # 1

The Farm

A family that had stayed with us in Oberammergau invited me to work on their farm for a few months during summer vacation, so in 1949 when I was fourteen, I took advantage of that offer. They had quite a successful operation with horses and cattle and field crops. Of greater interest to me was the machinery: several tractors and a lot of other equipment for harvesting, moving crops, and haying. They even had a machine that dug potatoes and loaded them into a trailer using a conveyor. Farming can be hazardous, and that was truer for me—an adventuresome fourteen-year-old—than for most people.

One day we finished working in the fields and returned to the house for dinner just as it was getting dark. I realized that I had left my jacket out in the field. Rather than walking all the way or taking a tractor (which the farmer would probably not have allowed), I borrowed their little motorcycle (which the farmer probably would not have allowed either, had he known about it). I was riding the little motorcycle down the lane to the field—throttle wide open, of course, the little bike going as fast as it could go—when at the last possible second, I saw a wire rope cable strung across the road right in front of me. There was no time to react, and the cable hit me right across the shoulders and pitched me off the bike flat on my back, knocking me out briefly and giving me a concussion. Had it been a few inches higher, or the bike a few inches lower, it would have taken my head right off. I slowly came to my senses, dusted myself off, and located and righted the motorcycle, which was no worse for wear. I collected my jacket and rode back to the house, never telling the farm family what had happened.

After that scary episode, as if to give an added warning, the farm tested me again: Later in the season, I drove a tractor out to one of the fields early in the morning. It had been cold overnight and there was a heavy frost on the grass. As I started down a hill toward the field, the tractor slid on the frosty grass and began picking up speed. Mid-slope, a road crossed the hill. When the tractor hit the road, it bounced me into the air. I hit my head very hard on the underside of the roof of the cab, and that knocked me out. The tractor continued its plunge down the icy hill, finally coming to a stop at the bottom. It was upright but I wasn't: I was unconscious in the cab.

underfoot to allow us to walk uphill on the slope. The nap of the sealskin would allow you to slide the ski forward easily, but would provide grip as you pressed backward to take a step. We'd remove the "skins" to ski down. Then we'd go home, have lunch, and do it again in the afternoon. The equipment was very primitive: leather, lace-up boots, and "long thong" bindings—bindings that secured the boot to the ski with leather straps up to forty-eight inches long that wrapped around your boot. At first, we had wood skis with no edges, then wood skis with edges that screwed on. I didn't own a pair of fiberglass or metal skis until I went to Canada in the late 1950s.

When I had a little money and the opportunity to ski in Garmisch, I would strap my skis and poles to my bicycle, put my ski boots in a backpack, and ride my bike the twenty kilometers through valleys and over a short mountain pass to Garmisch to go skiing. If I rode another ten kilometers or so around to Ehrwald on the Austrian side, I could ride up the tram for half what it cost to get to the top from Garmisch. If I left the house by bike at about 6 a.m. (still dark outside), I could make the 9 a.m. Ehrwald tram, or the next one. At the top, there was a tunnel about two-hundred meters long that I walked through. The large plateau surrounded by the high peaks and above the cliff band had excellent skiing served by a handful of lifts. I could ski all day in lift-served luxury, then catch the tram back down at 4 or 5 p.m., tie the skis and poles back onto my bike, and ride home in the dark, arriving in time for a well-deserved dinner.

I'm on the left with a friend on a ski mountaineering outing, about 1951.

My bicycle was my transportation, and it took me literally everywhere. I would chase the first snows of the year to find good skiing before we had gotten snow in Oberammergau—riding my bike with my skis tied to it—and then travel again in the spring, following the best spring skiing. Often, I'd ride my bike for two days into Austria just to ski. I'd carry a backpack with some clothes, a sleeping bag, and light provisions like teabags. Then I skinned up to a mountain hut operated by the Munich Mountain Club, and spent the better part of a week skiing the various peaks in the area before riding the bike home. The trip home had much more downhill, and I could sometimes ride the whole distance in a single day. At first, I stayed in a youth hostel in Landeck, Austria on the first night of the ride, but they charged a small fee and money was a very scarce commodity. One time when I was there, a guy told me, "You can stay free over there." He pointed to a building a block away. I went over to the building and told the man there, "Someone told me I could sleep here for free." He said, "You can, but I lock the door at 10 p.m. and open it again at six in the morning." I told him that would be okay, and spent the night there several times on my Austrian skiing trips. It was the Landeck jail.

The greatest adventure on my bike was an extended trip through Austria, Switzerland, and Italy in 1951. I put some clothes in my backpack, tied the backpack to my bike, and set off on my own, heading southwest. The route was almost entirely rural, and I could ride each day until I got tired, and then camp for the night. The first part of the ride was familiar—crossing into Austria shortly after Garmisch and climbing the Fern Pass toward Landeck. But as I climbed higher in the Alps, the mountains got steeper and the road narrower. My three-speed bike was no match for the climbs at the tops of the passes, and I spent many miles walking and pushing the bike on the edge of these narrow roads.

The weather in Switzerland was perfect, and I went through St. Moritz and over Maloja

With my siblings Marita, Toni, Hertha, Blanda and Norbert.

NEAR-DEATH EXPERIENCE #2

AVALANCHE IN INNSBRUCK

By the time I was sixteen, I was a passionate skier: I could not wait for the season to get started. That year, there was no snow yet in Oberammergau, but there had been a good bit of early season snow in Innsbruck, so I talked my older sister, Hertha, into asking one of her friends, a girl who worked at my grandfather's store, to drive us to Innsbruck to go skiing. Hertha's friend had a driver's license and a Volkswagen Bug—perfect ski mountaineering transportation— and she agreed to go along. My younger brother Toni went with us, too. At fourteen, he was an excellent skier. The Bug had a terrible heating system, so every additional bit of body heat made the ride over and back that much more comfortable.

There was good snow coverage, although the snow was wet and heavy—certainly less than ideal conditions—but after driving the distance from Oberammergau, we were determined to get a couple of runs in. Wearing leather boots and wrap-around long thong bindings that did not release—state-of-the-art gear—we skinned about halfway up the mountain. We came to a spot where we had to traverse across a steep, wide, untracked bowl. No one knew much about avalanche science in those days —least of all a handful of teenagers —but looking at the bowl and the route we needed to follow prompted a realization that we should traverse carefully so as not to trigger a massive snow slide, and ski single file, spaced apart so if the slope did slide, we would not be buried together in the snow. I was leading, and I had the others wait while I cut tracks across the bowl for them to follow. I was about halfway across when all the snow across the whole bowl above me let go. The snow under my skis started sliding as well. I was rolled over with my head downhill, and went under the snow instantly as the avalanche alternately picked up speed and slowed down with the changing terrain. It was a weird feeling to hear the sounds of the sliding snow change as the speed at which it was moving changed. The sound was enhanced because in addition to hearing the snow rolling and shifting within the avalanche, I was hearing crushing and grinding sounds beneath me as it slid over the dirt and rocks— the bowl had released all the way to the ground. The brightness of white around me grew darker as snow accumulated on top of me, and then it got lighter again as the snow covering me grew thinner when it tossed me over a knoll. On steeper terrain, the snow and I gathered speed again, and my vision became pitch black. They say that you should make swimming motions to try to stay on top of the snow, but my poles and skis were still on, and in this heavy rolling, I could not move my arms or legs. There was nothing I could do—nothing. I was totally helpless. When the avalanche finally stopped, I lay on my side. A few inches of space were available in front of my mouth, but it held little air. I was able to work my right hand free of the strap on my pole and reach toward what I thought was the surface. I had to figure out how deeply I was buried.

Meanwhile, Toni, who had been waiting with the others outside the boundaries of the area that had broken loose, had seen me go under, and instinctively followed the location where he had last seen me as that snow tumbled down the bowl. When the avalanche debris stopped moving, he skied down to where he thought I might have stopped. He ended up close enough to me—within fifty or sixty feet—that when my hand reached through the surface, he saw it. He yelled to the girls to come help dig me out. They did, and although I was thoroughly physically beat up and mentally out of it, we managed to get back down to the Bug and head for home.

Pass and into Italy. Once I came down out of the mountains north of Lake Como, there was a lot more agriculture then—orchards and pastures—and I could often pick my own free meal in an orchard or vegetable field by the side of the road. The farmers did not mind, although I got really tired of eating tomatoes after a few weeks.

Lake Como and Lake Lugano were fantastic—beautiful houses with elaborate landscaping, exotic cars and wonderful bicycling along the edge of the lake. I could always find a park to sleep in at night. I spent a week in Lake Como and another week or two in Lugano. It was very sophisticated and there was a lot of wealth. It seemed like everyone who owned a successful company in Milano lived in Switzerland at Lake Lugano because it was such a beautiful place with the mountains dropping right down to the lake. I rode over through Lake Maggiore, then back into Switzerland at the Simplon Pass, then over the Grimsel Pass to Interlaken and northeast to Lucerne. Then I went through Schwyz, Liechtenstein, and over the Arlberg Pass. I had been on the road for almost two-and-a-half months at this point and was looking forward to getting back to my mother's home cooking—eating fruit from orchards and tomatoes from farmers' fields was nourishing, but it was sure going to be great to get home.

I think having the opportunity to travel and live in unfamiliar situations as a teenager gave me a sense of adventure and comfort with other cultures and a confidence in my ability to adapt. Also in 1951,

My grandfather with Kathrin and Markus, about 1968.

I spent two months in Norway with a family, and the next year I went to Finland for May and part of June, then went to Sweden until the end of July. In August, I went from Sweden to Schleswig-Holstein, in the farthest north part of Germany—right by the border with Denmark—to stay with a family in a town called Flensburg. I had been there for a month and was ready to head home when my host family told me that my grandfather was coming up by train to accompany me home. This was completely unexpected. My grandfather had been in southern Bavaria all his life except for when he was in the army in World War I, and I was surprised that he would come such a long distance. When he arrived, he wanted to see the ocean, so we went to the North Sea, where the seashore is flat as a pancake and featureless—just water and sand. Grandfather was not too impressed, and wondered why anyone would want to live in such a place.

On the train trip home, we stopped in Hamburg and took a boat tour of the harbor, which was very impressive for the complexity of the waterfront, the amazing scope of the shipping industry, and the canals extending from the harbor into the city center. Then we continued back to Oberammergau. My grandfather later said that he had worried if he did not come up and get me, I would never come back.

Schooling in Germany uses a totally different approach than in the United States. Elementary school lasts seven hours a day, five days a week and is very intense with demanding expectations for behavior and discipline. The result is that a sixth-grade student performs at an academic level that would not be reached in the U.S. until eighth grade. After eight years in grade school, about 80% of teenagers start learning a trade and attend a trade school

Group picture with my class at Landsberg, about 1956.

one day every two weeks. Others go to specialty schools and then on to a college or university. Because of this model, tradesmen are afforded a greater degree of prestige and in fact perform at a much higher level in Germany and the European countries than in the U.S.

After working with my Grandfather in timber harvesting and riding lifts in Garmisch while skiing, I developed a profound interest in lifts and wire rope. People said I was "in love with wire rope" and they were not wrong. I was fascinated with it and wanted to learn everything I could about wire rope and lifts—that there was a technology that allowed movement up and down the side of mountain or across terrain that could not be tamed with a roadway was an amazing and powerful concept to me. It was almost like magic and in my desire to learn everything about it, I was like a sponge. I wrote to a few lift manufacturers and asked for their recommendation for a technical college or trade school where I could learn about lifts, wire rope, and lift construction. They replied that there was no school of any kind for that type of engineering—the only way to learn it was to work for them as an apprentice—something of a self-serving situation! The most appropriate university curriculum I could find was an agricultural machinery program at the technical college in Landsberg am Lech. Landsberg was only sixty-five kilometers (about forty miles) from Oberammergau, but I did not have a car. I paid the tuition myself using money that I had earned working for my grandfather, then rode my bicycle to Landsberg on Sunday afternoons, attended classes all week, and rode home after class on Friday evening. Classes lasted until 5 p.m. every day, a lot of the year the ride back to Oberammergau was in the dark. I used the light on my bike to see the road. I attended the technical college for four years and graduated in 1957.

Aerial Lifts and How They Work

Transportation systems operated by wire rope have many configurations that satisfy different needs worldwide. People are most familiar with those used for skiing and sightseeing but there are many, many other applications. The idea of transporting skiers using an aerial lift was inspired by ore tramways used in mining operations to extract precious metals and minerals from inside of mountains. Tramways were also used early in their history for moving animals. There are farmers in Switzerland who have small tramways for moving their cows from one pasture to another because the terrain is too steep for the cattle to safely traverse. Trams allowed the successful construction of huge public works projects, like Hoover Dam, which could only be built by using work trams to place concrete. Today, we see miniaturized tramways moving remote-controlled television cameras up and down (and across) the field to give a unique perspective to the coverage of all kinds of sporting events—football, ski racing, swimming, even baseball.

What all aerial lifts have in common is the use of wire rope to support and propel a carrier. In a chairlift, the carrier is the hanging "chair." (The name is a holdover from the first lifts of that type which looked literally like the seat and back of a chair dangling from the cable.) Today, that single chair has grown into double, triple, quad, six-, and even eight-passenger lifts that we still refer to as simply chairs, even though there are now so many different versions, including covered chairs, heated chairs, chairs

The first chairlifts in the United States were built at Sun Valley, Idaho in 1936 by Jim Curran working for the Union Pacific Railroad.

with or without footrests, chairlifts with automatic locking safety bars, etc. Enclosed passenger lifts are typically called gondolas. These originally came in a two-passenger version, then increased in size to four-, six-, eight-, and now ten- or fifteen-passenger cabins. Gondolas have three variations: a "mono-cable," in which the cabins are supported and propelled by a single cable; a "bi-cable," in which the cabins roll along one stationary support cable—called the "track rope"—and are propelled by a second cable called the "haul rope;" and the newest variation, called "3S," which uses two track ropes to support cabins accommodating up

Not all tramways are built to transport people.

to thirty to thirty-five passengers with a separate, continuous haul rope to move them.

Gondolas and chairlifts typically operate in a circular, non-reversible configuration where the haul rope moves either clockwise ("left up") or counterclockwise ("right up").

Aerial tramways have larger cabins and are always multi-cable, with at least a single (and much more frequently double) track rope and a haul rope. In addition, these tramways usually operate in a reversible "jig-back" configuration, in which one cabin ascends as the other descends. This was an early development—before the invention of electric motors or internal combustion engines. The jig-back was first developed with water held in a tank as a counterbalance to a load that a farmer needed to move uphill. Before water was used, the very first jig-back tram ever developed, built in 1644, was operated using horses.

In addition to chairlifts, gondolas and aerial tramways, there are several other systems utilizing wire rope as a means of motive power: funiculars, which have cabins or cars riding on rails propelled by a cable; funitels, where passenger cabins hang between a pair of haul ropes; and the funifor, configured with cabins between a pair of ropes like a funitel, but with track ropes to support the cabins in addition to circulating haul ropes for propulsion.

The vertical terrain of Europe lends itself to experimentation and innovation in aerial transportation technology, and new developments always seem to appear in Europe well before they are accepted in North America, but the United States has a rich history in cable transportation as well. The Cable Car system in San Francisco was invented by Andrew Smith Hallidie in 1873. Funiculars—cable operated inclined railways in which the cars roll up the mountain on a set of rails—have been in operation as urban transportation systems in the U.S. even longer than aerial lifts—for at least 150 years. There were four that operated in Pittsburg, Pennsylvania starting in the 1870s; two of those are still in operation. In the West, in addition to Hallidie's venerable San Francisco cable car system, there is an urban funicular—called the Angels Flight—which was built in downtown Los Angeles in 1901.

In terms of urban transportation, aerial lifts are gaining acceptance as practical urban transportation systems worldwide. In New York City, an aerial tramway has delivered travelers across the East River between Manhattan's Upper East Side and Roosevelt Island since 1976, and a tramway in Portland, Oregon serves the Oregon Health and Sciences University campus on Marquam Hill. There are several very large urban systems operating successfully in South America and new ones under construction in South America, Europe and Asia. The advantages of cable transportation are numerous: a minimal ground-level "footprint," virtually silent and emission-free operation, and continuous access for passengers.

Despite the many different types of lifts—and the fact that every installation is unique—they all have a great deal in common. Regardless of whether lifts operate with a circulating haul rope or in a reversible configuration, they all have a means of motive power (usually an electric motor) and a gear box to reduce the output speed of the motor to drive the haul rope, which wraps around a large pulley called a "bullwheel." There are brakes that slow, stop, and hold the lift as needed ("service brakes"), as well as braking systems that engage automatically in an emergency, for example if the traveling speed becomes too great or the haul rope starts to move in reverse. Because passengers are carried sometimes hundreds of feet in the air, and because aerial lifts frequently operate in a dramatically unbalanced configuration (much more weight is being pulled up the hill than is going down), braking systems are given a great deal of thought and are always configured with redundancy in mind.

The very nature of wire rope is that the rope is itself a machine made of parts moving in relation to one another. This complexity allows the rope to bend and flex over millions of cycles without stressing one part more than another, distributing loads evenly and preventing breakage. Just as any machine requires respect for its operating characteristics, what wire rope asks in exchange for this amazing performance is that it is treated with certain basic considerations.

There are so many fascinating things about wire rope—its simplicity, durability and amazing flexibility to solve so many kinds of transportation challenges. There is little wonder that the possibilities so captivated me as a young man and continue to do so today. For providing us with so many beneficial uses wire rope requires only a handful of conditions to be used safely and predictably:

1. It must be correctly sized and configured for the load(s) that will be imposed on it.
2. It must be installed and operated in a way that avoids factors that will mechanically damage the rope: abrasion, friction, excessive heat, twist or impact from an external source.

3. It must be flexed in a controlled and even manner without being bent too sharply.
4. It must be lubricated periodically to reduce friction between the individual wires and strands allowing them to move relative to one another.

If these requirements are met, wire rope will deliver consistent, reliable service for decades, but violating any of them is an invitation to disaster—a couple of examples of which will be discussed later.

To work correctly, an aerial lift needs to be tensioned, so that a haul rope will maintain adequate contact and friction on the drive bullwheel (not slipping as the load increases), and so track ropes will maintain the designed elevation between towers. Haul ropes and track ropes are tensioned independent of one another and may be tensioned at the top or bottom of the lift. Tensioning was traditionally achieved by using a weight—usually a large concrete block, although some early lifts were tensioned with a big container of rocks. Later setups used hydraulic tensioning systems that were equally effective, considerably more compact, and easier and quicker to de-tension when needed. The engineering process for a lift or other installation using wire rope determines the tension necessary to maintain the intended rope elevation between supports, the friction on the bullwheels required to avoid slippage and models these considerations while running, starting, slowing and stopping under a full range of load situations. Some recent aerial tram installations tension track ropes to a specific, engineered value at the time of installation, after which the tension is essentially static. The ropes move over the towers as the cabins ascend and descend, but there is no counterweight or hydraulic tensioning system. A couple of examples are the Zugspitze in Garmisch-Partenkirchen and the Jackson Hole aerial tramway in Teton Village.

Chairlifts are often described by the location of their functions— "bottom drive, top tension," "bottom drive, bottom tension," etc., or by their passenger use—"loading terminal" and "return terminal." Their loads are going in one direction—as skiers move to the top of the run. On the other hand, gondolas, funitels, aerial tramways and funifors tend to have their terminal locations noted as "top terminal" or "bottom terminal" (or "east" or "west") because passenger traffic tends to be more evenly distributed in both directions.

In addition to the main source of motive power—usually an electric motor—common sense and regulatory requirements demand a secondary means of operating an aerial lift in the event there is an interruption in line power or a failure of the main drive motor, which is usually a diesel engine that can operate the lift at a lower speed than the electric motor. This auxiliary power source can be engaged through a secondary gearbox input, a belt-drive system or hydraulically. Tramways and other large aerial lifts operating over inhospitable terrain will usually have several more means of evacuating passengers in the event of a mechanical problem.

The cable or cables are supported by towers located at intervals along the line from bottom to top. Chairlift towers are typically fabricated of steel tubing varying in diameter from eighteen inches to thirty-six inches or more. Gondola or funitel towers may be tubular or lattice, while aerial tramway and funifor towers are lattice due to the wider footprints required. Each tower has a ladder of some description attached to them providing access from the ground. A crossarm (or more than one) provides support from the tower for the line machinery that supports the cable or cables and there may be a catwalk to allow maintenance personnel access along the length of the line machinery. Aerial tramways, funifors, and bi-cable gondolas have longitudinal supports called "saddles" that align and support the track cables where they pass over the tower. The saddles allow the cables to move back and forth according to cabin position and load. They also have wheels, called "sheaves" (and pronounced "shiv") that support the haul cable. The towers have cable position detectors or derail switches for each cable that stop or prevent operation of the lift if the cable moves out of alignment for some reason. The location of that fault is indicated at the control room or drive terminal so that maintenance personnel can go to the tower and quickly correct the problem. In addition, towers typically have lifting frames above the crossarms and above the rope pathways to allow maintenance crews to temporarily lift the cables to replace sheaves, which have rubber liners to minimize wear on the cables and allow the cables to run quietly and smoothly over the tower.

The most significant difference between lift types is in the carriers. Chairlifts can be fixed to the cable or detachable—detachables have the advantage of offering a higher line speed (and a shorter ride over the same distance) while moving slowly through the loading and unloading areas. The other advantage found with detachable chairlifts is that slower loading speeds allow significant increases in capacity—it would be virtually impossible to get six people organized enough to load reliably on a fixed-grip chairlift, but it is easy and reliably done on a detachable. In some climatic zones, the ability to remove the carriers from the line at night while running the cable at a slow speed allows the resort to avoid rime ice buildup that would dramatically delay opening the lift in the morning. Fixed grip chairlifts, on the other hand, are simple, reliable, easy to maintain, and considerably less costly than detachables. A new development in fixed-grip chairlifts that simplifies loading is the use of a moving carpet—like a conveyor belt—that the skiers entering the loading area ski on to. The moving belt—the width of the chair—allows skiers to be moving at nearly the same speed as the chair as it approaches the point where they will sit down, reducing the effort of loading for both skier and lift operator and reducing loading mishaps and stoppage.

Gondolas typically use detachable grips and the carriers are propelled through the loading area by a conveyor system running at a speed proportionate to that of the line, but there are fixed-grip gondola systems as well where the line stops to allow passengers to enter or exit the cabins—the "Pulse" gondola at Squaw Valley USA was an example of this, and it had the odd distinction of operating in a jig-back configuration, as well. Detachable gondolas provide the operator with the opportunity to include mid-station loading and unloading or including a turn in the line. Gondolas are most popular with resorts looking to operate year-round, because they lend themselves to summer operation with mountaintop amenities for sightseeing and recreation like hiking or mountain biking. The tri-cable "3S" gondola with two track ropes can accommodate up to thirty-eight passengers.

Funitels offer many of the same advantages as gondolas. The added stability offered by their widely-spaced haul ropes allow operation in very windy locations and with passenger capacities of twenty to twenty-eight people per cabin. Funifors—the newest lift type on the scene, have large, aerial tramway-style cabins, but unlike traditional aerial trams with synchronous operation of the cabins, funifors operate independently with separate drives for each cabin, allowing a single cabin to serve a location without a need for high capacity, or a pair of cabins to share towers but operate autonomously.

Finally—aerial tramways, which for decades operated on a jig-back principle where the cabins were fixed to a haul rope that moved one cabin up as the other traveled down—are now being made so that the cabins can attach and detach from the haul rope, which is now one large, endless (spliced) loop rather than separate, individual upper and lower sections. This makes logistic sense for the resort operator, eliminating the need for trips with an empty cabin in bad weather, and reducing the risk of damage to a cabin parked at the top station overnight during a storm. The newest trend in scenic tramways is to have more than one passenger level, either an "upstairs/downstairs" arrangement or an enclosed cabin with an open passenger area on the roof.

Laber-Bergbahn

While I was still attending technical college in Landsberg, I worked on a small gondola being built in Garmisch-Partenkirchen. I had already decided that I wanted to work with lifts and wire rope, and the chance to get hands-on experience excited me. The pay was not great, but I would have done the work for free. Once I graduated in 1957, another opportunity landed literally in my lap—the construction of an aerial tramway in Oberammergau. The timing and location could not have been better: I was done with school and available for full-time work, and the project was in an area where my grandfather managed the forest for the landowner and that we had logged. I'd hiked and skied there. I knew it very well. A local contractor had been hired to do the concrete work at the upper terminal, but there was no way to drive there. They would need a lot of concrete at the site, and they needed a work tram to transport materials to the top of the mountain. A work tram would also provide the company building the passenger tramway a way to transport parts to the top terminal and tower locations.

Building work tram towers that would transport virtually all of the materials for the Laber Bergbahn project.

Cutting the line for the tramway was relatively easy through the lower section, which would be the only portion of the line in which the tram would be at or slightly below treetop level within the forest. The top section had a large span and was very steep, so a minimal amount of clearing was needed except right at the top.

I built a work tram that paralleled the line for the new tramway. The work tram's towers were made of the trees from the site. I cut them down, limbed them, and then attached rungs to them, so that I could access the tops. They were guyed off to large, strong trees left standing on either side of the line. I pulled up a steel cable after hiking a small rope from the top to the bottom. The small steel cable allowed us to winch the track rope for the work tram into place on saddles hanging from the improvised towers. The work tram's track rope was then anchored and tensioned and the smaller cable—which was spooled on the drum of a gasoline engine powered winch—became the haul rope for the work tram. A very simple carriage traveled up and down the track rope—pulled to the top by the winch and returning to the bottom by gravity, but with braking provided by the winch.

A single winch, powered by a small gasoline engine, operated the work tram.

The work tram allowed us to transport the raw materials: sand, gravel, cement, rebar—even the water with which to make concrete—to the top of the mountain where the contractor mixed it using a small mixer. The parts for the tramway—which were small and light enough to be transported by the work tram—were all moved to the top terminal in the same manner. It was the first time that I built a lift that would allow me to build another, larger lift, but it would not be the last—it was an extremely useful concept.

The Laber-Bergbahn project gave me the opportunity to learn a lot of project and site management aspects of lift construction, including surveying, organizing work for maximum efficiency, planning, and material staging. It was a lot of work, but I was really into it. I worked long hours and learned a lot, both directly and through observation. In many ways, it was a weird lift, and there were very few like it. It had a very narrow gauge at the top and bottom, but the track and haul ropes were farther apart in the middle of the line. It was not reversible—four small cabins circulated around the line and in the terminals the carriage rolled off the track ropes and on to a lever that moved the cabin around the bullwheel while the haul rope remained attached to the cabin. This meant that the lift had to stop each time a cabin entered the terminal, top and bottom, and the other two cabins on the line came to a standstill opposite one another on Tower 2, then very slowly resumed travel after passengers in the terminals had disembarked and the cabins reloaded and were transported to the other side of the line. The cabins had to be very precisely placed around the line to allow the terminal equipment to work correctly. It was an ingenious, but very intricate, system, which is probably why it never really caught on. Even so, the Laber-Bergbahn is still working today—using that original system—some sixty-four years after installation.

One of the cabins on the Laber nearing the top terminal, with Oberamergau and the Kofel in the background.

The Laber Bergbahn as it appears today—still in operation after over sixty years.

There is a single tower between the lower terminal and the tower at the exact mid-point of the line, then a long, steep span over a little valley before climbing to the top terminal. The overall elevation gain is slightly less than 800 meters (2,572 feet) in a length of 2,021 meters (6,630 feet or one and one-quarter miles). For a small tramway—the cabins only hold eight or ten people—it is a steep line, and it has an extremely limited capacity, only 130 passengers per hour, but it provided the area with a unique sightseeing and hiking attraction for summer visitors. In the winter, the skiing can be excellent, but it is ungroomed and steep: an "experts only" experience.

The Laber-Bergbahn project was a great learning experience for me and the opportunity to do a project that benefitted my hometown was rewarding as well. I was twenty-two years old and excited about the work. My fascination and enthusiasm for lifts and wire rope transportation was acute and my appetite to learn more had been whetted by the little tramway in Oberammergau, but though I would return to Europe again and again in the coming years, the Laber-Bergbahn project was really the last lift I would build in Europe. After all the travel I'd done in different European countries earlier in my life, I had a strong desire to go to North America and see a new world and an entirely different landscape.

◆ LABER-BERGBAHN

My work on the Laber-Bergbahn started by building a ropeway for moving materials and building the tower foundations and continued through the construction of the top and bottom terminals, pulling the track and haul rope and installing the cabins. Once the ropeway was operational, I was sent out to check the alignment of the line machinery that guides the haul rope over the towers. I was riding on top of the cabin to see where the haul rope was riding on the sheaves, but I was "protected" with a safety belt and lanyard that were attached to the hanger. As we approached the tower, however, the lanyard of the safety belt caught on the guard that keeps the cabin from hitting the tower, so, while the tram was still moving on, it was now attached to the cabin and was wrapped around the guard on the tower. We had no radios and there was no way to tell the control room to stop the tram. The safety belt got tighter and tighter on me until it snapped. The force flung me off the top of the tram cabin.

I fell about forty feet, landing on some soft dirt right between two large stumps. If I had landed on one of the stumps I would surely have been killed, and although I was knocked unconscious, I was otherwise not seriously injured.

As a twenty-two-year-old, my extremely lucky landing was wasted on me until some years later when I read a newspaper story about a movie stuntman who was attempting a stunt for a film that was amazingly like my fall. He was supposed to leap from inside of a tram car (not from the top of the cabin, as I had done), and the plan was for him to jump onto a tree and grab it. He somehow missed grabbing the tree and landed on the ground. He died instantly.

Sprung in den Tod

Der wuchtige Sprung zur Tanne geriet um einige Meter zu kurz. Der polnische «Stuntman» Fus zerschmetterte am Boden.

Die Tanne hätte den Fall von Fus aus der Seilbahnkabine auffangen sollen. So schrieb es das Drehbuch für den Film «Olympische Fakkel» vor.

Doch das Drehbuch des Lebens wollte es anders. Mit dem Tod musste der Stuntman seinen gefährlichen Beruf bezahlen.

How Lifts Are Built

Location is Everything

A new lift of any type is built to fill a need: It provides access to a presently unserved location for skiing, sightseeing or other recreation or activity or where existing transportation systems are inadequate or inefficient. Once a need (or in the case of a lot of lifts, just the desire for a new lift) is established, a whole host of other questions must be answered:

- Loading location (and the relationship of that location to existing or potential lifts, parking, trails, and other amenities)
- Unloading location
- The type of lift to be utilized: surface, chairlift, gondola, aerial tramway, funitel, etc.
- Anticipated or existing skier or vehicular traffic through the loading and unloading areas and along the line
- Avalanche risk for the terminals and potential tower locations
- Maximum snow depth along the line and its effect on lift operation and ski-under or vehicular clearance
- Crossing other lifts, roadways, utilities, streams, ponds, wetland areas, and cliffs
- Access to possible tower locations for construction and maintenance
- Rescue access and egress for skiers/passengers removed from the line
- The effects of wind, ice, and other climatic considerations
- Availability of power and other utilities
- Soil conditions
- Potential risks to the lift, which could include rock fall, soil movement/erosion, trees, and streambeds

Whew. Once all those factors are considered, and the approximate location of the terminals and the line are established, the terminals and line are plotted on a topographic map, from which a local engineer can develop an approximate profile of the ground surface along the proposed line. The topo map and profile may indicate areas in which towers are not feasible —such as in a streambed—and will narrow down the areas in which soil investigation and evaluation of clearances should be conducted.

Decisions must be made as to the location of the drive terminal and the tensioning system (top or bottom), rotation direction, carrier types, suspended or buried communications cable, tower head configuration (lifting frames, catwalks), tower ladders, auxiliary power unit, bolt-down or embedded tower footings—even the paint color. All this information is required to allow the resort operator to solicit bids for the work from potential vendors, who want to have as much information as possible so they can provide a detailed and accurate price and have some assurance that all the prospective vendors are bidding on the same project. A lift manufacturer may have its own installation crew, or may have installation contractors who install the equipment provided by the manufacturer. Prospective bidders will make a site visit to assess the details of installing the lift, although this is frequently done in the winter when the site is covered with snow and may give a less than conclusive impression of the difficulty of the work. Lift manufacturers typically bid on a lift project to an accuracy of plus or minus ten percent or fifteen percent, and resort owners are usually looking for a "turn-key" price, which requires only that they provide access to the site, parking lot space for staging equipment and materials and the required permits from any agencies having jurisdiction over such a project: county, state, and the US Forest Service in the case of resorts operating on National Forest lands.

On the Ground

A survey is done along the proposed line, providing the engineers for the lift manufacturer with precise elevations of the top and bottom terminals, the geographic features, and a general idea of the gradient along the line. Armed with this information, engineers can determine the number of towers, the proposed location of towers along the line, and the loading on each tower, which determines the configuration of the line machinery: the sheaves (pulleys) and surrounding structure that support the haul cable. When the profile of the lift is complete, drawings are transmitted to the resort for review and a final survey of the line, allowing the resort or installation contractor to mark tower locations and determine if any remaining issues will affect construction before the plan is finalized.

Bidding

The resort operator can now select a lift manufacturer based on pricing, previous experience with the company, the vendor's reputation within the industry, or the vendor's capability. Further reasons they might choose a particular vendor include: the vendor can deliver something that no other manufacturer offers; it may be the only vendor able to deliver within the window desired by the client; the vendor may extend attractive financing for the project; or the vendor might rise above the rest for some other reason.

Fabrication and Excavation

The lift manufacturer can then begin fabrication of the top and bottom terminals, the line machinery for the towers, and the tower heads. The manufacturer also can provide the installation crew or contractor with station (the exact distance along the line of the lift from a benchmark) and elevation of the top of concrete for the tower foundation, the required dimensions of the footing for each tower, as well as blueprints for the foundations of the top and bottom terminals.

If towers will be fabricated onsite (which is often the case), the lift manufacturer will provide specifications for fabrication of the towers, allowing the tower materials to be ordered. They can also order a length of wire rope to meet ANSI B-77 code specifications for aerial lifts.

The installation of a lift begins with marking the top and bottom terminal locations and tower locations. Once marked and laid out on the ground, tower footings and foundations for the top and bottom terminals can be excavated. Construction of a new lift nearly always begins right at the end of ski operations for the year (sometimes even before the resort has closed) because the new lift must be ready to operate when the season starts up again in the fall. Time is of the essence because there are only so many workdays to complete the work and there are no guarantees of favorable weather: Work must continue regardless. During our project at Mt. Bachelor in Oregon it snowed at least once every month we were there, from May to November. This is not at all unusual and while it may be uncomfortable and inconvenient at the time, some projects are unbearably warm through the summer and we would give anything for a few days of cold, snowy weather.

Access

On some projects, access to the tower and terminal locations is simple and straightforward. Installers can drive to every tower, excavate using heavy equipment, move materials by truck, and erect the towers and terminals using a crane. Other projects present greater challenges. If acceptable to the resort operator and following environmental review and approval, the installation contractor or crew may need to build roads to the terminal locations and towers. The most difficult jobs present access issues that cannot be solved so easily: Access to a terminal and/or tower locations may be strictly over the snow, and materials must be moved over the snow by foot or snow machine, or flown by helicopter. Most projects include a mix of access issues, and the installation contractor or crew comes up with a strategy for dealing with each location early in the project. One solution that I used in several different projects with difficult access (and have seen used only rarely by other contractors) is to install a temporary work tram constructed parallel to and not far from the line of the new lift. A work tram can be used for moving materials, fuel, and other items during construction that would be difficult or costly to move by foot or helicopter. It is a simple system using temporary towers assembled onsite to support a track rope. The towers can be made of trees or steel and they are angled to provide clearance for a carrier and tied off to trees or stakes. A large winch is moved to the top of the work tram's line. It pulls the carrier up and allows gravity to move it downhill. In a situation where every efficiency needs to be leveraged to keep a project moving smoothly, it can make a huge difference. It can move materials on bad-weather days when a helicopter may be unable to fly, or can bring in fuel for equipment. At Mt. Bachelor, we built a work tram over the snow early in the project because we knew that access to locations along the line would be more limited and difficult once the snow melted. The work tram was invaluable for moving fuel, tools, and materials to the tower locations, as well as the site of the top terminal. Once the snow receded from the top terminal in mid-summer, the crew had to walk to the top every day, and the work tram ferried their tools, lunches and fuel for the crane, air compressor, and other equipment at the top of the mountain.

Tower Footings

Excavation of tower footings can be done using heavy equipment—a backhoe or excavator—or by hand. Since concrete is often delivered to the tower locations by helicopter, it is important to make the tower holes the right size, but not too big, since each additional cubic yard of concrete comes at a premium price. Towers that are bolted down to the foundation require reinforcing steel (rebar) in the footing as well as accurately placed anchor bolts and a form is constructed to hold the anchor bolts and a tower base at ground level. Direct-embedment towers require a concrete base on which the tower tube will sit that align it on the centerline of the lift. A small concrete pad is poured in the bottom of the hole and an angle iron guide is embedded in it using an instrument so that the angle iron is perfectly centered on the line. The bottom of each tower tube is notched to fit the angle iron, assuring that when the bottom of the tube is placed on the guide and the tower is plumbed, the top of the tower will be aligned with the others up and down the centerline of the lift.

For bolt-down towers, once all the tower holes have been excavated and formed, concrete is poured to fill the tower footings and forms, the forms stripped, and the concrete given time to cure prior to installation of the towers. For lifts with easy access by road, this can be done by "tailgating" concrete from the chute of a concrete truck directly into the holes and forms, by pumping concrete into the footings or with a crane and concrete "bucket"—a large cylinder with a handle-operated trapdoor in the bottom that retains the concrete in the hopper until the handle is pulled, dispensing the concrete into the form.

The Flying Circus

It is much less costly to transport towers to their location by truck, erect them using a crane and pour concrete from a concrete truck than to perform those operations with a heavy-lift helicopter. It can also simplify the logistics of the job, because towers can be installed one by one as the foundations and steel fabrication progress and usually requires a smaller crew than installation using a helicopter. In some situations, access to tower locations is so difficult or limited a helicopter is the only way to get the work done.

Direct-embedment construction was designed for difficult access projects by using a heavy-lift helicopter to place the towers in the holes and pour concrete around them in rapid succession. The cost of ferrying the helicopter to the project site is minimized by combining tower and concrete placement in one or two days of work. Typically, placement of towers starts at the top of the lift: the helicopter brings the tower to the hole, the ground crew guides the base onto the angle iron guide on the pad in the bottom of the hole and—while the helicopter hovers holding the tower vertical—they attach guy cables to stakes driven into the ground, trees or other anchor points and tighten the cables with winches to keep the tower standing upright. The helicopter then releases by remote control the wire rope slings it used to carry the tower and flies down to get the next one. While it is gone, the crew moves downhill to the next location. That description makes the process sound a lot calmer and more controlled than it is in practice. Even with an experienced crew and an excellent pilot, doing anything with a helicopter carrying a heavy load and trying to place it precisely is potentially dangerous, unpredictable and close to chaotic. The noise of the helicopter makes it virtually impossible to communicate and the rotor wash makes work on the ground exceedingly difficult, as dust obscures vision and debris, tools and any loose construction materials blow around uncontrollably. Another issue is static electricity. Helicopter rotor blades moving through dust in the air or rain generate static electricity and a lot of it. The first crewmember making contact with a suspended load or the hook from the helicopter can get a powerful shock and if you let go and then grab the load or hook again, you get shocked again—the static will recharge instantly. When this is a problem, the ground crew will tell the pilot on the radio that the hook is "getting hot" and will have him touch the load to the ground to discharge the static electricity before they handle it or they'll tie a wire rope sling to a shovel and use that to ground the concrete bucket, tower or hook before making contact with it. Everyone working with a helicopter has made the rookie mistake of grabbing the concrete bucket and getting knocked on their butt by static electricity at least once—it's a rite of passage.

The helicopter pilot has his hands full also—he is flying a heavy load at the end of a long cable attached to the belly of the helicopter, his vision is also affected by blowing dust on the ground and he needs to not only keep the helicopter flying and the load in the right place, but to keep an eye on the ground crew scurrying around. There are plenty of other complications and potential obstacles: aerial power or communication cables, other lifts, bad weather, even other aircraft. Because helicopter time is so costly, we are always trying to give him a maximum-lift load but requiring maximum performance from the helicopter can make it more difficult to fly and allow less fine control than a lighter load with a greater margin of available power, making the process more dangerous for the ground crew.

The ground crew is well protected with helmets, goggles and radios with headsets for communicating with the helicopter pilot, but it is always a challenging and dangerous job. Work continues down the hill until all the towers are standing in the holes and securely tied off, then the crew starts at the top again, verifying that all of the towers are correctly aligned and plumb or at the designated angle from vertical, placing and tying rebar in the holes and making sure that everything is ready to pour concrete.

If placing the towers with a helicopter is difficult, pouring concrete can be even more challenging: because although the amount of concrete loaded into the concrete bucket can be varied according to the fuel load on the helicopter, wind and other factors, the pilot has to thread the bucket between the tower and the guy cables, assist the ground crew as they guide it into position to be poured and then compensate as the weight in the bucket decreases as concrete flows out of the bucket into the form or hole. He then flies the empty bucket back to the "landing," flies it into position behind the concrete truck and hovers while the crew exchanges it for the full bucket waiting there. The helicopter's external load hook usually has a load cell that provides the pilot with a digital readout of the weight of the load and as he departs the landing the pilot will call out the weight of the full bucket on the radio to the ground crew so they can fine-tune the amount of concrete in the next bucket to suit the decreasing fuel load of the helicopter or provide a little better cushion of available power if needed when hovering at the site where he is pouring the load.

Terminal Construction

Once the towers are standing, construction of the terminals is the next priority. In the case of a fixed-grip chairlift, it was a matter of installing a supporting structure and a handful of components, but with the advent of detachable chairlifts, the quantity and complex interoperation of a lot of machinery rivals that of a gondola. The construction of a gondola, funitel or aerial tramway typically require a crew or subcontractor dedicated to terminal construction, a crew working on towers and line machinery and a specialized crew for installation of terminal equipment and electrical systems.

The drive terminal for a fixed-grip chairlift is frequently delivered to the site fully configured at the manufacturer's shop, ready to be installed atop the supporting structure. Once the bullwheel is installed and the line power and communications line connected, it is ready to run. The much larger and mechanically complex drive and conveyor system of a detachable chairlift requires more installation work, alignment and adjustment. Once installed, power provided, and the tensioning system configured, the next task is to connect the safety systems on the towers.

Communications

The top and bottom terminals are connected to each tower using an aerial or buried multi-conductor cable called the "comm line," which integrates operational controls for the lift—starts, slows, stop and emergency stop commands—with verbal communications between the operators as well as the rope position detection or derail systems that will stop the lift in the event a malfunction or derail occurs on any of the towers.

Pulling the Haul Rope

Installing the haul rope is a major project and frequently occurs just as the weather is becoming problematic. Just moving the spool of haul rope to a location from which it can be installed on the lift is frequently a major project, because it can weigh ten tons or much, much more. The spooled haul rope is generally placed at the lower terminal of the lift, in line with the up line or downline so that it can be guided on to the sheaves as it is pulled off the spool. A fiber rope is hiked up (or down) and passed over the towers to allow a light pulling cable (usually called a "sand line") to be pulled into position, which is then connected to the haul rope. The spool of haul cable is set up on stands and anchored firmly to allow it to spool off in a controlled manner, including a braking system to keep the haul cable elevated while it is pulled carefully on to the line. One poorly understood, but essential consideration is that wire rope must always be taken off the spool in the same orientation in which it was put on—if it went on "over the top" it must be taken off the spool from the top—if this simple rule is ignored, twist and tension will be introduced into the rope which will inevitably cause problems later. The sand line is pulled around the line of the lift using a winch or a piece of heavy equipment while a crew member operates the brake on the haul cable spool. The braking system can vary from a very elaborate hydraulic damper to a large timber levered against the rim of the spool and tensioned using a "come-along." As the haul cable is being installed, the crew can align the sheave trains on the towers to keep the cable rolling on the center of the sheaves without the risk of derailing. Once it has been pulled all the way around, the haul cable can be tensioned and prepared for splicing. Installing the track and haul ropes for an aerial tramway, gondola, funifor or funitel is much more complex and demanding—in some cases huge spans are involved, with buildings, roadways and waterways below the line adding engineering and logistic challenge to an already difficult task.

Splicing

In most lift or aerial transportation systems, a continuous loop of wire rope is created by "splicing" the ends of the cable by crossing and interweaving the strands in a manner which does not change the rope diameter. Splicing wire rope is as much an art as a science, requiring years of field experience to achieve competence. Wire rope used for transportation systems typically has six strands, each strand made up of multiple wires and the strands wrapped in a helix around a core that is typically made of fiber that can hold lubrication. The dimensions of a splice are dictated by the diameter of the wire rope: the minimum length of a splice must be no less than twelve hundred times the rope diameter, so a splice in a one-inch haul rope must be no shorter than one hundred feet.

Different splicers use different techniques, but the two basic patterns of a wire rope splice are either "three and three" or "alternating strands." Wire rope used on lifts is either "regular" lay or "Lang" lay—which describe the manner in which individual wires are wrapped into strands. The different lays require different splicing techniques.

The splicer measures back from each end of the rope and "opens" the lay of the rope back the required distance, removing the core of the rope on each side. The six strands on each side are then cut back so that the ends of a strand from each end of the rope will meet at a calculated distance from the center of the splice, called the "marriage"—the longest strand on one end will meet the shortest strand on the other end, the next longest will meet the next shortest, etc. The two ends of the rope are now crossed, and the splicer will begin laying in the three strands on one side with the three on the other at the marriage point, then straightening the "tails." (Tails are the ends of each strand that will get tucked into the center of the reassembled rope from which the core was removed.) The tails are wrapped with cloth or plastic strips to bring them to the same diameter as the core that they replace, to support the outer strands. Working outward from the marriage, the two ends are gradually wrapped together, tucking the tails into the core at each location where the trimmed strands cross—there are a total of twelve tails that cross and are tucked into the rope at six locations, three on each side of the marriage. The tucks are painted a color that contrasts with the rope so that the splice can be easily seen and inspected from time to time. Done correctly, the only way the splice will be noticeable is from these paint marks—there will be no difference in diameter and the splice is every bit as strong as the cables it joins.

When the splice is finished, the finished rope placed in position on the bullwheel and towers, the tensioning rigging is removed, and the lift is ready to run.

Carriers

With the drive and return terminals completed, the towers installed and aligned, the protective systems operational and the haul cable installed and spliced, the carriers—chairs, gondola cabins (or, in some cases, a blend of the two) can be installed. On a fixed-grip chairlift, the distance between carriers is a function of the maximum line speed of the lift and the mandated timing between carriers, so the carriers are installed by the crew using a long tape measure to space them correctly. On a detachable, the line and terminal conveyors operate at speeds relative to one another and the carriers are launched automatically at intervals calculated by the logic system of the lift. With carriers installed, the lift is ready for testing and approval by the authority having jurisdiction—loaded with weight to simulate the load of a full complement of passengers then accelerated and braked under a variety of conditions to assure that it will respond appropriately once put in service.

Opening for the Public

The moment that everyone has been waiting for—opening for the public—is always a special occasion and a proud moment for both the resort operator and the installation crew. It is an opportunity to recognize and honor the dedication and hard work of the crew and to celebrate the improved capabilities of the resort and its commitment to customer satisfaction. The lift manufacturer or installation contractor will typically provide a person to train the resort's operations and lift maintenance personnel and to "babysit" the new lift for a month or so, fine-tuning the installation and providing timely correction of any problems that occur during that time.

Canada

In 1958, I was working on a short project for Bell Tramways of Lucerne, Switzerland when they offered me a job building a sightseeing gondola in Banff, Alberta the following spring. I got an inexpensive ticket from Bremen, Germany on an immigration boat sailing to Halifax, Nova Scotia. The boat was filled with poor and working-class people headed to Canada to make a new life. I did not speak much English, but after traveling in Europe though non-German speaking areas and living with families in Finland and Sweden, I could get by well enough in places where I did not speak the language. When we landed in Halifax, I noticed that there was a very strange twinkle or shimmer to the air—I had never seen anything like it and could not figure out what it was. It was a very weird

The SS Italia—more an inexpensive and efficient way to get to Canada than a "cruise", but the ship did have a band!

Picking tobacco in Canada.

thing, like the air itself was sparkling. I asked someone about this effect, and they said that Halifax had a huge fishing and fish processing industry. There was a factory where they processed the fish and then they burned the fins, tails, and other discarded parts, and the fish scales were carried into the air with the smoke exhausted from the plant. They would eventually settle to the ground like mist. That story made the sparkling effect a lot less magical: I could not wait to get out of Halifax.

I took the train to Toronto and found a simple, cheap room in a building downtown between King Street and Queen Street. I had no money. I'd left Germany with about two hundred Deutschmarks, which was the equivalent of about $47 in U.S. dollars at the time or about $400 today. I ate a lot of Corn Flakes—so many Corn Flakes that I never wanted to eat them again!

I met some German guys and they tipped me off to opportunities for work. I soon had three jobs. In the morning, I picked tobacco on a tobacco farm. It was sort of a piece-work job. We had to pick tobacco leaves until the little house where the leaves were dried was full; then we were done. In the afternoon and evening, I had a job working for a landscaping company. I could even work at night. Golf courses would water their grounds after dark when the golfers had left for the day. During the watering, the worms would come out of the ground. Afterward, I would go out on the golf course with a headlamp and a little bucket and fill the bucket with worms to sell to the fishing stores for bait! Between those three jobs, I was making good money. I saved enough to travel west to Alberta and then British Columbia, skiing in Banff and on the glacier in Lake Louise along the way, and doing some odd jobs from time to time.

Spring skiing on the glacier at Lake Louise.

At Banff I connected with John Brugger, whom I'd arranged to meet through the Swiss company that had hired me for the Banff job, Bell Engineering. John was about twenty years older than me, but we hit it off very well. Our first task was to build a work tram along the line where the gondola would be built, but the winch that we needed for the work tram had not yet arrived from Switzerland, so we were delayed. I told John that I'd like to go skiing while we waited, but the only area open this late in the spring (April) was Mt. Baker in Washington, which had lift-served skiing on the glacier at the top of the mountain. I asked John how I could go to Washington to ski, and he said that I'd have to go to Vancouver and apply for a visa, which would take some time to come through. That seemed like a lot of trouble for a couple of days skiing. I figured that if I tried to take the bus across the border I'd be required to show my passport and visa, because with my limited English, I was obviously not Canadian, so I came up with another plan. There was a little town in British Columbia called Chilliwack that was only a few miles north of the border, and I thought I could take the bus to Chilliwack and then just walk into the United States and hitch a ride to the ski area. I told John I would be back in a couple of days, but didn't tell him exactly what I had in mind. I put some clean clothes in a small backpack and got a bus to Chilliwack, which was a small town in farm country. From Chilliwack, it seemed like a pretty short distance to the border—eight or ten miles—and then a somewhat shorter distance to the Mt. Baker Highway. I walked south on farm roads out of Chilliwack, and had walked for quite a distance when it started to get dark. I came across a farm with a barn that was pretty close to the road. I had slept in plenty of barns while riding my bike in Europe, and I knew that farmers went to bed early and would probably be more annoyed if

I woke them up to ask if I could sleep in their barn than if I just went ahead and slept there. The lights were off at the farmhouse, so I went into the barn, had a good night's sleep on the hay, and woke up when I heard a dog barking in the morning. I was afraid the dog would alert the farmer to my presence, so I got out of the barn and back on the road in a hurry before the farmer came out to start work. I had walked for a couple of hours when I came to the Mt. Baker Highway and started walking east toward the ski area. Before too long a car came along and I stuck out my thumb to hitch a ride. The car slowed down and stopped and to my great shock, it was a Border Patrol vehicle. The Border Patrol officer opened his window and asked where I was headed.

I said, "Mt. Baker."

He said to get in. He started driving and asked where I was from.

For some reason, I said "Bellingham." I guess that was the only town I could think of in Washington—I didn't want him to think I had come from Canada.

"Where do you live in Bellingham?" he asked.

I told him something about staying with friends there, but it was a losing battle—he could tell that I didn't know anything about Bellingham and wasn't telling the truth. Before long we came to a large lodge on the side of the road and he pulled in and parked. We got out and went into the lobby.

There was a seating area on one side of the lobby and he said, "Go sit over there and wait. Someone is going to come from Bellingham and pick you up." Then he left. I didn't know what to do, but I figured I was in BIG trouble, and it was going to get really complicated, and that I'd probably never be allowed back into the United States.

The employees in the lodge didn't seem to be noticing me, and it seemed as if he hadn't said anything to them about keeping an eye on me. I figured it would take at least an hour for someone to get there from Bellingham. Watching to see if any of the employees were paying attention, I casually walked to the door and looked outside. No one took any notice, so I went outside and waited around to see if anything happened. After a minute or two, I crossed the highway quickly, avoiding the urge to run. I went into the woods and started walking north. I came across a dirt logging road that had quite a bit of log truck traffic on it. It was heading the right direction, so I followed it. I was worried that if the border patrol came looking for me, they would talk to the loggers, so I stayed off the road, walking parallel to it in the woods where I wouldn't be noticed. I walked for the rest of the day, passing the area where the loggers were actually cutting and loading the logs. I slept in the woods and the next morning walked north again. At one point, I came to a creek or small river and had to cross it, so I took off my clothes and shoes, put everything in my backpack and walked through the freezing cold water to the other side where I quickly dressed and started walking again to warm up. At last I came to the top of a ridge and could see a town ahead,

The finished gondola on Sulphur Mountain in one of the most magnificent settings in Canada.
[Banff Sulphur Mountain Gondolas], 1959, Bruno Engler/photographer, Whyte Museum of the Canadian Rockies,
Bruno Engler fonds (V190/I/A/i/b/3/na-19)

which was a very welcome sight, because I was hungry as hell. I figured that if my sense of direction in the woods had been correct, I had walked more than far enough to be north of the border again, although there had been no signs, fences, or other physical indications that I had crossed the border at any time going either direction. I walked into the town and was relieved to see that I had found my way back to Chilliwack! I caught the bus back to Banff without having made a single turn on snow, but with no further desire to ski Mt. Baker.

I did get to do a lot of skiing in Canada, where at least I didn't have to worry about the United States Border Patrol.

Work on the Banff gondola started in May 1959 and I could finally do the kind of work that I really wanted to do. We built a work tram for carrying materials first, then started work on the tower footings. John Brugger was a nice guy and quite knowledgeable, and I learned a good bit working with him. On Saturday nights, he liked to go down to the beer parlor in Banff. The odd thing about the place was that there were separate entrances for "Men with Escorts" and "Ladies." The Canadians liked to drink beer with a tomato juice chaser, which I found very strange. John drank more than I did and I always ended up having to drive us home.

While I was in Banff, I saw a notice for a race one weekend, the "Sir Norman Watson Downhill," sponsored by the Calgary Ski Club. It sounded like fun, so I entered. I did not have any race skis, so I just raced in my regular skis. It was a good course and I skied what I thought was a decent run, so I stuck around for the post-race party. To my great surprise, I won the race! There was a big trophy in the Post Hotel. My name is inscribed on it as the winner of the 1959 Sir Norman Watson Downhill.

When the Banff gondola project was finished, I wanted to go to the United States, but could not get a visa, so I got a ticket back to Genoa, Italy on a ship called the SS *Cristoforo Colombo*. I thought that maybe I could get a job teaching skiing and that would allow me to get a visa to work in the U.S. My Swiss friend Fritz Frey knew Stein Eriksen, and gave me Stein's phone number. I called Stein and asked about a job teaching skiing in his ski school in Aspen.

Stein spoke German pretty well, and when I asked about a job, he said, "Well, first I would have to see that you can ski. You know, everyone in my ski school is Norwegian…."

I told him that I thought I was a good enough skier.

He said, "Well, come to Aspen and we'll see."

I bought another transatlantic steamship ticket from Genoa to New York on the same ship I had just taken the opposite direction—the *Cristoforo Colombo*.

Banff Skier Places First

Hans Burhart of Banff posted a time of 3.2 minutes in taking first place in senior "A" division of the Sir Norman Watson trophy downhill ski race at Mount Temple.

Pat Duffey of Calgary covered the two and one-half mile course in 3:13.2 minutes to finish in the runnerup position while Erik Heumer placed third with a time of 3:26.2.

Rick Grandmaison of Banff took top honors in senior "B" division with a time of 3:36. Vern Futter was second in 3:49 and Peter Till third in 4:03.4.

Dave Pogue of Calgary won out in junior competition with a time of 3:10.3 followed by Bob Brown, who was timed in 3:16.4. Dennis Smith placed third with a time of 3:27.1.

Freida Clark won the girl's race in 2:59 while Ann Muirhead was second in 3:00.1 and Barb Brown's third-place time was 3:22.3.

NEAR-DEATH EXPERIENCE #4
THE OLDSMOBILE

While I was working in Banff, I bought an old Oldsmobile sedan for about two hundred dollars. It ran poorly when I got it, but I worked on it and got it so that it ran well. One night, I was invited to a party in Lake Louise. It was given by someone I knew vaguely and was an upscale affair—actual cocktails, not beer and tomato juice! We were all drinking heavily, and, in those days, there was a lot less concern about drinking and driving than there is today. I left the party and headed back to Banff in the Oldsmobile and somewhere along the way, I fell asleep. I woke up in the Oldsmobile out in a muddy field. It was pitch black, the middle of the night, and there was no way to get it out, so I hitchhiked back to Banff.

When I went back to get the car, I discovered that the tracks made after it left the road went right between two large trees close enough together that there were only about six inches on each side of the car. If it had hit either of those trees, I would surely have been killed. There were no seatbelts, and I was probably doing sixty miles per hour.

Stein

In the 1950s and 1960s, there was no more famous person in downhill skiing than Stein Eriksen. A Norwegian, Stein was the first ski racer from outside the Alps to win an Olympic medal in Alpine skiing when he won gold and silver medals at the 1952 Olympic Games held in Oslo, Norway. This made him a national hero. He won three gold medals (slalom, giant slalom, and combined) at the 1954 World Skiing Championships, and then retired from ski racing at age twenty-six. He leveraged his fame and charisma into a remarkably successful career as a ski school director and resort operator in the United States.

Stein's good looks and effortless technique established a prototype for the modern image of the ski instructor—the bronzed, blond god of the slopes—and made him into the first one-name celebrity of the ski world. When people said the name "Stein," everyone knew instantly whom they were talking about.

In the late 1950s, Stein was ski school director at Aspen Highlands—the perfect position for someone with his international celebrity and outgoing personality. His association with it lent credibility to the brand-new resort. At that time, the American ski industry had only been in operation for about ten years. There were a handful of ski resorts in the U.S. that had been established in the 1930s, like Alta, Sun Valley and Sugar Bowl, but the great majority of resorts in the United States started

Stein parlayed his Olympic fame, personality and good looks into a very successful career.

operation after World War II, many founded by returning war veterans exposed to the widespread popularity of skiing in Europe, who saw an opportunity to develop ski resorts back home. Many, like Pete Seibert at Vail and Bill Healy at Mt. Bachelor, had been ski troopers in the 10th Mountain Division and had trained in Colorado then fought in the Alps late in the war. Another 10th Mountain Division veteran, Friedl Pfeifer, partnered with industrialist Walter Paepcke to transform the sleepy silver-mining town of Aspen, Colorado into a ski resort. Aspen Mountain opened in 1946 and Aspen Highlands followed in 1958.

For official purposes, I first entered the United States when I landed in New York on the *Cristoforo Colombo* in 1959, then took the train to Denver and a bus to Aspen. "Auditioning" for Stein was an experience—more a test of survival than of teaching skill. Stein skied at top speed from hard-packed snow into deep powder, moguls, crud—basically every varying condition he could find—and I was expected to keep up with him. I guess the theory was that if I could ski any condition he could find with some measure of competence, I was probably capable of teaching people to do the same. In any event, I survived the test, and Stein offered me a job on the ski school, which was composed of a bunch of Norwegian guys and young women, an Austrian, Hans Forstner, and an American, Peter Brinkman, who later became ski school director at Heavenly Valley.

It is unusual for Hollywood to give an accurate impression of a particular job or a lifestyle, but when it comes to the life of an Aspen ski instructor in the late '50s and early '60s, they pretty much got it right. Aspen was, then as now, the winter home of a great many extraordinarily rich people, many of whom were from Texas. There was a considerable population of wealthy married women from Dallas, Houston, and Midland whose husbands had shipped them off to their Aspen homes for the winter to "learn to ski." They accounted for a lot of steady private lesson business for the ski school, and were eager to socialize with the ski instructors when not on the slopes. The instructors, being a young, outgoing bunch, were in party mode pretty much all the time. When you went to a party, it was expected that you would bring something to drink, and a lot of the time there would be a large punch bowl into which everyone's contribution would be emptied. Beer, wine, whiskey, gin—it did not matter. It all got poured into the bowl, combined into one terrible but very alcoholic brew that was usually served up in coffee cups. This was not favorable to getting up early the next day looking and feeling your best; but being young and resilient, we all managed most of the time.

Stein's ski school at Aspen Highlands attracted well-to-do clients whose skiing ability ranged from poor to pretty good. Most did not want to work too hard at becoming better skiers. They were content to take long lunches and end the day early and have drinks with their instructors. They loved the fact that most of the instructors were European—an accent gave an automatic impression of skill, charm and sophistication. We were occasionally called upon to go above and beyond our mission of just teaching people to ski. I had one student who was very determined to become a better skier, and never wanted to quit early and have a drink, unless it was chocolate milk. She was four years old, and I gave her private lessons for a week so her parents—who were very good skiers—could ski on their own without any concern for her. I was basically a nanny for a week, but the little girl and I had a lot of fun each day. By the end of the week, she could ski anywhere on the mountain. She was so appreciative that a few weeks later I got a wonderful card from her.

For My Hans Who Can Ski Backwards

I was very pleased to receive this thank-you card from my little student.

Thanks to Aspen's great snow and international atmosphere, a steady stream of top ski racers from around the world came through town to ski and party. Stein knew them all, and would introduce them around to the mutual delight of the young athletes and the bored ladies from Texas. The Olympian and four-time Hahnenkamm winner, the Austrian skier Anderl Molterer, was one, and another was a young Karl Schranz, a phenomenal downhiller who had already won the Arlberg-Kandahar several times on his way to nine wins over the course of his career, as well as four victories in the Hahnenkamm and an equal number at the Lauberhorn. He was terrifically talented and strong. One of my most distinct memories of my time in Aspen was skiing with Karl Schranz one day and (foolishly) following him down a steep, bumpy run which he, of course, took straight. We had only just dropped on to the run when I realized I had made a huge mistake and that I was in way over my head; but I held on, barely keeping it together, and finished the run upright out of sheer luck. Another instructor had watched the two of us from the lift and word got around that, "That Burkhart guy is crazy!"

In the winter of 1960, the Olympic Games were being held in Squaw Valley, California—a reasonably short trip from Aspen—so Stein and I went to Squaw as spectators. I do not know how Stein got there—he probably flew—but I took the Greyhound bus. One of the Norwegian Nordic skiers was a no-show, and Stein managed to procure their athlete credential for me, so I could walk into any of the venues to watch the events and could even go to the evening entertainment in the Athlete's Center. This would no doubt get you thrown in jail today and would prompt an investigation into the failure of the security and credential system, but in 1960 the athlete's passes were simple printed cards with no pictures on them:

It was a much simpler time. I went to the opening ceremonies and could see the U.S. Vice President Richard M. Nixon sitting in the front row with Avery Brundage, president of the International Olympic Committee, and Alex Cushing, the owner of the Squaw Valley ski resort. I went to the hockey game where the United States played the U.S.S.R. The arena was packed and deafeningly loud as the U.S. tied the score in the second period, then scored the go-ahead goal with five minutes to play and hung on to win—a shocking upset of the Soviets, who had been heavily favored to win the gold medal. This set the U.S. team up to win the gold medal if they could defeat Czechoslovakia, which they did the following morning in a similarly thrilling fashion. Trailing 4-3 at the end of the second period, they scored six unanswered goals in the third period to beat the Czechs 9-4.

Olympic Opening Ceremonies in Blyth Arena with Red Dog Ridge in the background.

Stein was friends with the Bogner family, who were famous as ski competitors but even better-known for their skiwear company. Willy Bogner Sr. had been a successful cross-country ski racer and had outfitted the German Ski Team in his clothing for the 1936 Olympic Games in Garmisch-Partenkirchen. He'd also taken part in the Olympic Games as a competitor. (He won sixth- and twelfth-place finishes.) In the early 1950s, his wife, Maria, had invented stretch pants, revolutionizing the ski apparel business—but the pants were also favored as street clothes by movie stars like Ingrid Bergman, Jayne Mansfield, and Marilyn Monroe. This created international sensation and demand.

Willy Bogner Jr. competed in the Squaw Valley Olympic Games with mixed results. Stein and I were with the senior Bogners on the afternoon that the men's slalom race was being held on Exhibition run. After the first run, Willy Jr. was in the lead, and the German spectators were thrilled at the prospect of taking home a gold medal to add to the gold collected by Heidi Biebl for her win in the Ladies' Downhill early in the Games. Willy's mother had no illusions. "Watch," she said to Stein. "He's going to go out in the second run." Maria was right. Willy Jr. missed a gate in the second run and was disqualified. He also DQ'ed in the giant slalom, but had a respectable ninth place finish in the Men's Downhill. Willy Jr. had a modestly successful career as a ski racer, but found greater success as a film-maker and cinematographer, with several ski movies and James Bond skiing sequences to his credit.

Willy Jr.'s career as a filmmaker has an unfortunate black mark on it. In 1964, while making "Ski Fascination," he was filming with a group of world-class ski racers near St. Moritz when an avalanche buried several members of the group. Bogner's girlfriend Barbi Henneberger (who'd won a bronze medal in Squaw Valley) was killed, as was Buddy Werner, generally considered to be the first world-class ski racer from the United States and winner of the 1959 Hahnenkamm downhill. Bogner was tried in a Swiss court for homicide by negligence because he had disregarded avalanche danger warnings for the area. He was initially acquitted, but later found guilty of manslaughter by negligence after the prosecution appealed the first verdict. He received a suspended sentence.

PLEASE REFER TO THIS FILE NUMBER

UNITED STATES DEPARTMENT OF JUSTICE
IMMIGRATION AND NATURALIZATION SERVICE
437 Post Office Building
Denver 2, Colorado
February 3, 1960

A11 937 072

Mr. Hans Anton Burkhart
200 East Cooper Street,
Aspen, Colorado.

Dear Sir:

This office is pleased to advise you that your application for status as a permanent resident of the United States has been approved by this Service.

A Form I-151, Alien Registration Receipt card, evidencing that you are now a lawful permanent resident of the United States, is being prepared and will be forwarded to you under separate cover in the near future.

Yours very truly,

John T. Clingan
District Director

By: Walter F. Weir
Walter F. Weir
Immigrant Inspector

Enclosures.

Stein was so well connected that when I mentioned that I would like to get a "green card," he made a few calls and told me to go to Denver and fill out an application. A month or so later I got this letter telling me that my application had been approved!

Lake Tahoe

At the end of the 1960 ski season, I left Aspen and headed west to California and Lake Tahoe. My experience at the Olympics had left me with a good impression of California and the Sierra, and I wanted to stay in the United States and work, so it seemed like a good destination. The Squaw Valley Olympic Organizing Committee had brought in a crew of sailors from the U.S. Navy's Construction Battalions—the "Seabees"— to build various infrastructure projects for the Games, which were to take place the next

Olympic venues with the compacted snow parking lots in the meadow at the upper left of the picture.

season. The Seabees had earned a great reputation for problem solving during World War II, and they brought that same creativity to helping to produce an Olympic Games in the High Sierra. Faced with the need to build huge parking lots to accommodate tens of thousands of Olympic Games spectators, they concocted a mixture of snow and sawdust (available, free, in virtually unlimited quantities from the sawmills in Truckee, Loyalton, and Quincy) that could be compacted to build an enormous temporary parking lot in the Squaw Valley meadow. The resulting surface was more durable and resistant to melting in the sun than compacted snow alone—at least until a few weeks before the Games, when a warm Pacific storm brought torrential rain to the valley, washing away all the Seabees' hard work. Fortunately, subsequent storms replenished the snowpack, allowing the Seabees to import additional loads of sawdust and rebuild the parking lot, which provided excellent service through the Games.

When winter ended, thousands of cubic yards of sawdust in the meadow needed to be removed—double the amount that should have been required, thanks to the pre-Olympic deluge. On flat areas in the meadow, the State of California brought in heavy equipment to scrape up and remove most of the sawdust, but in the creeks and drainages, it had to be shoveled out onto the flats by hand for removal. I got a job shoveling sawdust for the state for five dollars an hour, which was an exceptionally good wage for 1960, when minimum wage was one dollar and fifteen cents an hour. Five dollars an hour in 1960 was equivalent to about forty-three dollars an hour in 2020.

I was always looking for a job—I liked to have two or three jobs at the same time—and I heard about a job helping to take care of the boats at the Kaiser Estate on the West Shore of Lake Tahoe. I did not really know anything about boats, but an older guy who took care of the boats worked there. We hit it off and he hired me. Sometimes you meet someone and find that you have a good rapport with them right away, and this was one of those situations. I showed up on time every day and kept the boats immaculately clean, and that was enough. One day, the boat mechanic needed to go to Tahoe City to get a part and asked if I wanted to go along. We took one of the boats, motored over to the marina in Tahoe City and picked up the part. As we were coming back, he asked if I wanted to water ski. I told him I had never water skied and had no idea how to do it. "It's easy," he said, "and you're a ski instructor—you'll figure it out right away." I agreed to give it a try and—even though I was not a good swimmer—jumped into the lake and got my feet into the skis. He tossed me the rope. I got up on the first try and waterskied all the way back to the Kaiser's dock.

In the fall of 1960, I returned to Aspen Highlands and Stein's ski school, but for me the experience and lifestyle had lost a lot of the excitement of the first year. I had a girlfriend and had grown tired of the party scene, so a lot of the initial appeal of the ski instructor lifestyle had diminished. One day while teaching a private lesson, I broke one of my poles, so when we got to the bottom, I went into the ski rental shop (another of Stein's enterprises) and asked if I could borrow a pole. They were only too happy to help one of the instructors, and passed the word to Stein that they had done so. Although I returned the pole at the end of the day, Stein charged me for it. I knew it was time to move on. I gave Stein a week's notice and quit.

I headed back to California in my VW Bug, eager to find work. Hot on the heels of the Olympics at Squaw Valley, a brand-new ski area was in the works in the valley to the south of Squaw Valley. John Reily—who'd worked on a plan to build a ski area at the headwaters of Bear Creek since 1957—had set up the corporation called Alpine Meadows of Tahoe. He'd secured long-term leases on private land and a special use permit from the U.S. Forest Service to build a chairlift, several surface lifts, and base facilities. The installation contractor for the Alpine Meadows lifts was Lowell Northrop, who had built several of the lifts at

NEAR DEATH EXPERIENCE #5

HEAD-ON COLLISION IN THE VOLKSWAGEN BUG

I had driven west to Lake Tahoe from Aspen in my Volkswagen Bug and had several jobs during the summer of 1961—including removing sawdust from the Squaw Valley Meadow for the State of California and working on the boats at the Kaiser Estate. Fritz Frey was teaching skiing at Mammoth Mountain in the winter and was living in Tahoe for the summer. Fritz and I were working on the sawdust project together and one weekend went to Reno to look around. On the way back, we drove through Truckee and decided to go to Tahoe City. As we were driving south on California State Route 89—just about where the Alpine Meadows turnoff is now—we were hit head-on by a pickup truck coming the other way. The passenger side door popped open and Fritz was ejected from the Bug. I was knocked unconscious and was stuck in the car. The fire department came from Tahoe City, along with an ambulance from Truckee, and they extricated me and took me to Tahoe Forest Hospital in Truckee. When I came to, the nurse told me where I was and that I had been unconscious for a day and a half. I had broken my shoulder, had a bad concussion, and was bruised, but was otherwise okay.

Squaw Valley and managed lift maintenance at Squaw for the Olympics. The plan was to build a Riblet chairlift and two Poma surface lifts.

Although Alpine Meadows of Tahoe had permits to build the lifts, the amount of stock sold had not yet reached the threshold at which funds could be released, so work did not begin until July 1961. Fritz Frey and I were hired to dig holes for the towers. Lowell had detailed specifications for the tower holes, some of which had to be angled because the tower installed in that hole would be at an angle instead of vertical, and Lowell didn't want to use a spoonful more concrete than the specification required.

The road from California State Route 89 to the ski area site was terrible: It took an hour to drive the three miles. To save time, Fritz and I camped at the construction site so that we could get an early start every morning. We were paid $160 per hole, which was (for us, anyway) a lot of money. We would get up in the morning and one of us would cook breakfast while the other went to the hole we were working on to start the day's digging. When the food was ready, the cook would eat and then take over digging while the other went to

NEAR DEATH EXPERIENCE #6

ALPINE MEADOWS

As Alpine Meadows of Tahoe was preparing to build the first lifts, Lowell Northrup was building roads and doing infrastructure work. I was a laborer and general helper for Lowell—fueling the equipment, shoveling—whatever needed to be done. One day, Lowell was running a bulldozer and asked me to move a pickup truck so that he could move the dozer farther down the road, below where the truck was parked. I got in and backed the pickup down the road, but did not see a large hole below and behind the truck. When the rear tire of the truck went into the hole, it tilted the pickup sharply, and the truck rolled sideways off the edge of the road and down the slope below the road. One of the other guys on the crew was watching from farther down the road, and he later said that the pickup had rolled over seven times. When the truck came to a stop, I walked out through the popped-out windshield, much to the surprise of the other guys on the crew who thought I was probably dead. Even though there was no seat belt, and I was rattling around in the cab while the truck was rolling, I was completely fine; a few scratches, but I worked for the rest of the day.

camp and ate breakfast. We dug as deep as we could by ourselves (six or seven feet) and then teamed up—one of us in the hole shoveling the dirt into a bucket and the other pulling the bucket up with a rope and emptying the spoils. We could each dig a hole every day, so the project was moving along on time and Lowell—a man who was sparing with his praise— was pleased with our work.

That winter, I returned to Aspen, but I had no interest in working for Stein, and perhaps would not have been offered the opportunity after having quit the previous spring. That winter, I skied at Aspen Mountain instead of Aspen Highlands, and got a job working nights at one of the ski shops tuning skis. I had made a good bit of money the previous summer, and while the ski shop job did not pay that much, I had a season pass and paid my expenses. It was one of the only times when I was able to live something of a "ski bum" life-style. The night job allowed me the ability to ski every day.

I had gotten to know the Olympian, Anderl Molterer, while working for Stein. After retiring from competition in 1960, he had become the Ski Racing Director for Aspen Skiing Company. While he had been Austrian National Champion eleven times and had medaled in downhill and giant slalom at the 1956 Olympics in Cortina, his ability to ski moguls was what fascinated me. One of the iconic runs on Aspen Mountain, "Ruthie's Run," was the site of Aspen's World Cup courses for decades. One day Molterer and I took a run on Ruthie's, which was deep in moguls. Molterer skied it in his usual smooth and elegant style, and I followed him, eager to soak up the nuances of his technique. Even though I was in over my head, I skied the moguls better than I ever had before, and made it to the bottom without crashing. It was the greatest skiing challenge I had conquered up to that time, and I could not help but be proud of myself for pulling it off.

There was some rivalry between the Aspen Mountain Ski School and Stein's ski school at Aspen Highlands, and I kind of exploited that. I let the people at the Aspen Mountain Ski School know that I had worked for Stein for a couple of winters, but was kind of fed up with him. I let them know that I would be happy to teach private lessons if someone were interested. It paid off when someone came looking for an instructor to teach private lessons for their friend for a week.

I arranged to meet my student, "Jim," the next morning, and was impressed right away. Six feet seven inches tall, he was a guy who really stood out in a crowd. I saw right away that people took notice of him. When we were in a lift line or near other people, everyone looked at him—but I chalked it up to his size and that he was very handsome and had a nice smile. We got along well: He was a friendly, nice guy who had a good sense of humor and a big laugh. He had some difficulty skiing because of his size and had been wounded in the leg in the amphibious landing on Anzio Beach during the war. (They ordered him out of the landing craft first to see how deep the water was.) But he honestly did his best and got to be a decent skier in the week that I gave him lessons. I did not watch television, so it took a while to find out that the reason people were so fascinated with him was that he was a very well-known actor and that the show that he starred in was the most popular show on television. The big guy was James Arness, who played U.S. Marshal Matt Dillon on Gunsmoke from 1955 until 1975.

I had been contacting lift manufacturers in Europe, asking if any that were planning projects in the U.S. were looking for someone who spoke German and English and had a green card allowing them to work in the United States. This relieved the manufacturer of a good bit of potentially aggravating effort, so it was a good pitch. In response, I received a letter from a German company, Pohlig Heckel Bleichert (PHB), which had sold two gondolas in the U.S. Valuing my experience on the projects in Banff and Oberammergau, they offered me a choice of working on a project in Park City, Utah or one in Squaw Valley. The catch was that the Squaw project would not start until the following spring. I told them I wanted to work at Squaw Valley.

You can see both types of cabin in this photograph—some have a more angular shape to the bottom of the cabin, while others are rounded.

At the end of the winter of 1962, I headed west to work on the PHB gondola project at Squaw Valley. PHB was strategic in organizing the project, and in some ways was way ahead of its time in the use of sourcing parts and particular subcontracted work. PHB hired me to be the local on-site contact well ahead of the start of the work, so I could provide any surveying needed by the concrete subcontractor, receive and stage parts shipments from Germany, and coordinate the project on their behalf.

That season had experienced heavier than normal snowfall, so the surveying and work on tower foundations was delayed somewhat until we could access the tower sites and get up the road. I had a profile and a topographic map. The major survey benchmarks for the lift had been set by a surveying company, and an engineering company in Reno drew up the tower foundation specifications according to calculations provided them by PHB. This solved the problem of having the engineering stamped by an engineer licensed in the local jurisdiction. A concrete subcontractor formed and poured the foundations using blueprints from the engineers and PHB. They got most of the twenty-three towers finished that fall, leaving only a few to be completed the following spring. PHB had the towers manufactured in Salt Lake City and used cabins manufactured by a company called Atlas in Utah. The Squaw Valley Ski Resort owner, Alex Cushing, did not like the first cabins we received, and PHB was able to get Atlas to revise the design and provide a different model for the remainder of the order. That is why the gondola had two different types of cabins.

The PHB gondola transformed the skiing experience at Squaw Valley.

I stayed in Squaw Valley that winter and started receiving parts shipments in the spring of 1963 ahead of the arrival of the PHB crew. I hired some local laborers to work on the project. Les Guilford, who worked on the Squaw Valley gondola crew for a few years, was one. Another was a college student named Paul Minasian, who then went to law school and became one of Squaw Valley Ski Corporation's attorneys. Once the PHB crew arrived, we assembled the towers; installed the drive, return equipment, and line machinery; and pulled the haul rope. It was really a reasonably easy project. Distributing the work over two building seasons made it possible to work at a reasonable pace without undue stress.

Looking back, it is easy to forget that—for the time—the PHB gondola at Squaw Valley was an advanced, state-of-the-art lift. There were other gondolas in the U.S., but most—like the "Magic Carpet" at Sugar Bowl—had been constructed with repurposed ore transport machinery from defunct mining operations, and they tended to be somewhat crude and rough. The first purpose-built passenger gondola in the United States had been constructed only five years earlier at Wildcat ski area in New Hampshire. The PHB lift was quite sophisticated. Alex Cushing was concerned that his lift maintenance crew did not have the skills to maintain the new lift, and asked PHB if they could provide someone to stay for the winter to babysit the new lift, train the operators, and instruct the lift maintenance staff. The other guys working for PHB were married and were looking forward to returning to Germany at the conclusion of the project, so they suggested that I do the operational and maintenance training, which was fine with me.

The gondola was an ambitious project and greatly improved the resort's customer experience. With a lower terminal attached to the main base lodge and a top terminal within a mid-mountain lodge, the gondola brought Squaw Valley to a level of sophistication available at only a handful of other resorts in North America. This was very satisfying to Alex, who loved nothing more than being able to boast about having the most advanced, biggest, and best lifts. Skiers loved the four-passenger gondola, and Alex could host black-tie parties at the top of his mountain where guests could literally get into the gondola cabin at the bottom of the mountain in formal wear and emerge inside the mid-mountain lodge, which was called "Gold Coast" after the ultra-wealthy North Shore of New York's Long Island, where, coincidentally, Alex's family had a home. Gold Coast had a restaurant, a bar that overlooked the North Bowl on Headwall, and a semi-circular observation room on the second floor looking out over Squaw Peak and Siberia Bowl.

It's difficult to overstate the impact of the 1964 PHB gondola on the development of Squaw Valley as a resort. It allowed skiers to travel nearly two miles up the mountain protected from wind and snow and, with the construction of the Gold Coast Lodge, would create the dual-elevation resort concept that we take for granted today.

The gondola with Olympic House and Blyth Arena in the background. The circular Rotunda off the Olympic House deck offered radiant heating for outdoor dining in the winter—very, very chic by ski resort standards in the 1960's.

Alex Cushing and the 1960 Olympic Games

Born in 1913, Alexander Cochrane Cushing was the grandson of a wealthy Boston tea merchant and the son of a fine art painter. He grew up on the Upper East Side of Manhattan, attended Groton, Harvard University, and Harvard Law School. After graduating from law school, he practiced law, working at the U.S. Department of State and the U. S. Department of Justice, where he argued a case before the U.S. Supreme Court—the youngest lawyer to have done so at that time (although his argument to the Court must have been less than persuasive, because he lost)—and then went into private practice with the Wall Street firm Davis, Polk. With the outbreak of World War II, Alex enlisted in the U.S. Navy, serving in South America and the Pacific. He left the navy at the end of the war with the rank of Lieutenant Commander.

Following the war, Alex resumed his law practice at Davis, Polk, but the life of an attorney—even one working for a prestigious, old-line firm—simply did not measure up to the adventure that he had experienced while in the navy, and he began seeking a business and lifestyle that would offer excitement and reward. American GIs serving in Europe had seen the well-developed Alpine resorts there, and had come home from the war with dreams of building ski resorts in the United States. Cushing saw the opportunity to get into the ski business as a way of escaping the lucrative but predictable life of a lawyer. On a trip to the West, Cushing and his best friend and brother-in-law, Alexander McFadden (they were married to sisters) were skiing at Sugar Bowl. Alex had twisted his ankle the day prior and was playing the piano in the bar, entertaining the après ski crowd, which included Wayne Poulsen. From Reno, Nevada, Poulsen was a veteran ski racer and ski jumper at the University of Nevada. When asked by Cushing where the best ski terrain in the West could be found, he replied that he owned land near Lake Tahoe that he believed had the potential to be the best ski resort in North America. Cushing, McFadden, and Poulsen hiked into Squaw Valley from State Route 89 to look at Poulsen's land and the mountain. Cushing and

Alex in 1959.

McFadden were impressed—McFadden telling his friend, "you could fit *two* Sun Valleys in here…." Wheels were set in motion that would lead to the development of a world-class ski resort at Squaw Valley. Sadly, McFadden would not live to see his friend's success in the ski business. In February 1948, McFadden and Cushing were vacationing in Aspen with their wives and engaged the director of the Aspen Ski School and one of the instructors to take them skiing off-piste on Independence Pass. Although the local professionals cautioned of avalanche risk, Cushing and McFadden insisted they wanted a real "test of their skill."[1] Skiing late in the afternoon, the party triggered a slide and McFadden was caught in it and vanished. The ski instructor skied down to the highway and had a passing motorist drive into Aspen and spread the word that there had been an avalanche. The village responded by sending over one hundred searchers—skiers, townspeople, and sheriff's deputies—who searched by torchlight for fourteen hours, probing and digging trenches in the avalanche rubble before finding McFadden's body buried under ten feet of snow.

Although heartbroken by the loss of his best friend (for the rest of his life, Alex couldn't speak of the event without breaking down in tears), Alex raised all the money that he and his wife, Justine, could get their hands on, a total of about $400,000—the majority of which was her inheritance—and, working in partnership with Poulsen, built a Heron double chairlift, a rope tow, and a modest lodge. Squaw Valley Ski Resort opened for skiing on Thanksgiving of 1949.

In the first several years the resort was beset with all kinds of disasters. Alex always wanted the biggest and the best of everything, and while the Squaw One chairlift was billed the "largest in the world," and had been optimally located for skiing and sightseeing, avalanche activity had not been given adequate consideration, so in the first few years of operation, the lift was repeatedly damaged by avalanches that closed it for weeks at a time. The fickle Sierra Nevada climate produced copious snowpacks; but warm, wet storms from the Pacific Ocean could also bring heavy rain during the winter, washing out the bridges on the only road up the valley, and flooding the Squaw Valley Lodge. There was no technology to groom the ski slopes other than slide-slipping, so the skiing was much better suited to experienced, athletic skiers than beginners. Alex's small lodging operation, the Squaw Valley Lodge, had only a few rooms, so most skiers drove in from Tahoe City, Truckee, or Reno to ski. Nevertheless, the ski area was modestly successful, and Alex, who believed that the role of a ski area oper-

During the first several years of operation, Squaw One, the only chairlift, was buried repeatedly by avalanches—the only way it could be reopened was digging the line out by hand.

ator was to be in the "uphill transportation business" hired a world-renowned skier, Emile Allais, to run the ski school, and enjoyed the fruits of his labor. Cushing's relationship with Wayne Poulsen had never been good—the two had vastly different visions for the resort—and the partnership soon dissolved with Cushing taking the ski resort and six hundred forty acres of land that Poulsen had brought to the partnership and Poulsen winding up with land in the valley that could be subdivided and sold for residential lots. The rancor between the two would never resolve.

One morning in 1954, Alex read in the *San Francisco Chronicle* that the City of Reno was submitting a bid to host the 1960 Olympic Winter Games. Alex had a keen eye for a promotional opportunity and realized that putting in a similar bid would generate considerable free (and needed) publicity for Squaw Valley, so he made a few calls. Just as anticipated, the unlikely notion that Squaw Valley could play host to international competition created a lot of attention. Alex had intended to float the idea only as a publicity stunt: "I had no more interest in getting the Olympics than the man on the moon," he said, but others took the idea seriously. Ski instructor Joe Marillac—a national hero in France for his exploits as an Alpinist and resistance fighter during World War II—was a believer: "You have the mountain, and the rest can be built!"

Skiing at Squaw Valley in 1950-51 seems like a bargain at \$4.00 per day on the world's longest chairlift or \$36 for four nights lodging, meals and lift tickets!

Encouraged, Cushing decided to ride the publicity tsunami for all it was worth, and prepared a presentation for the U.S. Olympic Committee, going up against well-established resorts like Lake Placid, Sun Valley, and Aspen. Although he got a frosty reception—one Olympic Committee member called Squaw Valley a "figment of Cushing's imagination" and another said the fledgling resort was "a glorified picnic area"—Cushing convinced the committee members to make Squaw Valley the United States' nominee for the 1960 Olympic Games.

His salesmanship was called upon when the International Olympic Committee convened in Paris to award the Winter Games, but Alex was well prepared. The materials describing each prospective host resort's bid had traditionally been prepared in English, French, and German, but Alex realized that all the German speaking countries were proposing their own resorts as hosts, so he had the Squaw Valley bid documents prepared in English, French, and Spanish. He hired a friend to meet with the South American delegates in their home countries ahead of the Paris meeting and pitch them on an Olympic Games in the Western Hemisphere, sealing the deal when they saw to their delight that, for the first time, the Olympic bid was being presented in their native languages. Alex had a huge scale model made of the mountain and the proposed Olympic facilities, and shipped them to Paris, but discovered on arrival that the model was too large to fit through the doors of the hotel in which the Olympic presentations would be made. He rented space down the street where the model could be displayed, and found that the few minutes he spent with each of the delegates while they walked to look at the model gave him an opportunity to develop a relationship with them that eventually paid off: The committee members—after several rounds of voting—awarded the 1960 Winter Games to the most unlikely of host sites, Squaw Valley.

Much has been said and written about the 1960 Olympic Games. Many people believe that the Squaw Valley Games were the best Winter Games ever held, because most of the events were held in a concentrated area—ticket holders for a skating event could easily watch an Alpine skiing event or ski jumping. Unlike previous Winter Games held in Europe, the athletes and officials were housed together in dormitories and ate in a congregate dining hall, which encouraged social interaction between athletes from different sports and nations. There was no "Italian Hotel" or "Swedish Hotel." Although the Cold War between the United State and the USSR was at its peak, there was a true feeling of comradery among

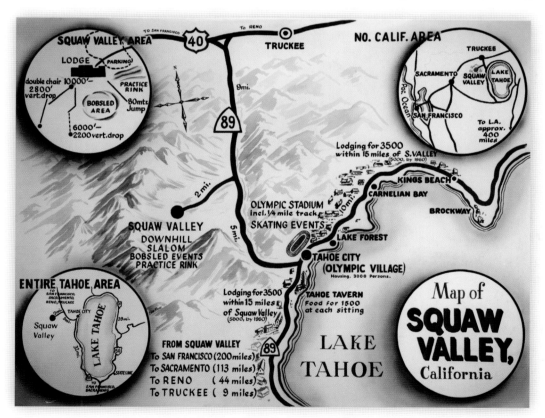

The early planning for the Games included bobsled competition and proposed building a stadium and holding the skating events in Tahoe City.

the athletes. After the United States hockey team beat the USSR and was preparing to play Czechoslovakia for the gold medal, the Russians advised them to have a tank of oxygen in the locker room that would allow them to more efficiently recover between periods—because at 6,200 feet elevation, the air had less oxygen in it. Athletes with more oxygen in their blood could compete more efficiently.

Characteristic of any enterprise with which he was associated, Alex's involvement with the Olympic Games was not without controversy. In September 1955, he'd been appointed president of the Olympic Organizing Committee, and presided over the first meeting of that committee, but in early January of 1956, he resigned as president and as a member of the committee board of directors. Several other members of the committee resigned as well, "to eliminate problems of dual interest," as the final report of the organizing committee stated. A European account was more candid: "On September 7, 1955, the Organizing Committee was established in San Francisco. Alec Cushing became the president. The "Father of the

This rendering of the mountain and base facilities gave an accurate representation of the courses and venues.

Games" proved to have a good nose as a land speculator, but his tendency to use the approved funds for his own interests was his undoing. After serious disputes, Cushing was forced to resign on January 5, 1956."[2]

Raising the money to build facilities for the Games was taking longer than anticipated and International Olympic Committee president Avery Brundage, an American, threatened to withdraw approval for the Games and award them by forfeit to Innsbruck, Austria unless additional money was committed by April 3, 1956. The Organizing Committee turned up the heat on the California legislature and, amazingly, on April 3—hours before Brundage's deadline—California Governor Goodwin Knight signed the state budget including an allocation of $4 million for the Games. On April 4, Brundage stated that the Games now "officially" belonged to California.

In total, the State of California committed $8.99 million for the Games, the federal government $3.5 million for the construction of Blyth Arena, the State of Nevada $400,000. Corporate cash and in-kind donations totaled about $2.5 million. The U.S. Department of Defense was authorized to spend $900,000 to assist in staging the Games. The total public expenditure was about $15,290,000. The California Olympic Commission had established a policy that public funds could be used to construct permanent facilities only on public lands, which complicated the alignment and ownership of the lifts and buildings constructed for the Games, but Alex managed to come out of the Games with a greatly improved and now internationally famous resort. Not a bad outcome for what started as—literally—a publicity stunt.

Alex was a complicated and interesting person, and my relationship with him—starting in 1963 and continuing for nearly 40 years until 2002—was a remarkable experience that encompassed the full range of emotions. Together, we built one of the greatest ski resorts in North America, and we did things that no one else in the American ski industry had done. But as much as each of us complemented the other and brought their game to a new level, we had deep disagreements that, more than once, wound up in court—and he always lost.

Our backgrounds could not have been more different. Alex came from generations of wealth and privilege—the term "Boston Brahmin" was coined to describe families like the Cushings. His family lived in Manhattan, just off Park Avenue, literally two blocks from Central Park. His father died when he was three and his mother was sickly, so he was largely raised by nannies and his older siblings, and went off to boarding school at a young age. He had an excellent education and the social and professional connections that virtually guaranteed success and continued wealth.

My childhood in a small town in Germany, by comparison, was unsophisticated and rooted in my extended family, anchored by my grandfather's store, which had opened in the 19th century and is still in family operation today. Oberammergau was—and is—a village, where practically everyone knows everyone else. My family was not "poor;" we just did not have any money. From the time I was a young boy, I was always working—it was simply the culture of my family and our community. After the eighth grade I paid for my own education, using money I earned working at my grandfather's store. When I was able to work outside the family, I did whatever I could to make a living. My fascination with lifts started early and I used every opportunity to learn everything I could and develop my skills and understanding by working on a variety of lift projects.

Alex had a story he loved to tell about how we met. In 1963, as construction of the PHB four-passenger gondola at Squaw Valley was nearing completion, Alex became uneasy about the capacity of his employees to operate and maintain the new lift. It was considerably more demanding and complex than the existing lift inventory, which consisted of a handful of fixed-grip double chairlifts and a few rope tows. He wandered over to the lower terminal, found the superintendent for the installation, and asked if there was anyone whom he could hire to stay on when the project was done to run and maintain the gondola. "Yes, there is," was the reply. "Who?" asked Alex. "That man: Burkhart," said the superintendent, pointing to a rock face below Tower 4. I had rappelled down the cliff and was drilling into the face while dangling from the rope. Alex, apparently, was impressed and made it a point to track me down later and lay out his proposal. With that I became a Squaw Valley employee.

Squaw Valley in the 1960s

When I took the job operating and maintaining the gondola, I could hardly have anticipated that my relationship with the Squaw Valley Ski Resort and Alex Cushing would continue for nearly forty years. The first few years were a clear indication of Alex's management style, but at the time I was too young and inexperienced to recognize it. Alex's attention to the ski area and to specific elements of the operation was highly variable. He lived in the valley some of the time, but following the Olympics, he had become something of an international celebrity, and enjoyed that renown when he traveled. He entrusted operation of the business to John Buchman in his absence. John was a unique character and an odd choice to help operate a ski resort and make management-level decisions on a day-to-day basis, because as far as I know, he had never skied. John had worked in a lumber yard and was part-owner of an auto repair business in New Jersey—a far cry from the life he would soon be living in California's Sierra Nevada.

John and Alex met when John was a taxi driver in New York City and picked Alex up as a customer. John was looking to make a change in his life, and it is a good indication of Alex's charisma that he could meet a cabdriver and, over the course of a taxi ride, convince him to move 3,000 miles west, leaving everything familiar behind, to help a total stranger open a resort dedicated to a sport he had never tried and in which he had no interest.

John had absolute loyalty to Alex, however, and from the time he came to work at the resort, he lived on the premises, worked seven days a week, and rarely took a vacation. He was a great fan of the San Francisco Giants baseball team and knew the team's owner at the time the team moved to California from New York in 1958. He lived with his little dog, Gus, in a small house that was constructed prior to the Olympics to promote the Winter Games that were scheduled to be held in 1968 in Grenoble, France. John managed the Squaw Valley Lodge. He held that title after he and Alex had bought a handful of surplus military barracks, and had them trucked to Squaw Valley then reassembled into a no-frills lodging property available for rentals when the ski resort opened. Prior to the Olympics, John scored a major coup by securing deposits from the major news outlets—*Time, Life, Look, Sports Illustrated, New York Times*, CBS television, etc.—for lodging their reporters and photographers during the Games. The deposit money was then used to almost double the size of the hotel.

John was also, briefly, the "Mayor of Squaw Valley" (even though the valley was, and still is, an unincorporated area in Placer County that has no mayor or city government). During the International Olympic Committee meetings in Paris to award the 1960 Games, a representative of a competing site raised the objection that Squaw Valley was nothing more than a ski resort (which was true) and stated that when the IOC designated an Olympic site, the agreement was with a town or municipality, not a commercial entity. Alex hurriedly found a telephone and called John in Squaw Valley—waking him up in the middle of the night—and said, "John—if anyone calls, you're the Mayor of Squaw Valley. Got it? The mayor."

"Whatever you say, Alex" replied John, hanging up and going back to sleep, probably wondering how he had been elected without ever running for office.

John was a steady presence in the office for decades, making sure the secretaries did not take too long a lunch and making the lift maintenance guys wipe the mud off their boots so they would not mess up the carpet. In the end, he probably knew more about running a ski area than anyone else who had never skied.

All of the operations of the mountain: lift operations, guest services, dispatch, lift maintenance and grooming were crammed into this tiny compound under the Squaw Peak and Cornice one lift terminals.

Alex believed that, as a ski resort owner, he was in the uphill transportation business and nothing else. The ski school was operated as a concession, as was the rental shop and the food and beverage operation—elements that other resorts had found to be important to the guest experience and potentially very profitable. For a while, Alex had two ski schools competing for customers at the resort—a "French technique" ski school operated by Stan Tomlinson and Declan Daly, and a "Graduated Length Method" ski school operated by the inventor of that instructional concept, Clif Taylor.

Alex was always keenly interested in new lifts, but once they were built, he didn't understand the need—and was reluctant to spend any money—to maintain them. "It's a brand-new lift," he would say about a lift built three years prior. "Why should I have to spend anything on it? It's fine." The lift maintenance crew had no workshop space, no tools, no air compressor or welding machine. They were good guys who worked hard, but there was little they could do without the tools and equipment to do the work. There were no radios, which made maintenance work on the lifts difficult and more dangerous than it needed to be, to say nothing of avalanche control or grooming.

One summer morning, Alex and I had driven up the mountain and were standing outside the upper terminal of the gondola at Gold Coast looking over toward North Bowl when we heard an odd noise that occurred at a particular interval, kind of a "click" then a thud. There was a tower on the Siberia lift a hundred yards or so away and the lift maintenance guys were running the lift. As each chair on the up-line got to the tower, it would hit the crossarm with the "click" sound and then fall off. Since we had no radios, I had no way to tell the guys at the lift to what was happening and that they needed to stop the lift.

Alex turned to me and said, "Is that how they take the chairs off?"

I replied, "No—I'll be right back." I jumped in the pickup and raced down to the bottom of the lift to tell them what was going on. The cable had derailed to the inside and as each chair reached the tower, the hanger would hit the first sheave and stop and the clip attaching the chair to the cable would be ripped out of the cable. By the time the lift stopped, more than twenty chairs were piled up around the base of the tower.

Every time I went to John Buchman to ask for money to buy tools or radios, his response was always, "Oh, we don't have any money." In the mid-1960s a young salesman for IBM in Carson City contacted the Squaw Valley Ski Corporation accounting department to tell them about IBM's products. He made a great sales pitch for us to buy a computer, a Model 40, which was about the size of a commercial refrigerator. He explained in detail all the amazing things we would be able to do with a computer. The accounting people found this compelling, indeed. I was a little skeptical, but I appreciated the accounting group's genuine desire to have the tools to be able to do their job better. I supported the idea, but of course we ran into John Buchman's favorite phrase, "Oh, we don't have any money...." I went to Alex with the idea and, although he thought I was out of my mind, he eventually gave in and allowed us to buy the computer. One of the burdensome tasks that the acquisition of the computer would allow us to do was processing our own payroll. (Previously, we'd paid employees by providing their hours to the Bank of America at the end of the pay period, and the bank delivered the checks. Although the accounting department had been willing to take this on, Alex was adamant about continuing to use Bank of America.)

The accounting staff—eager to put the new computer to the test—started doing a parallel run of payroll figures and comparing their results to those done by Bank of America. They

Gold Coast was the top terminal of the gondola and the only mid-mountain lodge in the 60's.

found that the bank was frequently incorrect—and the errors never seemed to be in our favor. After we brought that to Alex's attention, the pitch to buy the computer seemed a lot more sensible, and we brought the payroll processing in-house.

The gondola was working well and had transformed the resort operation. It opened an enormous amount of mountain-top skiing to beginners and intermediates, who could ride up the gondola, enjoy the views from the top of the mountain, and ski terrain that was well suited to their ability.

Alex was always looking to improve the lift network and in 1964 skiing on the upper mountain expanded to the west with the installation of the Emigrant and Shirley Lake lifts. The Gold Coast mid-mountain lodge was built in 1965 at the upper terminal of the gondola. The resort was taking shape as a large, modern operation with a lot of varied terrain. Slope grooming was virtually nonexistent, however. We had a couple of small crawler tractors made by Oliver Corporation that were about the size of a sedan with wide tracks that could drive reasonably well on snow. They had blades and could move snow up to a point, when they would simply run out of traction or flotation. We would take them out in pairs because they were constantly getting stuck, and if you were working with a buddy, you could pull each other out. There was a particular bottleneck on the trail from the top of the Squaw One lift to the bottom of the mountain—the "Tower 20 Traverse"—that accumulated a lot of snow in each storm and had to be plowed to keep the beginner and intermediate skiers from skiing down a difficult face and possibly going into a creek. To keep the traverse open, another Squaw Valley employee, Dick Reuter, and I would take the Oliver tractors to Tower 20 and plow for hours—in aggregate moving less snow than a single modern grooming machine could move in a half-hour. Often, the visibility was near zero and we were in an area that was dead center in the Headwall avalanche path, but the traverse had to be plowed. If you pushed the blade full of snow too far over the edge, the front of the Oliver would go off the compacted area and tip forward until you could not back up, then you would have to be pulled out by the other machine. If you got too aggressive and tried to push too much snow at once, the tracks would start spinning and you would have to back up and take another pass to fill in the hole you had created. It was an incredibly slow and inefficient process, but it was all we could do.

Dick Reuter soon became a legend at Squaw Valley as the consummate mountain man. A tall man with incredible strength, he had worked as a logger, and was tremendously skilled with a chain saw: The larger and more difficult the tree to be cut, the better he liked it. He was also a tough and reliable lift maintenance man who had a talent for keeping the finicky and primitive lifts in adjustment using what we called the "Dick Reuter Tool Kit"—a big adjustable wrench, a small adjustable wrench, a pry bar, and a big hammer: It was all he needed.

Dick worked at Squaw Valley for many years, and was wooed away by the opportunity to build a new ski area (with lots of big trees to cut) at Kirkwood, California south of Lake Tahoe beyond Carson Pass on California State Route 88. Kirkwood was remote—there was no power to the area and, even today, power for the entire community is generated onsite—but Dick did a terrific job of laying out the ski trails, building the lifts, and creating the ski resort from scratch. For that job at Kirkwood, Dick moved his young family to Woodford's, California, a tiny town south of Lake Tahoe, and made a daily commute over Carson Pass to the new ski area location. Eventually, as Kirkwood developed, the Reuters built a home there, but Dick would make a trip back to Squaw Valley every fall for deer season. He had a secret spot on the back side of Granite Chief Peak that he would hunt. Although other people owned Kirkwood, that ski area will always be thought of as Dick's unique creation.

There were many others who worked at Squaw Valley at that time who made indelible contributions to the lore of the resort. Leroy Hill worked for the California State Department of Beaches and Parks, and managed that agency's oversight of the state's assets in the valley. Leroy worked at Squaw Valley for fifty years, later as a ski instructor and Ski School Director when we started operating the ski school as a company department rather than a concession. Tom Nored did lift maintenance and later worked for Jan Kunczynski at lift engineering. He then built a successful pier construction business on Lake Tahoe. Danny Sprague was another mountain man who started working at Squaw as a teenager and could not get it out of his blood. He became a masterful welder/fabricator and a highly skilled heavy equipment operator. He worked at Squaw for decades on virtually all our major projects.

I met a Swiss girl named Hedi who worked at the Hofbrau, the restaurant and bar at the base area that operated in the building that had been the California Visitor Center during the Olympics. We were married in March of 1964 and had a son, Markus, before the year was over. I bought a lot on Squaw Valley Road from Sandy Poulsen for $6,200 and started building a house there in my spare time—evenings and weekends.

In 1965, I got word that my old employer, Bell Engineering, of Lucerne, would be building a new aerial tramway between the east side of the city of Albuquerque and Sandia Peak in New Mexico. An ambitious project—almost 4,000 feet of vertical and nearly two miles long—it would rival the most significant trams in Europe. Being obsessed with wire rope and lifts, I wanted to work on the project and was being offered the opportunity to do so. I met with Alex one evening, explained that the gondola was operating smoothly, we had a good crew who understood how to run and maintain it, and now was a good time for me to leave to work for Bell on the project in Albuquerque.

"What? But you do a great job," Alex said. "I don't want you to leave. If you want a tram, we can build one here. You could run the project instead of being just one of the workers. What if we did that? Would you stay?"

I told him I would think about it, but I was skeptical. "You don't really have the mountain for a tram," I said, "Where would you put it?"

"Meet me tomorrow morning and I'll show you," he said.

The next morning, we stood at the intersection of Squaw Valley Road and Squaw Peak Road and Alex pointed at the corner where the Austria Haus stood. The Austria Haus had been constructed for the Olympics as Austria's promotional venue for the upcoming 1964 Winter Games in Innsbruck.

"We'll build a big, impressive building for the lower terminal right there," he said, "and put the first tower up there." He pointed to the top of the 1,200-foot-high rock outcropping that dominates the west end of the valley.

"Okay—then where does it go?" I asked.

"I don't know—you'll figure that out," he replied. "You're in charge."

I had watched Alex in action long enough by now to recognize an opportunity. "Very well," I said. "But if I'm going to be in charge, I need to have total authority for the project. You provide the money and let me do everything else."

Alex posing in front of he Rockpile—he wanted to put the first tower "right there."

He agreed, which was a key to getting the project done on time and on budget. I had his promise of complete authority for the execution of the project, and I must give him a lot of credit for living up to it. I was twenty-nine years old.

"What's the biggest tram in the world?" was Alex's next question.

I replied that there was a recently completed tramway in Palm Springs that carried 80 passengers, and another in Europe of similar capacity.

"I think we should build it for 120 passengers—leapfrog ahead with the world's largest. It would get a lot more attention that way," he said.

I told him I would investigate it. He was insistent on a large, impressive building for the lower terminal—something that would be the focal point of the base facilities of the resort. Tram terminals in Europe were generally utilitarian looking buildings—not architecturally striking—in keeping with the European affinity for function over flash. Alex could not be moved from wanting a grand building for the lower terminal.

"I know a great architectural firm in Boston," he said. "I'm going to call them and ask them if they know anything about trams."

Within the next few days, I hiked up to the top of the Rockpile with a transit and looked at Alex's idea for a tower location. If you drew a line from the corner where the Austria Haus sat through the prominence of the rock outcropping, and continued almost due west, there was a knoll on the north shoulder of the next little ridge where you could place a second tower, and then a wide, deep canyon before a large plateau. It was a very good alignment. Alex wanted to angle the line differently and put the top terminal on Emigrant Ridge, but I talked him out of it—the terrain was too flat, and the top terminal would have been in a location that was constantly windy. The plateau on the west edge of that deep canyon had aerial tramway written all over it, and the view of Lake Tahoe from the top terminal location was spectacular. I drove Alex up and showed him where the top terminal could be located with the line that placed the towers in the most favorable locations.

He was ecstatic: "It'll be perfect. The world's largest tram and a view of Lake Tahoe—I can see the cover of *Ski Magazine* already."

The next step was to lay out the line on a topo map, which I did in preparation for a trip to talk to potential manufacturers. I also got good elevations at the tower sites, which would speed up the engineering process.

I arranged a trip to Europe to meet with potential manufacturers and to look at some recent projects. I flew over first, made appointments to meet with all the potential vendors, and made hotel reservations in all the places we would be staying during our trip. Alex was planning to fly into Geneva, then get a train to Zermatt. We planned to meet at the train station in Zermatt and have a look at an eighty-passenger tram constructed by a Swiss company called Garaventa—a newcomer to building passenger trams. An eighty-passenger cabin was very large by European standards, so it was worth a visit.

When Alex arrived in Zermatt, he was accompanied by an attractive woman wearing skintight leather pants and tall boots. He introduced her as his friend Harriet Shaw. This was a big surprise, and when we got to the hotel, I scrambled to arrange another room for Harriet—fortunately, one was available. Alex, Harriet and I had dinner, and Alex and I talked shop until it was late. He wanted to get an early start the next morning and told me to come get him when I was ready to go to breakfast. The next morning, I was dressed and ready to go early, and I went to Alex's room to let him know I was ready to go down to breakfast. I knocked several times, but there was no answer—maybe he had already gone downstairs? I decided to try Harriet's room to see if he had told her he was going to breakfast. When I knocked on her door, Alex answered. After that, I told him that I would just leave the room reservations at two rooms—there seemed to be no reason to get three.

The three of us were very compatible. Harriet had mentioned that she liked Swiss pear schnapps and wanted to see if she could buy some to be shipped home. We were close to a distiller that bottled their product with a pear in each bottle. Alex was not interested, so Harriet and I drove out to the farm and got a tour of the orchard, where the pear trees were festooned with bottles tied over the blooms that would eventually mature into a full-sized pear right inside the bottle. Harriet bought a case and arranged for it to be shipped back to the U.S.

Trips to Europe with Alex always included long, leisurely lunches.

The following day we chartered a private plane to fly us to St. Moritz to meet with Von Roll. It was a perfect, clear day and a beautiful flight over the Alps. The scenery was simply fantastic, although the flight saved us a lot of time as well. (It would have been a 300-kilometer drive.) We were staying in a very, very fancy hotel. That which delighted Alex, but made me feel distinctly out of place. We were joined by Bob Gebhardt, who, after working at Squaw Valley for a few years, had started his own contracting business. To make the project more efficient, we were planning to have Bob do the foundations and concrete work for the towers and upper terminal so I could concentrate on installing the drive equipment in the lower terminal and coordinating the work of the other contractors. Bob was accompanied by his wife, Salty, which turned out to be an exceptionally good thing. While we were in St. Moritz, Bob's back went out and he was unable to stand or walk without terrific pain. Salty

Lunch with Harriet and Alex at the Zugspitze.

rented a station wagon, and we carried Bob from the hotel to the car and put him in the back. Lying flat in the back of the car, he was comfortable enough that Salty could drive them to the Munich airport for a flight back to California. How he tolerated sitting in an airplane seat for that long, I have no idea, but they managed, somehow.

From St. Moritz, Alex, Harriet, and I went to Garmisch-Partenkirchen to meet with representatives from Pohlig Heckel Bleichert (the company that had built the Squaw Valley gondola). We were met by three guys in black suits and ties who came in a limousine. We rode up the Zugspitze and met the director of the company who

On arrival at the top of the Zugspitze, PHB served us glasses of champagne. Mr. Smith, the General Manager of the Zugspitze entertained Harriet while the PHB people pitched Alex and me.

was waiting at the top terminal with an attractive girl bearing a tray filled with glasses of champagne. PHB really knew how to woo prospective customers, but they were another big steel company with a small lift division, and Alex and I were both uncomfortable being so obviously "sold."

"We can't go to breakfast at the hotel," he said after the meeting and lengthy sales pitch. "If we do, they'll be waiting for us. We have to go somewhere else."

"Like where?" I asked.

"How about the train station?" he said. So, we went to the dirty little train station for coffee in the morning to avoid the guys in suits.

Harriet had run out of time, so she took the train to Munich to fly home from there. Alex and I were a little burned out from having looked at trams all over Switzerland, Austria, and Germany, and it was discouraging that so many of them were big steel companies with small divisions, only, for lifts. It made me uncomfortable to think that our project would be one of many handled by a smaller division of a large company. There was the risk of a delay because of a job in a larger division taking priority. When we met with the vendors, it seemed like we were mostly meeting with salespeople who knew how to sell lifts but had no idea how to build one, which was disconcerting. One exception had been the small Swiss company Garaventa, but they were new to passenger trams and had never done a project in the United States. Unlike the others, when we met with Garaventa, I talked to their chief mechanical and structural engineers, guys who knew what they were talking about instead of salesmen. After meeting with all the major players, I had a good feeling about Garaventa

Squaw Valley of the 1960's had a distinct style that leveraged the abundant snow and sunshine of the Sierra Nevada compared to the colder climates found in other parts of the country. Skiing was booming in popularity and skiing under perpetually sunny skies in California was a great counterpoint to the state's image as a surfing mecca.

and had confidence they would be responsive if I had any questions or ran into a problem. I told Alex that I thought Garaventa was our best option, and he agreed, so we headed back to Switzerland.

On the way, we stopped for the night in a small town, Oberstdorf. There was one more tram there that I wanted to look at. I called ahead to reserve rooms and the owner said that this was the staff's day off, the "Ruhetag," so there would be no services or restaurant, but there was a restaurant just down the street, and we were welcome to stay. That was fine with us. When we arrived, we picked up our room keys and a key to the front door from the owner. Alex wanted to go to his room, and I wanted to get a beer, so I told him I would be down the street at the restaurant, and to come down whenever he was ready. I was in the restaurant a little while later when the local sheriff came in and said, "You know, I just came down the street and there's a guy trying to climb out the window at the hotel. I don't know if he's trying to get in the window or get out of the window, but he was kind of stuck in the window." So, I walked up the street and there was Alex on the windowsill.

He said, "Well, I don't know—it's kind of too far down and I don't want to fall to the inside…."

I said, "Alex, you have a key!"

He said, "I know, but I can't find it…."

The trip to meet with tramway vendors was eye-opening for me in many ways. Alex, it seemed, was always hungry, and at about 11 a.m. he would start talking about having lunch. When we went to a restaurant to have lunch, he would always ask for the wine list and order a bottle of wine, usually something expensive. I drank a lot of excellent wine while shopping for lifts with Alex. He always liked to have dessert, too. Lunch would last a couple of hours, which was very much out of keeping with my practice of eating a quick lunch and getting back to work.

A rare photograph of the night lighting (strictly decorative...) that was used for a while in the 1960's and 70's. The "Light Tower Chutes" on Headwall got their name because of the lights originally installed there.

When we arrived in Goldau to meet with Garaventa, they suggested staying at a hotel on Lake Lucerne, the Hotel Vitznau. We drove over to the hotel, which was very elegant and right on the shore of the lake, and the first thing Alex said to the woman at the desk was, "How long are your beds?" She took him away to inspect the beds, which he must have found satisfactory, because he spent the next week hanging out at the hotel while I worked through all the technical discussions with the Garaventa engineers in German. He later told me, "That bartender at the Hotel Vitznau absolutely makes the best martini in the world!"

Alex had hired a high-powered architectural firm in Boston to design the lower terminal of the tram, Shepley, Bulfinch, Richardson & Abbott (Richardson was one of his class-mates at Harvard). Although the firm did a great job and won awards for the design of the building, working with architects on the other side of the continent in the 1960s wasn't an efficient process. We made several trips to Boston to discuss the design and work out details of the interface between the tram equipment and the building. More than once, we took a red-eye flight from Reno to Boston, arriving early in the morning, meeting all day with the architects, and then catching another overnight flight back west. Alex seemed to have no problem with this, and it was not because he was good at sleeping on the plane—he would buy a stack of magazines in the airport and read them on the plane. The day before each flight, I had been up early and worked all day, so I would be tired and ready for some rest, but every time I woke up, he would be wide awake and reading. I do not think he ever slept on the plane. On one trip, we had been at the architect's office all day and got to Logan Airport in Boston in the evening for our flight home. We were both tired and hungry. We checked in with the airline and went to a restaurant to have dinner. We got a table and menus, and I asked Alex to just order something for me while I went to the men's room. I came back to the table to find a large, elaborate platter covered with totally unfamiliar objects: Alex had ordered us a dozen oysters each. I had never seen—much less eaten—an oyster before and it was probably not an ideal appetizer before an overnight flight, but that was Alex.

Building the Squaw Valley Tram

O nce we had established which manufacturer would supply the equipment for the new Tram, and the architects started on a design for the lower terminal, I was able to begin the groundwork that would allow us to do the installation in one building season once the equipment arrived from Switzerland.

I built a road to the ridge where the towers were located. Not an easy task: It was steep terrain and the road to the Tower 2 site was a climbing traverse. It seemed like the mountainside was either solid granite or sandy, decomposed granite with little in between,

Site of the lower terminal in Spring, 1968. The Austria Haus and French Pavilion— constructed for the Olympics to promote the forthcoming Games—had been moved behind the Lodge and we were ready to build, right on the spot Alex had picked almost two years before.

so the dozer work was slow. Having a road to the tower locations was critical because we needed to deliver concrete for the tower footings and needed to truck the tower components to the sites. The use of helicopters for lift construction—universal now—was unknown in 1968, and being able to drive to the tower sites would be a distinct advantage throughout the project and afterward. Once the road was constructed to Tower 2, the road to Tower 1 was a spectacular and narrow descent with a steep drop off on either side—not a road for the faint-hearted.

Pouring the footing pad at Tower 1 with the small 'transfer' concrete truck.

I surveyed the line and established benchmarks at each tower and the terminal locations that would be used throughout the job to locate the exact position of each piece of equipment. I set the exact centerline of the lift and calculated the station (distance along the centerline from the bottom terminal) and elevation for each of the critical points. Once this was done, we were able to mark the exact locations for the tower foundations and test the quality of the soil and rock that would anchor the towers and foundations. Bob Gephardt had recovered from his back trouble, and his crew formed and poured the footings that would anchor each leg. There was no way to get concrete trucks from the local concrete company to the tower sites—and their drivers would probably have refused to drive the road—so we rented a small concrete truck and built a transfer site on the Summer Road by the lower terminal of the Headwall lift where we could pour the concrete trucked from the batch plant into our smaller truck that would then deliver the concrete to the tower sites.

Unlike most lift towers that rely on the mass of the footing and the pressure against the compacted earth surrounding them to provide support for the tower, aerial tramway towers tend to be anchored deep into solid rock. The footings Bob's crew built for each tower leg did little more than give us something to bolt the steel structure to—the real strength was—and IS—provided by the anchor bolts permanently connected to bedrock below the towers. The footings had sleeves through which we drilled into the rock below them, then inserted 40-foot-long anchor bolts which were pressure-grouted, then hydraulically tensioned a week later. By "pulling" on them with a hydraulic cylinder and then locking that tension in the bolt, we could be certain of their ability to withstand the force that the tower would exert. The bolts are checked periodically to verify that they are still tensioned and, therefore, that they are still safely anchoring the tower structure.

Pressure grouting the anchor bolts at Tower 1.

A house mover moved the Austria Haus and French Chateau (which, as I mentioned, were built for the 1960 Olympic Games to promote the 1964 Games in Innsbruck and 1968 Games in Grenoble) from the site for the lower terminal of the tram at Squaw Valley Road and Squaw Peak Road to locations along Squaw Creek, behind the lodge. John Buchman lived in the French Chateau, and the Austria Haus became the club-house and pro shop for the tennis club at the lodge. Both buildings would be moved again in 1981.

I did as much of the site preparation and preliminary work as I could in the summer of 1967 in anticipation of the arrival of the Garaventa crew in May of 1968. Once the homeowners on Granite Chief Road learned about the project, a handful of them started a clamor about "aerial rights", because the Tram would go over their lot, if not their home. Alex offered to give each of the affected property owners a couple of free season passes and that was enough to buy the aerial rights over their property.

I rented a house on Granite Chief Road in Squaw Valley—literally a block from the site of the lower terminal—that would house the crew. The location allowed the crew to go back to the house for lunch each day—lunch together gave a sense of camaraderie, and everyone enjoyed it. Campbell Construction had started excavating the site of the lower terminal—although it had been a very normal winter for snowfall, the lower elevations lost snow quickly once the weather turned warm and the days got longer. The tower locations and top terminal would take longer, but they had good exposure to be clear of snow by the time the Swiss crew arrived. Getting the road plowed all the way to the top would be another project, but it had to be accomplished to

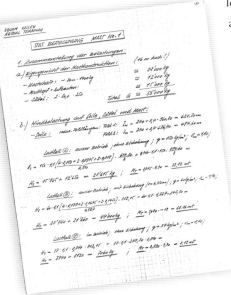

The Garaventa engineers did a truly monumental job in producing over 200 pages of meticulously calculated and handwritten engineering notes for the project.

allow the concrete subcontractors to start work.

The Garaventa crew arrived on May 17, 1968, accompanied by Karl Garaventa. Since this was the first project for the company in the United States, Karl and his brother, Willi, were determined that everything would be perfect—on time, on budget, everything running like a Swiss watch—and they were planning to manage the job themselves

Pouring concrete for the foundation and machine-room level of the lower terminal. Photo by John Corbett.

to make sure that was the case. Karl had some funny ideas, and he was frankly kind of cheap. There was a Swiss girl, Emmy, who was going to cook for the crew, and I asked Karl how he planned to have her do the shopping. He said we could get her a bicycle with a trailer and she could ride into Tahoe City. This was long before the bike path that now connects Squaw Valley and Lake Tahoe, and while it was only about a six-mile trip, State Route 89 was a lot narrower then, with cars and trucks zooming past at 50 miles per hour—the poor girl was going to get killed. I found a way to let her use one of the pickup trucks to do the shopping, because shopping and cooking for the Garaventa crew was a serious undertaking. The Swiss-Italian guys would have a big water glass of red wine with lunch, so Emmy bought Gallo "Hearty Burgundy" by the gallon. At one time, there were thirty Hearty Burgundy jugs lined up against the wall of the house.

One day, my son Marcus, who was about four, was fishing in the little stretch of the south fork of Squaw Creek that ran in front of the rental house. To his great delight, he actually caught a little trout. It was only four inches long or so, but he was very proud of it and when Karl Garaventa asked for the fish, Marcus handed it over. To his shock and horror (and ours), Karl popped the little fish into his mouth and swallowed it whole!

Sometimes in the morning, the Swiss crew would ask, "Hey, have you seen the guy from the state?" They were talking about Leroy Hill, the ranger for California State Parks, and the question meant that the Swiss guys were hoping to have marmot stew for dinner, but they did not want Leroy to catch them killing the marmots. There was a large marmot colony that lived in a rock retaining wall near the bottom terminal of the Headwall lift, along

Cabin 2 loaded on a truck at the Port of Sacramento for the trip to Squaw Valley.

The saddles for the towers were a particularly large and heavy load—this is one of eight sections of saddle that had to be transported to the tower sites....

the side of the summer road. They would drive very slowly in a pickup truck to where the marmots would be sunning or grazing on the opposite side of the road from their burrows in the rocks. A couple of guys would sit on the tailgate with shovels. The slowest marmot would get whacked with a shovel and taken down for the long-suffering Emmy to clean and cook for dinner.

The ship carrying all of the parts and equipment for the project arrived at the Port of Sacramento and everything was loaded onto trucks to be hauled to Squaw Valley. Overseas transport by container was much less common than it is today and there was a great deal that could not be packed into a container, but the materials were all moved without incident. The cabins—which had been enclosed in crates after they were finished in Switzerland—were nearly fourteen feet wide and had to be hauled as an oversized load, so we had to hire a pair of CHP cruisers to act as pilot cars for the trip from Sacramento to Squaw Valley. The cabins couldn't fit through the "Mousehole" under the railroad in Truckee, so we had an impromptu parade down Commercial Row and across the grade crossing, before bringing the little convoy down West River Street to the home stretch down Highway 89 to the Valley. It turned out to be a great way to get the locals excited about the project and generate some publicity.

Karl Garaventa objected to spending money to rent a crane to build the towers and upper terminal, and had shipped over a bunch of sections of "needle" and several heavy-duty winches with gas engines with which to do the steel erection. The needle was a tall, upright mast assembled from triangular sections that bolted together, so it could be extended as needed by adding more sections. It was supported by guy cables that the operator could adjust with a winch to vary the position of the tip. A pulley hanging at the tip supported a cable with a hook operated by a separate winch: there were sometimes three winches—two positioning the needle and one providing the lifting power. .

The crew working at the tower used the needle like a crane, with one man hooking up steel pieces to be hoisted into position and another operating the winches. Although the needle had a modest lifting capacity compared to a crane, most individual pieces of the towers were relatively light. The basic method had been used by the Swiss for centuries, and while it was a lot slower than a hydraulic crane, the components of the system were lightweight and could be transported into a remote location where you could not drive a crane—you could use the winch to drag itself into position as I had on the Laber-Bergbahn project.

It was an effective (and cheap) way to build a lattice tower, and the Swiss guys were very skilled at rigging the steel pieces so that they hung at the correct angles, allowing them to be moved into position and bolted in place by the men climbing the steel. The Garaventa crew had been doing this for so long that they knew where each piece fit

The Garaventa crew assembling Tower 1 using the needle—the slender boom leaning in from the left.

Tower 2 under construction using the same method—although it is considerably taller than Tower 1.

Squaw Valley Tram

In 1966, when I was writing the specifications for the proposed tramway in Squaw Valley, every manufacturer capable of providing the equipment for the project was in Europe. We talked to several companies in Austria, some in Germany, and a couple in Switzerland before settling on Garaventa in Goldau, Switzerland as the company we would use. As a result, all the documentation for the project—blueprints, engineering calculations, manuals, everything—was written in German. That was no problem for those of us building the tram—we were all fluent in German—but it was a big problem for the U.S. Forest Service, the State of California Department of Industrial Relations (which has regulatory authority over all lifts), and the Placer County Building Department. In 1968, we were about three-quarters of the way through the project and the State of California was very anxious to have the load-test procedure and the maintenance documentation translated from German into English. I was not fluent enough in English to do the work so I found a translator in Oakland who could do it, even though it was very technical language. I told the crew that I had to drive down to the Bay Area, and I would be back late that evening or the next morning at the latest. The contractor for the lower terminal building—Campbell Construction—was from the Bay Area, and their job superintendent on the project overheard this conversation. He said, "You don't have to drive all the way down there—that's going to take a lot of time. I can fly you down in my plane—it's in Truckee. I can fly you down; you can drop off the documents; then when the translation is done, we can fly down again and pick it up."

It was a nice day, and we had a smooth flight from Truckee—until we got to the little ridge that forms the back side of the Oakland Hills. There we got into heavy fog. We could see no more than a hundred feet ahead of us. I said to the pilot, "What the hell are we going to do now? You can't fly in this fog." He said, "If I go back a few miles then fly low and follow the freeway into Oakland. We can just follow the freeway under the fog." That made sense to me, so we turned around, flew back a few miles, then gradually flew lower until we were below the fog and over the freeway. The strategy was working well, right up to the time that we both looked up and saw the front of the Caldecott Tunnel. I figured, "Well, that's the end of us…," The pilot pulled the plane up as much as he could, and we cleared the ridge above the tunnel by about twenty feet.

We turned around, landed at an airport near Concord, rented a car and drove into Oakland. I did not take him up on the offer to fly down to pick up the finished translations: Once was enough.

without having to spend a lot of time poring over the blueprints, so the work went quickly. Each tower was unique. Tower 2 was quite tall at almost 140 feet. Tower 1, while lower, was longer to accommodate the long saddles, which together had a fifty-meter radius to allow operation at ten meters per second over the tower. This needed to make the breakover from the steeper span on the front of the mountain to the flatter section leading to the top. The tower construction moved along rapidly at the same time as Bob Gebhardt's crew did the concrete work at the upper terminal, preparing it for installation of the tramway equipment by the Garaventa crew. Karl insisted on using needles to erect that as well. Campbell Construction, building the lower terminal building, had no such limitations on their activity. They had installed a tower crane that could reach any part of the building, and were using it to full advantage. The lower terminal was a thoroughly modern building and the construction techniques—with extensive use of post-tensioned concrete—were state of the art for the time. Campbell was doing a great job and was right on schedule, which was a relief for me.

The blocky concrete construction of the lower terminal building disguises the complexity of the building. This picture, taken at the rear of the lobby level, shows cables for the sophisticated post-tensioning system. There are two floors below the lobby, with office space and the motor room for the aerial tramway and three floors above with additional office space, the loading platform and tram control room and the tram maintenance shop. The section of the floor blocked out in the foreground is an elevator shaft for a 120 passenger elevator—one of two elevators in the building.

Upper terminal ready for installation of track ropes and haul rope. The cable that has been installed is the rescue rope.

Kathrin at the upper terminal with one track rope in place. The stairs on the left and right were the original means of egress from the unloading area.

After a couple of months of installing structural elements, I started to get a little concerned about the installation of electrical systems. I spoke with Karl about getting an electrician on the crew so we could be prepared for installation of the drive machinery and control system: It did not seem like there was anyone focused on that. He checked into it, and said they had two guys who would be capable of doing the work, and one was interested in coming to California. His name was Erhard "Hardy" Herger. Hardy's arrival in Squaw Valley in 1968 would turn into a lifelong friendship for the two of us, and a permanent fascination with the United States for him. Hardy was a wonderful person and a fantastic worker—always dedicated to doing things better. When "better" did not meet his high standards, he would frequently invent a new and greatly improved way of addressing the problem. The phrase "good enough" was not in his vocabulary. Hardy was a great addition to any crew. He had a great sense of humor and a relentlessly positive attitude. He was a fantastic addition to the Garaventa crew in Squaw Valley, because he got along well with all the Swiss guys, and worked effectively with Campbell Construction's electrical subcontractors. (Although they were probably a little intimidated by the Swiss maniac who got two or three times as much done in a day as they did.)

While Hardy was a totally competent and enthusiastic guy to have on the crew, his arrival—or rather that of his wife—created some issues. A few weeks after

Hardy arrived, his wife turned up one day from Switzerland. She was a flamboyant woman, and the only spouse of the Swiss crew to make the trip to Squaw Valley. That alone probably would have been okay, but a week or so after she arrived, her boyfriend showed up—a flashy flight attendant from South America. The Swiss guys on the crew hated him on sight, and after a week or so, a couple of them came to me and told me that if the "gigolo" did not get out of town, something bad was going to happen. I passed the word and within a couple of days, he left… along with Hardy's wife, who was never to be seen again.

When the towers and top terminal were finished, and the lower terminal was far enough along to have the lower terminal docking saddles, counterweight deflection sheaves, and counterweights for the track ropes in place, we were able to start pulling rope. We hiked a pair of lightweight manila ropes down from the top, carrying them up and over each tower, and throwing them down the cliffs. Then we used those ropes to pull up a pair of lightweight cables, which pulled heavier cable until we had wire ropes in place that were sturdy enough to pull the track ropes. We had to pull up four ropes on each side: two track ropes, the haul rope, and the rescue rope, which was the lightest by far and came last. The track ropes were pulled into place, wrapped around the bollards at the top, and clamped temporarily. Then we made sockets at the bottom that would attach the lower end of the track ropes to the counterweight ropes.

Rico DiGiacomo and Karl Garaventa at the lower terminal in the process of pulling track rope #1.The peeled log Karl is sitting on is the brake for the spool of rope: one end is tied off and the other end is pulled against the rim of the spool with a come-along to exert tension on the spool and the rope being pulled toward the top.

On the work platform over the Tram Bowl preparing to tension Track Rope #2.

Tensioning the track ropes was a major project. It involved sliding the cable clamps and an 80-ton-rated, multi-part block down the cables from the upper terminal. We built a special work platform for the crew that hung from the track ropes. It allowed them to install the rigging while dangling out over the cliff. We could reel them back in using a winch. Once the track rope was tensioned to the correct specification, the rope had to be laboriously advanced around the bollard and finally clamped, with the additional, extra cable taken up on a circular rack. It was a difficult and labor-intensive task, and we got very adept at it after performing it four different times. Once the track ropes were installed and tensioned, we were able to install the slack-carriers between the towers, and pull the haul rope to the top, through the tensioning system, and back down to the bottom, where it was pulled through the drive. The carriages were set on the track ropes, the hangers and cabins installed, and the haul rope attached to the cabin with sockets at the uphill and downhill ends of the cabin.

Now we had a one-cabin tramway that would move. The cabin was driven to the top terminal, we pulled tension on the haul rope, cut it, and made sockets to attach it to the other cabin. Once the sockets were attached to the carriage of that cabin, we had a two-cabin reversible tramway.

The Garaventa crew at the house on Granite Chief. Back row, L to R: Emmy Legler, Fritz Legler, Hardy Herger, Toni Forster, Angelo Marieni, Hedi Burkhart, Karl Garaventa. Front row: Sepp Rickenbach, Franz Voneu, Markus Burkhart, Hans Burkhart, Kathrin Burkhart, Sepp Immos.

"Mit dem Bau der Luftseilbahn in den USA ist der kleinen Goldauer Firma der Durchbruch im Weltmarkt gelungen."

("With the construction of the aerial cableway in the USA, the small company from Goldau made a breakthrough on the world market.")

Willi Garaventa, on the impact of the Squaw Valley Tram on his company

The load test is always a somewhat tense event for everyone associated with the installation of a lift. By code, the carrier—whether it is a chair, gondola, funitel, or aerial tramway cabin—is loaded with weight equivalent to the rated passenger capacity times 175 pounds plus ten percent. For the Squaw Valley Tram—which would be the world's largest, once it passed the test—that was 120 people, so 120 x 175 pounds plus 10 percent = 23,100 pounds. We would use water, so we needed 2,770 gallons of water—about fifty fifty-gallon drums per cabin. The cabins were loaded up with drums of water and the testing started. The testing went well—standard stops, emergency stops, overspeed tests—the system functioned flawlessly. The one test no one wanted to do was a track rope brake application from full speed. This was a good thing, because the cabins probably would have swung far enough to hit the haul rope and maybe the track ropes. The State of California's Department of Industrial Relations was satisfied, as was Chuck Dwyer, who had come in from Denver to observe the load test on behalf of the Forest Service. We had a permit and were ready to operate right on time.

Alex Cushing believed in taking advantage of any opportunity to have a big, splashy party, and the 1968 grand opening of the world's largest aerial tramway was the biggest celebration in Squaw Valley since the Olympics. The difference from the Olympics was that this party was completely Alex's. He did not have to share it with the International Olympic Committee, and if he wanted elephants for this party, there was no one to tell him he could not have them. So, there were elephants.

The individual tram cabins were named after the two financial institutions that had loaned him the money for the tram—Bank of America (their cabin was called "The A.P. Giannini" after the founder of Bank of America) and "Connecticut General" after the insurance company providing the balance of the funding. Alex invited California Governor Ronald Reagan, Mrs. Reagan, and their family to attend, but the Reagans never appeared. He invited a bunch of Placer County officials and a lot of his friends from New York and San Francisco, as well as a great many members of the ski industry press, national sports magazines, and national news media. The grand opening garnered a lot of attention in the ski magazines, as well as stories in *Sports Illustrated* and all the California newspapers. There

The finished lower terminal—with the track rope counterweights flanking the entrance—is a striking piece of architecture that won many awards. Among tramway terminals worldwide, it may very well be the most handsome and it remains a iconic structure even after more than a half-century.

was a christening of the tramway cabins with champagne—just like the U.S. Navy would do for a new battleship. And we gave tours of the motor room, describing the operation of the drive system. The elephants came from John Ascuaga's Nugget casino in Reno. An adult elephant performed in front of the tram building, and a baby elephant greeted passengers at the loading platform. The original idea was to have the elephants ride in the tram cabins, but no one was sure how the elephants would react to the ride, and we did not think having a nervous elephant in the cabin would be a good idea for several reasons.

The Squaw Valley Tram (or, as Alex always called it, "The Cable Car") opened to the public on December 18, 1968— seven months to the day after the Swiss crew had arrived to start work. The project was done on time, and on budget, and it gave Squaw Valley bragging rights as not only the site of the VIII Olympic Winter Games, but also the most technologically advanced ski resort in North America and the owner of largest aerial tramway in the world… for a year. In 1969, a larger tram was built in Europe, but that never kept Alex from referring to his tram as the "World's Largest."

Hardy Herger

One of the best and most unexpected benefits of the Squaw Valley Tram project was making the acquaintance of Hardy Herger. Hardy was an outstanding electrician—that was what he came to be—but his talents went way beyond the electrical aspects of the project. Hardy was a relentlessly curious and innovative person, and he was always looking for a way to do things better—there simply was not an ounce of "good enough" in his character. He was also a positive and cheerful person, and incredibly hard working, so he was a great person to have on a project when conditions were tough or the work was not going well, because he never complained and would find a way to get things done. When the tram project was finished, the rest of the Garaventa crew went home to Switzerland, but Hardy liked the United States and wanted to stay. He moved in with Hedi, me, and our kids, Markus and Kathrin, and stayed for five or six years.

Hardy was born in Urnerboden, Switzerland, a tiny settlement (the 2003 population was 40) set in a magnificent high valley in the Alps at the foot of the Klausen Pass. The pass is usually open from May or June until October when it is closed due to snow, so Urnerboden is quite isolated during the winter. About eight miles east and 2,300 feet lower in elevation, Linthal is the "big" town, although the population of Linthal is a little over a thousand. Hardy's parents, Maria and Josef, were farmers and, typical of farm families, had a lot of children: Hardy was the fourth of ten. In 1939, when Hardy was four, Josef and Maria bought a farm on the slope of the Rigi, a mountain surrounded on three sides by water not far from Lucerne. Hardy and his siblings had to walk to school—an hour's walk each way—but they loved exploring the mountains when not working on the farm.

With mentoring from the director of the power company in the town of Arth, Hardy studied to become an electrician. He graduated with honors, then continued his studies in other areas of technology. He started his own company and through his work in

Hardy Herger

low voltage electronics and communications, became associated with Garaventa, which was located nearby in Goldau.

A universal trait among the Swiss is that they are tremendously proud of being Swiss. As far as they are concerned, the Swiss are the smartest, hardest working people on Earth—and likely the best looking. Also—although it is little known outside of Switzerland—a long, long time ago it was the Swiss who hung the moon. Hardy was no exception to this. He had extraordinary pride in his national heritage. If you had not guessed his nationality, within five minutes he would make sure that you knew. My wife, Hedi, was Swiss, too—although not as rabidly Swiss as Hardy—and they got along well, spoke their odd dialect of German, and probably compared notes on how terrific they were because they were Swiss. Other than this odd obsession, shared by his countrymen, Hardy was a modest and generous man.

Perhaps because he had grown up in a small country, when he got to the U.S.—which must have seemed enormous—Hardy developed a love of driving long distances. He was an avid driver. While we were working at Snowbird, Hardy decided one Sunday morning that he should drive to Las Vegas for breakfast—over 400 miles. He drove from California to Alaska on the Alaska Highway, much of which was gravel. To protect his beloved Citroen DS sedan from the spray of rocks thrown up by passing big rigs, Hardy covered the hood with carpet and made a protective cover for the windshield with Plexiglas. The Citroen DS was an eccentric choice of car, but Hardy loved the engineering of the front-wheel drive, unusual at the time, and the hydro-pneumatic suspension system, which allowed him to adjust the ride height and even change a flat tire without a jack. It was the perfect car for someone in love with innovation. His other car—a Lancia—was less of an engineering marvel and more of an Italian hot rod. Both the Citroen and the Lancia offered less-than-stellar reliability, however, so it was completely unsurprising that Hardy became a huge fan of Subarus. He drove one more than 300,000 miles. The all-wheel-drive Subaru was the perfect choice for exploring the backroads of Nevada, which Hardy loved to do. He knew every gravel road, every ghost town and every abandoned mining operation across the Silver State—the Swiss guy knew Nevada a lot better than most native Nevadans. Once he had his mind set on a destination, he was very reluctant to stop.

We were driving from Squaw Valley to Snowbird once, and after many hours, I said, "Hey, Hardy—let's stop in Elko and get some coffee."

He said, "Do we *have* to?"

I forced him to go to Elko, otherwise he would have happily driven all the way from Tahoe to Snowbird, non-stop.

When the Snowbird project was done, I had some money I wanted to put into real estate, and I spent the day with a realtor looking at lakefront lots on Lake Tahoe. I thought if I could find one that was steep and difficult to build, I could pick it up cheaply and install a little funicular between the house and the Lake, and do well on the investment. We had looked all over and not found anything suitable, but there was a house on the West Shore between Tahoe City and Sunnyside that was for sale and it had a long and well-built pier. It looked like it had been on the market for quite a while. The lot was a mess with a couple of abandoned cars thrown in to add to the ambience. The house was okay—it had large windows and was balloon-framed, which meant that it must have been quite old—and there was a separate guest house that was newer and looked comfortable. The asking price was $150,000, and I told the realtor that I would pay the seller $152,000, but I needed an answer within twenty-four hours. This was long before "over-asking" offers in real estate were common. They accepted the deal quickly. I got to work cleaning up the lot, and towed the abandoned cars out to the street. The place looked presentable. By now, Hardy had been living with my family at our house on Squaw Valley Road for more than a few years. He would go to Switzerland in the summer and come back with a new girlfriend each year who would stay with him in our guest room. This arrangement was driving Hedi crazy. She finally said that Hardy and his girlfriends had to go. Buying the house on Lake Tahoe allowed me to move Hardy and his girlfriend into the guest house and keep the peace with Hedi. One day I was working in the yard at the Lake Tahoe house when a couple drove in the driveway. The asked if the house was for sale. I told them that it was not on the market and they said, "That's too bad; we'd give you $400,000 for it." Hardy ended up marrying Nellie, the girlfriend with whom he moved into the guest house at the West Shore property,

so it turned out to be a good investment all the way around.

Hardy had a lot of great expressions, but his most frequent and all-purpose phrase was, "Boy, oh boy!" I have no idea how he picked this up, but it was a constant and could be used for virtually any occasion, substituting for "Wow", "No kidding?" or "Too bad…" or any one of dozens of other expressions. If he was really fired up, it might even become "*Boy*, oh boy, oh boy." He was never at a loss for words, although he never used bad language (at least not in English) and "Boy, oh boy" was usually gleeful. He called a banana a "monkey sausage," and when he ate an apple, he ate the whole

Hardy and me posing on the newly finished Solitude triple chairlift for a Marketing Department photo.

thing—core, seeds: the works. In addition to his vast technical knowledge and love of innovation, Hardy was an expert and enthusiastic ballroom dancer—so accomplished that he had received his international ballroom dancing certification. Hardy and Nellie had a daughter, Cornelia, who was adorable and charming and—at least according to Hardy— as smart as her brilliant mother and father combined. She made his life complete.

As a result of his keen interest and research into energy-saving technologies and applications in Europe (especially Switzerland, of course…), Hardy became an expert on energy conservation and renewable sources of energy. His house was one of his laboratories for experimenting with different ways of creating energy and using it efficiently and Squaw Valley was the other. At home, he had solar-heated hot water and hydronic heating long before it was commonly seen in residential settings. He had photovoltaic panels that swiveled to follow the sun so that their electrical output was optimized all day. He made more power

Hardy with his friend and co-worker, Freddie Strolz.

than his home consumed, and sold solar-generated electricity to the power company. At Squaw Valley, he had an even larger canvas on which to create, and he installed an innovative ground-source heating system to take advantage of the consistent temperature of the ground to heat the large Children's World building. At Gold Coast, he installed an incinerator that dramatically reduced the amount of wastepaper that had to be hauled down the mountain each day, while producing heat and hot water for the building. There were many less dramatic, but equally effective installations—super-efficient boilers for heat, hot water, and hydronic snow-melt systems; efficient lighting systems; and heat generated by the funitel's large electric motor to heat the building and melt the snow on the exterior walkways. Hardy may have been considered something of a "mad professor" by the people at the electric utility, but he won academic awards for his innovative uses of technology to save energy in creative and unexpected ways.

In late middle age, Hardy's restless mind took an unexpected and unlikely turn to religion. As he did with everything, he threw himself into it wholeheartedly, so much that he very quickly became a minister and started pursuing a master's degree and then a doctorate in divinity. He went to school in Sacramento and would work all day at Squaw Valley, change his clothes, drive the hundred miles to Sacramento, go to class, then drive home. It was a regimen that only Hardy could endure.

After I left Squaw Valley, Hardy and I had a daily 'meeting' every morning at the Starbucks in the Village. We would have coffee, talk about our projects and he would fill me in on the latest activity on the mountain. He had a lot going on and the company depended on him and gave lip service to how much he was appreciated, but it was frustrating for him that he couldn't do things as well as he knew that they should be done. Our meetings were his daily therapy session with someone who understood the situation and the challenges that it presented.

In 1986, Hardy bought a small house in Urnerboden, the village where he was born, and spent his vacations traveling to Switzerland, renovating his house and hiking. In returning to that tiny village in the mountains, he was completing the circle of his life, and he was proud and happy to have a permanent connection to Switzerland and a place to call home in his homeland. Sadly, while hiking alone near Urnerboden in September of 2012, he had an accident. A farmer, tending to his herd of cows in the mountains, was alerted by his dog's barking and found Hardy's body below the trail he had been hiking at the bottom of a two-hundred-meter cliff. The farmer called Hardy's neighbors who had been worried when he had not returned from his hike the previous day. Hardy was seventy-seven.

Hardy's house in Urnerboden, Switzerland.

Hardy was an enthusiastic and tireless hiker.

We had a memorial service at Squaw Valley that was attended by several hundred people—Nellie came from Switzerland and Cornelia from Portland, where she works as an architect. There were a lot of people from the Sierra Swiss Club in Truckee. Hardy had—of course—been an active part of that organization and was loved and appreciated by all the Swiss Californians who belonged to it. The tributes to Hardy were many and heartfelt; his work at Squaw Valley for more than forty years spanned more than one generation, and it was clear not only that he had quietly made Squaw Valley a better place, but also that his remarkable work in energy-conservation had impacts across the region, showing how a large business could be a more responsible citizen of the world. Hardy was a great person who did exceptional work and helped the people around him to learn, grow, and succeed. He had a wonderful sense of humor. He loved a good meal with a glass of wine, a little schnapps, and good friends. He was a good man and a great friend, and he is remembered with great fondness by everyone who knew him.

MAUI

Early in 1969, with the Squaw Valley Tram up and running, I had a call from a man in Hawaii who asked if I was interested in building a sightseeing gondola on the slope of Haleakala—the volcano on the island of Maui. I really did not have time for the project, but he was insistent that he would like me to come look at it, and I had never been to Hawaii, so I accepted. I got a red-eye flight from San Francisco, and flew over to Maui. The Hawaiian fellow picked me up at the airport in the morning and described the concept while we drove to the mountain.

A visit to the top of Haleakala is a popular trip for tourists visiting Maui. There is a long, winding access road about twelve miles long between the community of Kula and the entrance to the Haleakala National Park at about the 6,500-foot level. The road continues another ten miles to the top of the mountain—the 10,000-foot level—where there is a visitor center and observatory. There were bus tours, and tourists liked to drive up the mountain, but the road was narrow and twisting and the drive took the better part of an hour. While the views were excellent, traffic on the road was an increasing issue for the residents, and was expected to get worse as tourism to Maui increased in the future. A sightseeing gondola would provide a comfortable, relaxing ride to the summit—much faster and more fun than the drive. It would relieve some of the traffic and would be a potentially profitable enterprise. There was an alignment for the lift that would all be on privately owned land—skirting the National Park and several other public reserves of land. It was the property of a Christian missionary organization that had owned the land for a long time and could benefit from the income produced by the gondola.

We got to the site for the lower terminal, but it was impossible to see the top of the mountain from there, and I could not tell what the line would look like or where it would go, so we drove up the access road. For the first mile or two, the landscape was lush and heavily treed—jungle, really. As we climbed, the vegetation became scrubby and low, then became just ground cover, like a meadow. The views toward the rest of Maui and the ocean were sweeping and spectacular, but I still could not see the top or visualize where the top terminal would be located, so we drove farther up and into the National Park. Finally, after about twenty miles of switchbacks, we reached a plateau with the visitor center and, a short distance away, the observatory. At this elevation, the landscape was nothing but lava rock and sand—a moonscape well above the clouds. We looked at the proposed site for the top terminal and discussed what the alignment would look like. Because the landscape was so featureless, it was hard to pick out landmarks along the line to see where the lift would go. I could not tell anything about it from the top. I said, "I'm going to walk downhill and look it over. I'll meet you at the bottom."

I started walking down, following what I thought was the intended lift line. It was difficult to keep going straight, because the landscape on the volcano was totally barren and from the mountain at that elevation, you could see only ocean to the horizon—no shoreline. For the first hour I was walking, there was nothing—not a plant, not a bird, bug or fly—absolutely nothing but rock and sand. It was weird. I had binoculars, and after a while was able to pick out a buoy in the ocean. That was enough of a reference to keep me going straight and give me some feel for the profile of the line.

About halfway down—after the landscape had changed back to the low vegetation that covered the mid-slope section of the volcano, I came across a flock of wild goats. They did not seem fearful or very curious about me, but they kept their distance. The lower I got, the taller and denser the vegetation and trees became, until toward the bottom I had to do some serious bushwhacking to be able to wend my way through the jungle. It took five hours to walk down, as I kept to as much of a straight line as I could. It was an awfully long walk, and it would be an exceptionally long lift. It could be done, but it would have to be two sections with two separate drives in the middle and a terminal that the cabins passed through. They could come off the line for the lower section, roll onto a conveyor, and then launch onto the upper section. The owner would have to bring power into the middle, because there was not enough power at the top—or maybe any power: it was possible that the facilities at the top were all run on a generator. It could be done but was going to be an expensive project.

We drove back to the airport for a 6 p.m. flight back to San Francisco. As I boarded the plane, the flight attendant said, "Hey, didn't I just bring you over this morning?"

I said, "That's right, and now I'm going back!" Hawaii seemed like a great place, and the next time I went, I thought it would be nice to spend more than twelve hours there.

Unfortunately, while it was a great concept and would have been a unique and probably very popular tourist attraction, the project was never constructed. The Christian missionaries were unable to persuade anyone to finance construction.

12

"I Need One of These"

I was doing some work at the lower terminal of the Squaw Valley Tram one day in the early fall of 1969 and a guy I did not recognize was lurking around and looking at things. I heard a voice behind me say, "I need one of these." It was an odd comment for someone to make, so I totally ignored it, but a few hours later, I heard the voice again: "This is what I need—I need one of these." I turned around and it was the guy who had been hanging around; he was about forty years old and had a big smile.

"What do you mean?" I asked. "A tram? Why do you need one of these? Are you serious?"

"Yes, I'm dead serious—this is what I need," the guy replied, sticking out his hand. "My name is Dick Bass."

"Why do you need a tram, Dick?" I asked, shaking his hand. "And where?"

"I have a mountain in Utah—Snowbird—and a tram like this would be perfect," he said.

"I'm not familiar with that. Where is it?" I asked.

"Little Cottonwood Canyon—just before Alta," he replied.

I had been to Alta. It was a small ski area that had been there since the late 1930s.

"It's not built yet," said Bass. "But it has the potential to be the best ski area in North America."

I have never met a ski area owner who did not think this about his resort.

"You have to come over and look at it," Bass continued. "I have the tram line all figured out. I just need someone to build it. Just under 3,000 feet of vertical in a little over a mile and a half. A tram is the only way to go with our terrain."

"Who is the manufacturer?" I asked.

"We don't have one yet. I could really use your advice on that."

I was far too busy at Squaw to take on such a large project. "I really don't have time to get away from here right now, Dick. Sorry."

"It's a short trip. Fly over to Salt Lake after work one evening. I'll pick you up in the morning. Go look at the project, you could practically be back here for lunch the next day. I really think you're the guy I need."

Another tram project was really tempting, and he seemed to know what he was talking about.

"Okay, I'll come take a look."

Bass gave me a business card: "H.W. Bass and Sons, Dallas, Texas." He wrote his Salt Lake City phone number on the back with the name of a motel near the Salt Lake City Airport.

"Just call me in the morning and let me know you'll be in that night. Get a cab from the airport to the motel. I will pick you up in the morning. We can drive up the canyon, look at the project and I'll get you back to the airport for your flight. It's perfect for a tram; you'll see."

I had part of a free day the following week, so I made an airline reservation to Salt Lake City for Wednesday evening, returning Thursday afternoon. I called Bass in the morning on Wednesday and told him I would be in that evening.

He was enthusiastic. "I can't wait to show you Snowbird, Hans," he said. "It's fantastic."

The next morning, Bass came to the motel, picked me up, and drove me up the canyon. Steep walls on each side flanked the narrow, winding road. The slopes leading down to the road—where they were not rock walls—were obviously avalanche terrain, with nothing larger than scrubby, low trees in many places. After a few miles, it opened on the right and higher, and more distant peaks came into view. Bass parked on the side of the road. Pretty soon, Ted Johnson walked up from his little cabin a short distance away—it was the only building there. From our spot on the highway, Bass pointed out Hidden Peak, and said, "I want the top terminal right there, and the lower terminal goes down there."

"Dick," I said, "this is a beautiful mountain, but it's a mountain for experts. You cannot make money from experts; they all want to ski for free. Where are the beginners and intermediates going to ski? And besides—the base area is a gully; you have no room to build!"

"We're going to build high rises," he replied, "and we'll figure out where the beginners and intermediates are going to ski."

Actually, Dick and Ted had already figured out where the beginner and intermediate lifts were going to go, but they were smart enough not to tell me they planned to have me build three chairlifts at the same time as the tram….

Dick drove me back to the airport and I flew back to Reno, but the brief tour of the site with him had convinced me of his seriousness about building a tram at Snowbird. It was a nearly ideal location for an aerial tramway. The amount of terrain accessible from the tram would be enormous, and between the vertical and the mostly northerly aspect, it would be great skiing. The tram would require four towers with a lower terminal in the very center of a village and a top terminal on a plateau with a commanding, 360-degree view into Salt Lake City as well as Little Cottonwood Canyon and the surrounding peaks. It was beautiful and dramatic terrain, perfect for a tram, but at the time I had no idea what a challenging job it would be.

Dick, Ted, and I traveled to Europe together. As I had done with Alex Cushing, I took them to see a few different tram installations, and we met with potential manufacturers. Garaventa had met all our expectations for the project in Squaw Valley, and they were eager to expand their base in North America, although I hoped that they would take a somewhat less active role in managing the project in Snowbird than they had at Squaw. Dick and Ted decided that Garaventa was the best fit for the project, although we visited all the other tramway manufacturers so that when we met with Garaventa we could get a competitive bid. With this bit of gamesmanship complete, they signed a letter of intent.

It was an ambitious project, and I knew that it would take more than one building season to get everything done. There was simply no way—even with favorable weather—to build a four-tower tram and top terminal and install the drive equipment in a lower terminal in a single summer in the Wasatch Range. I was very frank with Dick, and explained that to meet the deadline of opening for the 1971–72 season, we would have to use every possible logistic advantage. I would be bringing a crew from Switzerland to build the towers and install the machinery, and, while they were terrific, experienced workers, we would need to find lodging for the whole crew close to the project site in a place where we could have cooks prepare meals for them every day. We would probably need to transport them to the tower sites by helicopter. I was going to have to push them hard, but if they knew that we were doing everything possible to make them comfortable and allow them to work as efficiently as possible, they would repay our investment. Dick and Ted agreed right away, suggesting that we house the Swiss crew at the Gold Miner's Daughter, a large lodge in Alta. There was a helicopter company—Hoskins Helicopters—that had a small helicopter skiing operation out of Alta, so they were familiar with the area and with mountain flying: We could use them to transport the crew.

I told them that as soon as Garaventa finalized the tower locations and engineering, I would need to start building roads and working on tower footings to get a head start on the project. Roads to the tower locations and upper terminal were critical

Looking over the Tram line at Snowbird, Summer of 1970.

because all the materials for the towers and terminal—forms, rebar, concrete, steel, everything—would be moved by truck on the roads. Ted and Dick were happy and excited to get started on the project.

In early June of 1970, I drove a pickup truck to Salt Lake City, worked for the weekend, then left the truck in long-term parking at the airport and flew back. My schedule for the remainder of the summer and fall was to work Monday through Thursday at Squaw Valley, get on a plane Thursday evening to Salt Lake City, work Friday, Saturday, and Sunday at Snowbird, then fly back to Reno Sunday night. Every time I got off a plane, there was a pickup waiting in the parking lot.

One weekend when I was working in Snowbird, a young guy came up to me and said his name was Kent Hoopingarner; he was a ski patroller at Jackson Hole, and wanted to work on the tram project. I told him that the work was going to be done using a crew from Switzerland and I did not have anything for him. A couple of weeks later, I was in Squaw Valley and he showed up again. I thought, "This guy really gets around," but I still did not have a job for him. The next time I was in Snowbird, he showed up again. He must have been attacking this problem on multiple fronts because the next thing I knew, Ted Johnson had rented a bulldozer and hired Hoopingarner to widen and improve the old mining roads that would give us access to the upper terminal. Hoopie's persistence and creativity in getting a job on the project was an indication of how far he would go. It was the start of a long and very successful career at Snowbird and in the ski industry for Kent, who became Ski Patrol Director and General Manager at Snowbird before holding management positions at Purgatory and Alpine Meadows ski areas in later years.

Sometime during my trips to Snowbird to prepare for the installation the following year, Dick and Ted let it be known that they wanted to build some chairlifts as well as the tram. I told them I did not know how I could manage that. It was basically another full project, and the demands on the crew would be approaching the superhuman. I thought that maybe I could hire a crew to do the fabrication work for the towers, have the dirt work and concrete done by a subcontractor, and then use the Swiss crew to do technical assembly and erection one day a week. It would mean working them seven days a week much of the time, but it was the only way.

Dick and I traveled to Europe again, this time to meet with prospective chairlift suppliers and this time with his kids—two boys and twin girls—in tow. The kids lived in Dallas, and I could not disagree with the opportunity for them to tour through the Alps and the Dolomites, but bringing Dick's family along meant that we had to rent and travel in two cars rather than one. Dick took the two boys, and I had the girls, Bonnie and Barbara, who were twelve or thirteen years old. We met with all the major lift manufacturers to see who had the ability to deliver three chairlifts the following summer at the most attractive price. The trip involved driving through most of the most renowned ski resort towns in Europe—beautiful, historic places—and some of the most breathtaking scenery in the world: fantastic passes with mountain peaks stretching as far as the eye could see and lush, picturesque valleys. It was the kind of European tour that many Americans would spend years planning and anticipating. For kids from Texas, I thought it would be an opportunity to discover and appreciate a spectacular part of the world, but the two girls spent the entire time reading comic books and giggling. I do not know if they ever looked out the window.

Dick and I were both favorable toward Doppelmayr, but when we met with them at the factory, Dick did not think their standard chair design was comfortable—something about it just did not hit him right. The Doppelmayr people offered to change the design and build a prototype that he could try, and they did—twice! Dick liked the twice-revised prototype chair, and the Doppelmayr people looked relieved to have met the challenge. We signed an agreement for three chairlifts and headed back to the U.S. with a great deal more work ahead.

Once the dust settled on the revelation that we would build three chairlifts as well as a tram, I knew we would need some additional help. I hired a ski patroller from Squaw Valley named Liam Fitzgerald to work on the Snowbird project. Liam moved into the campground down the canyon from Snowbird with his wife. He did a little bit of everything and did a great job. Like Hoopie, Liam had a long career at Snowbird and was a widely respected ski industry professional.

Werner Auer had worked on the Squaw Valley tram and was a talented fabricator and welder, so he was a great asset in keeping the chairlift project moving along efficiently with minimal impact on the tram project. Since space at Snowbird was so limited and would be fully utilized for staging the components for the tram, we had only enough area in which to unload and stage the parts for the chairlifts coming from Austria—no room to fabricate towers. I was able to find an industrial yard that I could rent in Salt Lake City where we could receive loads of tower tube and do the fabrication work, then truck the structural pieces to Snowbird for final assembly and installation. It was an efficient use of space and although offsite fabrication of the towers added an intermediate step that would normally be unnecessary, in this case it was unavoidable.

The dozer work on top of Snowbird's Hidden Peak had largely been completed, and roads were constructed to the tower locations. Working with a concrete contractor from Salt Lake City, I had built the footings for the towers, inserting sleeves into each where we would drill, grout, and tension the anchor bolts that would transfer the loads on the towers to bedrock. All the preparatory work was complete when winter set in. As heavy snows blanketed the Wasatch Range, I headed back to the Sierra Nevada and Squaw Valley for what would be a challenging and turbulent season.

Who was Dick Bass?

Dick Bass was born in Tulsa, Oklahoma, the son of Harry Bass Sr. who had started as a bookkeeper for an oil drilling company and had become a shareholder in the company when it incorporated. Harry Sr. started his own oil and gas company— Goliad Oil and Gas Corporation—and made a fortune in oil and gas drilling and processing. Dick and his older brother, Harry Jr., grew up in Dallas, Texas. Dick enrolled at Yale at age sixteen, and graduated in 1950 with a degree in geology, then served two years in the U.S. Navy during the Korean War.

Dick was introduced to skiing in Vermont during college, and later took his older brother skiing at Aspen. "I skied in 1953 and hated it," said Harry. "I skied again in '54 and hated it. It was excruciating."[3] Despite Harry's initial dislike of skiing, the brothers each invested in Aspen in 1955, owning as much as seven percent of the company at one point.

Dick Bass

Harry went on to become chairman of the board and majority shareholder of Vail Associates, after turning down the opportunity to "get in on the ground floor" of Vail when founder Pete Seibert approached him in 1960 for start-up funding. Dick Bass made a modest investment in Vail in the early '60s and built a large home there which he later loaned to Gerald Ford for use during Ford's presidency in the 1970s. Dick also served on the Vail Associates Board of Directors from 1966 to 1971.

Ted Johnson had skied Alta—just up the road from Snowbird—since the 1950s and had a dream of building a ski resort at Snowbird, the site of an 1860s-era silver-mining boomtown-turned-ghost-town. Johnson tracked down the owners of the abandoned mining claims and quietly bought them up, then embarked on a barnstorming tour to secure funding to build the resort.

Dick Bass met Johnson at a party in Vail in 1969, and the next day watched Johnson's thirteen-minute promotional movie (filmed by Warren Miller and featuring Johnson skiing) about Snowbird. Johnson's enthusiasm for the area's potential was so compelling that, as Dick put it, "...he hooked this 160-pound large-mouthed Bass!"[4]. With Johnson's conceptual plan for Snowbird and Dick Bass' capital, they opened the resort in 1971. In 1974, Johnson sold his holdings to Bass, who owned and operated the resort for another forty years, until 2014.

The other great achievement of Dick Bass' life was in mountaineering. In 1985, on his third attempt, Dick Bass stood at the summit of Mount Everest, becoming the oldest person (at age fifty-five) to summit Everest and the first person in history to complete the "Seven Summits Challenge," a quest he had started with his friend Frank Wells (later President of the Walt Disney Company) to climb the tallest peak on each of the seven continents. The two men had arrived at the idea of climbing the highest peak on each continent independently. After this idea was communicated through mutual friends, including Clint Eastwood, the two met for the first time in 1981 and climbed six of the seven peaks together in 1983. They had been members of unsuccessful Everest expeditions in 1982 and 1983, and Bass had been denied a climbing permit in 1984; he was finally successful in 1985 after Wells had been forced to abandon the quest due to business pressures. Bass and Wells wrote a book about the experience, "Seven Summits," which was published in 1986.

Dick was a great character and, despite a lifetime of wealth and amazing accomplishments, he was still capable of laughing at himself. A story that a friend told about him—that had to have originated with Dick—was that Dick had been on a flight on which he sat next to a pleasant man who listened to him go on about the treacherous peaks of Everest and McKinley, the time he almost died in the Himalaya, and his upcoming plan to re-climb Everest. Just before the plane landed, Dick turned to the man sitting next to him and said, "After all this, I don't think I've introduced myself. My name is Dick Bass."

The man shook his hand, and responded, "Hi. I'm Neil Armstrong."

Dick Bass died in 2015 at eighty-five.

Without you, I truly believe Snowbird could not have opened on December 23, 1971 considering the earliest, heaviest snowfall on record and with all the lifts we had planned for that first phase—particularly the Garaventa aerial tram. I don't get to see you very often, but I feel a great friendship for you as a person and admiration for what you're able to accomplish in the mountains.

Snowbird Founder Dick Bass, May 12, 1999

Bad Blood at Squaw Valley

Even before the tram project was completed at Squaw Valley, Alex had been trying to get me to take on more responsibility for the operation of the mountain and maintenance of the lifts. From my perspective, it was an impossible job and a thankless one—there were no facilities with which to do the work, no equipment, no tools, and no money—but Alex, as usual, was relentless in his efforts to get me to take on the mountain operations and maintenance roles. Finally, in August of 1969, I accepted the task, subject to several specific conditions that would allow me, I believed, to gradually transform a disorganized, ineffective, and underfunded operation into one that would provide a safe and enjoyable experience for our guests. I proposed a two-year moratorium on new lift construction (so needed funding and energy could be devoted to reorganization and rebuilding), a consolidation of administrative operations in one building, careful budgeting with regular, consistent reporting, and financial accountability. Most of all, I needed to have complete authority over the operational elements of the business to be successful. One sentence toward the end of my proposal stands out, even today: *"PLEASE NOTE: There is a great lack of satisfactory human relations here, between factions in the community, between the personnel and our customers, and among the employees themselves."* Although this was written on August 31, 1969, it would continue to be true for decades thereafter.

At the time of our agreement in August 1969, Alex agreed to spend $615,000 on improvements to the lifts, equipment, tools, vehicles, and work on the slopes, which was the minimum amount I thought I would need to make significant progress. He also agreed to a reorganization of the operation, but his actions fell far short. I did my best under the circumstances and tried to be cooperative and agreeable, but following the 1969-70 season, my frustration was evident in a memo I sent Alex. It referred to the August agreement and read, in part:

"You have in no way lived up to all the agreements and have, in fact, relegated your responsibility to someone else, who has in no way followed through in these commitments to me. Against my better judgement, I kept quiet and compromised with the situations that developed. This was a mistake."

I was ready to quit at that point, but Alex agreed to a budget of $225,000 to be spent over the next six months and I thought we could just do the most urgent improvements using that. Unfortunately, Alex again failed to live up to his word, providing only about $75,000 of the promised funds for lift repairs, maintenance, and other off-season activity, so going into the 1970–71 ski season, we were way behind where we needed to be in terms of lift repairs and maintenance. This was significant because during the previous several years, Squaw had racked up more than its share of black marks regarding lift safety. In 1967, the Shirley Lake lift had experienced a rollback. This is a situation in which a lift starts moving in reverse due to a failure of the brakes to hold the much heavier load that exists on one side of the line than the other. Rollbacks are extremely dangerous and can result in many fatalities and injuries, and although no one was seriously hurt, it was a red flag about the conditions of the safety systems on the lifts. In 1966, Squaw had been accused to operating Headwall without a functioning bullwheel brake, and in 1969, the State of California Department of Industrial Relations (which has regulatory authority over lift safety) had written the resort up for a deficiency in the same brake. Alex brushed off the state recommendation and in March of 1970, Headwall had rolled back, injuring a handful of skiers.

Exhibition closed 1:20 by John, top terminal bearing problems, opened again with doubts at 2:00. Red Dog closed 3:05 because 2 depression sheaves were about to come off Tower #3, opened again 3:40. Broadway stopped 3:30 with full line on bottom stop button, would not restart. 4:15 Cornice II derailed on top—6 people on line. Broadway started 4:55 and cleared by 5:00, small speed motor had something wrong also slow button on top at same time. Cornice II cleared at 5:00 by running slowly—cable was between guide sheaves before bullwheel on top—no injuries.

The handwritten dispatch log from a single day of operation—lift reliability was obviously a major problem...

The 1970-71 season got off to a terrible start when at the beginning of December, Dick Reuter fell off a lift tower, landing on the steel tracks of a Tucker Sno-Cat parked below. Almost anyone else would have died, but Dick was a strong and gritty mountain man and although he broke a lot of ribs, collapsed a lung, and had other internal injuries, he lived through it and, amazingly, was back at work in about a month.

On February 3, a thirty-nine-year-old woman from Canada died after she slipped off the run between the top of KT-22 and the Saddle in icy conditions, slid down, and hit a tree. Another expert skier had died after a similar accident on the same run in 1967. I had proposed a blasting and grading project to widen the run and had been allowed to do a little work, but Alex had refused to spend any more. After the first death, he said in an interview: "Under certain conditions, that area can be very slippery. If you fall off that mountain, nothing can stop you from rolling all the way down. I have fallen from top to bottom myself, and I'm a fairly good skier. Now, I won't go near there when it's slippery." His comment after the second death was, "That's only our fourth fatality in twenty-one years." True enough, but not exactly a reassuring commitment to skier safety.

On February 5, the top terminal of the Emigrant lift—a weird "floating" bullwheel system that was slated to be modified in the proposal that Alex had denied—had a structural failure, resulting in a situation in which the cable derailed off the bullwheel and wrapped around the bullwheel support shaft. The resulting shock and immediate stop damaged the lift and caused several skiers to fall from the lift, paralyzing one man. I told Alex right away that the lift needed to be repaired correctly and the top terminal reconfigured according to the plan I had submitted and that he had agreed to almost 18 months before—there were reasons that the lift had failed that needed to be corrected. The haul rope had been kinked by wrapping around a shaft only

Squaw Valley —'Junk'

SQUAW VALLEY (AP) — The Squaw Valley ski resort, with the prestige of the 1960 Winter Olympics behind it, was living with controversy Wednesday after a departing employe called its lifts "pieces of junk."

Hans Burkhart, Swiss-born engineer who had been mountain manager at the ski area, resigned last Sunday

"Everyone knows the lifts there are pieces of junk — they're all falling apart — and there's no money available for improvements," Burkhart said Wednesday

Alex Cushing, president of Squaw Valley, called Burkhart's allegations "absurd" and added.

"He was about to be fired. I didn't want this to come out, but now it has to."

Burkhart, who says he will become mountain manager at the Snowbird resort in Utah next month, criticized the Squaw Valley facilities in an interview

Burkhart assumed responsibility last spring for all 26 lifts. He had worked at Squaw Valley eight years.

"Mr Cushing promised me a half-million dollars to make major improvements for this season. Instead, I got only $60,000, and this was barely enough to do the minimum preventive maintenance," Burkhart said.

"The exact figure was $269,536," Cushing said Wednesday and added that 21 of the lifts are less than eight years old.

A lift accident in late January injured several skiers, and Burkhart charged Wednesday that the chairlift "collapsed simply because it was no good. They put it back together in a hurry, but it was no better than before."

Cushing rebutted, "That's simply absurd," and said he will discuss the accident next Wednesday in a news conference in San Francisco.

"We've been getting a rash of bad publicity I want to reverse the trend," Cushing said.

Attendance has fallen off sharply since the accident, he said. The ski area has handled more than 8,000 skiers on its busiest days, but Cushing estimated that the best February single-day attendance was between 4,000 and 5,000.

"Up through January, we were 50 per cent ahead of last year In February, we were 50 per cent behind last year," he said.

eight inches in diameter and then shock loaded: the damaged section of rope needed to be removed and a replacement section spliced in. Rather than accepting this plan—which would have put the lift back in operation according to the requirements of the B-77 Code—Alex had a crew from Lift Engineering (which had installed the lift) replace the bolts that had sheared off in the bullwheel support structure, lever the haul rope back onto the bullwheel, and put the lift back in operation.

That was enough for me. The haul rope had been damaged, and it was clearly unacceptable and a code violation to put it back in service with nothing more than a casual, visual inspection. I wrote Alex a letter of resignation, effective at the end of February. When contacted by the press about the incident, I told the truth: The lifts had been demonstrated to be unsafe on multiple occasions; I had submitted a plan to bring them up to a standard of safety that would be acceptable to both the regulatory agency and the ski resort's insurance carrier; Alex had agreed to that plan, but later had withheld the funding required to do the work. He had taken a $615,000 proposal for lift improvements, reduced it to $225,000—and included ordinary maintenance in that amount—and then only been willing to spend a total of $75,000. I said that it was unacceptable and that I could no longer be a party to this substandard method of operation.

Alex, of course, fired back, calling a press conference at the Clift Hotel in San Francisco. My lawyer, Paul Minasian, and I attended the press conference, much to Alex's chagrin. His statements at the event ranged from confusing to blatantly false, alternately expressing complete confidence and satisfaction in my abilities and claiming that serious financial irregularities had been discovered and that I had quit just before I was going to be fired. He said that he had filed suit against me but was unclear just what the suit was for. He claimed in one sentence that he had "given" me $296,000 with which to do lift maintenance and in the next breath the amount had become $636,000. It was a typically bizarre performance by Alex. He could easily have anticipated what questions would be asked and prepared his answers, or at least had the documentation at hand to refer to, but he looked to be winging it, and that was not lost on the journalists who attended the event. At one point, one of them asked if I would be allowed to answer questions, and Alex replied, "No—if he wants to have a press conference, let him rent his own hall!"

He did a radio interview and cited a totally different amount of money that he claimed to have spent on lift maintenance and repair—an amount about four-and-a-half times the actual figure. One particularly fanciful claim was that Squaw Valley was so successful that "we pay our stockholders regularly…." In later years, he would boast that the company had never paid a dividend. He again claimed that I had stolen from the company. He said that Squaw Valley had the best lifts in the world, but that you could turn the best equipment into junk if you did not maintain them; but then he said that he was not saying that I had not maintained the lifts properly. It was contradictory and confusing at best.

He claimed that we agreed that I was to be paid $18,000 a year: $13,000 in cash and $5,000 in stock. This was news to me. I had never agreed to take stock in the company in lieu of payment and Alex's claim that I asked for stock seemed calculated to show a level of confidence in the company that I did not have. Alex stated this "agreement" several times, each time citing a vague date for when it had been discussed, "six months ago" and "oh, three or four months ago…." He claimed that the board of directors had just agreed to the transfer of stock and the Corporation Commissioner for the State of California had yet to approve it. It was a moving target and I doubted that the board had ever heard of the idea. Not surprisingly, I never saw a share of the stock.

Despite his inconsistent and evasive claims, he had filed a lawsuit against me claiming that I had stolen from the company. While Alex said at the press conference that there was rampant financial irregularity and made it sound like a considerable amount of money and property was missing, the supposed theft turned out to be a surveying instrument worth $1,400 that I had arranged with the Squaw Valley accounting department to buy and pay for using payroll deductions and toward which I had already made several payments.

I filed a lawsuit for slander, because Alex's untrue accusations had the potential to seriously damage my reputation and ability to earn a living in the future, and to recover the salary that he had agreed to but had not paid. The lawsuits were consolidated so that discovery and depositions, as well as the trial, if we got that far, would be handled as a single event.

I gave a deposition in Salt Lake City while working at Snowbird. Fortunately, the trial was not scheduled until the following spring, when the work at Snowbird had been completed. On May 23, 1972, the cases went to trial in Placer County Superior Court in Auburn, California. Although they blamed everything that had ever gone wrong at Squaw Valley on me, the issue for the jury to decide was whether I had stolen the transit, because that was the crux of their case and, if untrue, proved that Alex had slandered me by making the accusation. Although Alex denied any knowledge of the purchase of the transit, the head of the company's accounting department testified that he had told Alex about the purchase and that Alex had instructed him to bill me for it on an installment basis and subtract payments from my earnings. I had copies of payroll check stubs on which two payments had been deducted from my wages. There was also a copy of the original invoice for the instrument with a hand-written note to Alex on the face of it from the accountant, who testified that Alex had such a fantastic memory that there is no way he would have forgotten about the installment payment deal at the time he made the accusatory statements in March of 1971.

There were some simply bizarre accusations that came up in the trial. John Buchman testified under oath that there was carpet in my house that I had stolen from the company. I did have carpet in my house that had been purchased by Squaw Valley—that much was true. When we moved into the house on Squaw Valley Road, the floors were bare plywood: I did not have the money to have carpet installed. Markus was a baby and was crawling around on the plywood floor, getting splinters in his knees. There was a remodel being done in the Lodge and they had stripped out the old carpet and put it in a dumpster and I took several large pieces out, took them home and carpeted part of the house with them.

Now, eight years later, Mr. Buchman was claiming that I had stolen carpet that they had discarded. When the jury heard the truth of the situation, this story was an especially obvious example of the deceptive claims that they were making about me. Paul asked me if I had carpet in my house that had been in the Lodge and I admitted that I did, telling the jury how I had built the house with my own hands, putting in five or six hours of work on it in the evenings after having worked all day at the mountain, working on weekends, then moving in and not being able to afford to have it carpeted and how baby Markus had gotten splinters in his little knees. By now the jury was thinking that I *had* stolen it but was sympathetic because I was struggling to provide for my family. Once they realized that the carpet that John Buchman was claiming I had stolen was used carpet from hotel rooms that I had fished out of a dumpster, you could see the shift in attitude on their faces. The idea that I had "stolen" it was ridiculous, and it greatly diminished any credibility that Alex or John might have had with the jury.

The trial lasted eight days and the jury deliberated for only hours before returning with verdicts on the three issues. They found in my favor—awarding me $10,000 in damages in the slander lawsuit and $7,700 for unpaid wages.

Within a week, Alex and his lawyers had filed a motion for a new trial in Placer County Superior Court, claiming that the $10,000 that the jury had awarded me in damages was "excessive", that the evidence was insufficient and claiming an error in the original trial. That motion was denied by the judge in August. As we were leaving the courtroom after receiving the judge's ruling, Alex asked me if I wanted to go down the street and get some lunch. Over lunch, he started asking me about lifts and it seemed clear that he had put all the drama of the lawsuit behind him as soon as he left the courtroom. He was ready to move on.

In hindsight, it is mind-boggling to consider how much time and money—I would guess nearly $100,000—was wasted in the pursuit of this lawsuit. All over a $1,400 transit.

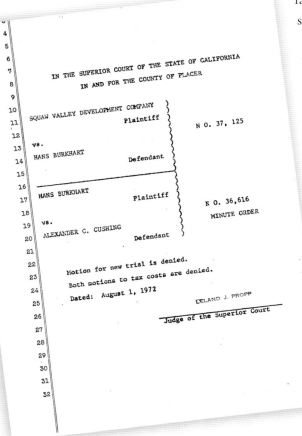

IN THE SUPERIOR COURT OF THE STATE OF CALIFORNIA
IN AND FOR THE COUNTY OF PLACER

SQUAW VALLEY DEVELOPMENT COMPANY

           Plaintiff

N O. 37, 125

vs.

HANS BURKHART

           Defendant

HANS BURKHART

           Plaintiff

N O. 36,616
MINUTE ORDER

vs.

ALEXANDER C. CUSHING

           Defendant

Motion for new trial is denied.
Both motions to tax costs are denied.
Dated: August 1, 1972

LELAND J. PROPP

Judge of the Superior Court

15

Snowbird Tram

The personal turmoil that accompanied quitting at Squaw Valley and being sued by Alex Cushing had to be forgotten as I prepared for the start of the installation work at Snowbird. It was a normally heavy winter in Utah—almost 500" of snow had fallen at Alta and Snowbird—and there was a lot of work to be completed before the Garaventa crew would arrive from Switzerland in May. I had rented a cabin for my family in the canyon between Snowbird and Alta and had arranged to rent the entire Gold Miner's Daughter lodge in Alta for the summer to house the Swiss crew—the owners had agreed to allow our cooks to use the kitchen so we could prepare three meals a day for the workers. The crew would want to have a place to hang out together in the evening, so this was an ideal situation with room for everyone. I hired the contractors who had lowered and flattened the top of Hidden Peak to bring their dozers back and start removing snow on the roads to the tower sites and the top terminal. It would be a long process, but the sooner we gained road access to those locations, the sooner we could begin assembling the towers on the foundations that were already in place.

The dozer operators started working on opening the roads and, predictably, progress was slow, because in places they were plowing twenty feet of snow off the road and in some locations the work took place on a steep slope. One of the operators, Jeff Johnson, came to me one evening and said that he was approaching a section to be plowed that was below a steep bowl and he was concerned that when he made the cut for the road, it would slide and sweep the Cat off the road. I thought he was being overly cautious, but the next morning I sent a kid we had hired as a laborer along with him with a radio to be a spotter. I told the kid to keep an eye on the situation and call me if he saw anything that looked troublesome. This was intended as reassurance enough to keep Jeff working, but sure enough, a few hours later the laborer called and said we had better come up.

"What happened?" I asked.

"It slid all right," said the kid. "The Cat's totally buried."

"How's Jeff—is he OK?" I asked.

An aerial view of Snowbird with the line for the tram superimposed.

The amount of snow that needed to be removed from the roadways presented a real challenge—and a significant hazard— to the dozer operators. The crane is dwarfed by the road cut in this image.

"All I can see is his hard hat sticking out of the snow," said the kid.

We fired up the helicopter, flew up and dug Jeff out and then put him in the helicopter and flew him to the hospital in Salt Lake City to be checked out. He was unhurt, but we never saw him again.

The Swiss crew arrived on May 17, 1971, along with my younger brother Toni who had joined them for the flight over and was going to help as a crane operator. Also joining the crew was Joe Suter, a teenager from a Swiss family in Truckee, California who would be spending his summer break from school helping Hardy with the electrical systems. We had received the first few containers of parts and set to work right away unpacking them and separating the tower pieces from the terminal machinery. We needed to remove the snow from around the tower footings and most of that work would have to be done by hand so that the footings would not be damaged. The top terminal site was less buried and was the easiest place to land the helicopter, so it made sense to start there and see how much we could get done.

Snowbird had hired a subcontractor, Cannon Construction, to build the lower terminal building, and Ted Johnson was supervising that work on behalf of Snowbird. The Cannon Construction employees were union members, and they made an issue of working with a bunch of foreigners who did not speak English and who were not in the union. Within a month of the arrival of the Garaventa crew, Snowbird had to hire an attorney to help smooth over the issues with the union. The union ironworkers, working for Cannon, felt that they were being cheated out of work by the non-union Swiss crew building the tram towers (although the union crew had plenty of work building the lower terminal building and other base-area facilities). The union allowed that it would be willing to issue "temporary work permits" to the Swiss workers if the Swiss crew paid dues to the union as well as a "health and welfare" contribution, and if a shop steward were assigned to work on the project to keep an eye on things for the union. The Iron Workers Union said that they had been contacted by the unions for the millwrights and carpenters, who were also "concerned" about the work at Snowbird. The unions were, with little to no subtlety about it, threatening to slow things down unless they received a thinly disguised payoff to "permit" the Garaventa crew to do their work—work that the union iron workers had never done, had no idea how to do and, frankly, had no interest in doing. It was all about money. Snowbird settled the issue—I wanted nothing to do with it.

Liam Fitzgerald was a 24 year old ski patroller working at Squaw Valley when he met Hans Burkhart. Liam's first impression was that "… he seemed a little gruff and aloof and didn't have a real good rapport with his Squaw Valley staff. Somehow I managed to get on his good side, and it was a real great experience: Hans was one hell of a guy! He was probably the hardest worker I've ever seen in my life, absolutely determined nothing was going to stop him from getting the job done. He set the standards! If you wanted a day off it was looked on as disloyalty to the cause. We worked 12 hours a day. He worked an additional two on either end."

Walt McConnell in *The Snowbird Tram, One of the World's Great Tramways*

The weather at Snowbird was so unrelenting that the Swiss crew—normally indifferent to snow and cold temperatures—took to calling it "Snow Hell." Werner Auer had driven to Utah from Squaw Valley across the Nevada and Utah deserts in blazing heat—yet when he reached Snowbird, it was snowing.

The parts and equipment coming to Snowbird from Garaventa in Switzerland had a long and complicated journey. Smaller parts and equipment were carefully crated, labeled and packed into shipping containers which were trucked to the railroad station in Goldau and then taken by rail to Basel, where they were loaded onto barges. Large pieces that would not fit in containers were loaded onto flatcars on the railroad or, in some cases, trucked to the port in Basel to be loaded. The barges floated down the Rhine River to Rotterdam, where the containers and larger parts would be loaded on a ship for the voyage to the U.S. The containers were unloaded at the Port of Los Angeles, loaded on rail cars and transported by rail to Salt Lake City, where they were unloaded from the train and trucked to Snowbird. That was the plan, anyway. In the middle of the project, the dockworkers went on strike, interrupting the flow of containers and larger parts out of the ports. The containers and structural parts had mostly arrived by the time the strike began, but the shipments of wire rope—track ropes, haul ropes, and rescue rope—came from Fatzer in Romanshorn, Switzerland and did not come on the same ship as the Garaventa parts. The ropes had been shipped through the Panama Canal and were scheduled to be unloaded in San Pedro, California, but because of the strike, they could not be unloaded there and were diverted to Vancouver, British Columbia where the port was in normal operation. Ted Johnson had alerted Union Pacific

Drilling for the tower anchor bolts pressed on regardless of the weather—even in the snow.

Railroad of the size and weight of the spools of track rope (99,400 pounds each, in a very concentrated footprint) and the railroad had sent four specially configured railcars to San Pedro to transport the spools of track rope, but when the ship was diverted to Vancouver, one of the special rail cars disappeared between Southern California and Canada. The railroad tried loading the spool onto another rail car, which collapsed under the load, but finally modified another rail car for the purpose, which succeeded.

When the track ropes reached Salt Lake City, they were loaded onto special heavy-haul tractor-trailer rigs. At the bottom of the canyon, a second power unit was brought up behind the trailer to push the load from behind. This was in addition to the tractor pulling the lengthy trailer. Even so, the trucking company was afraid that if they had to stop for any reason on their way up the canyon, the rig would not be able to get started again—it would just sit in one place and spin its wheels. With the road closed to other traffic by the Utah Highway Patrol, the four spools of track rope were hauled the ten miles up the canyon and unloaded onto a concrete slab behind the lower terminal that we had constructed for that purpose.

The little Bell utility helicopter bringing a load of parts to a tower site.

The haul ropes—which were shipped from Switzerland after the track ropes—managed to avoid the longshoremen's strike and came through the port of Galveston, Texas, and were shipped by railroad to Salt Lake City.

The little helicopter from Hoskin Helicopters expedited the commute to the tower locations and the top terminal. They were ready to go every day at 6 a.m. to take the first load up, and within about 40 minutes everyone was at their work site and hard at it. The helicopter could carry two men in addition to the pilot, and there were cargo baskets on the outside for their extra clothing, tools, rigging, small parts—whatever would fit in the basket. I found out the hard way that you had to be careful what was put in the basket, though.

Although we had a fast and efficient way to move the crew, moving materials was laborious. Although the access roads had been plowed, at first, they were extremely muddy and difficult to navigate. I had a Mercedes-Benz Unimog with all-wheel drive and large, knobby tires that we chained, and a flatbed trailer that we used to move a lot of the steel for the towers and top terminal structure. Then I rented a truck designed for delivering steel that had tandem rear axles and a one-man cab on the left side. On the right, the bed was flat all the way to the front of the truck, so you could carry long pieces that would overhang both the front and rear ends of the truck. Chained up, the truck would make it up the road until it hit the steeper, muddier parts, then we would tow it with the Unimog or a dozer.

NEAR DEATH EXPERIENCE #8

Snowbird Helicopter

One of the most valuable tools on the Snowbird project was Hoskins Helicopter's little Bell 47G—one of the first successful utility helicopters. If you have ever seen an episode of M.A.S.H., you know the helicopter with the lattice tail-boom and the Plexiglas bubble. Hoskins had a heli-skiing operation out of Alta in the winter, so their pilots were experts at mountain flying, and knew the area well. Although it was not large enough to fly large parts or much concrete, we had the helicopter standing by for the whole job. It flew the crews up to the tower sites each morning, brought them hot lunches, and made the job a lot more efficient because you could go look at something anywhere on site very quickly. I even had the pilot drop me on the top of a tram tower a few times, although he did not like doing that too much because the sudden change in weight in the ship made it unstable. I frequently took my kids (who were seven and five) along when I went somewhere in the helicopter, and they loved it.

Dick Bass was a great "idea guy" and was always looking at different ways to improve Snowbird. Even before we had finished the tram from the base area to Hidden Peak, he was thinking about adding a tram between Hidden Peak and White Pine Peak, which would open terrain to the west of the area served by the Hidden Peak location. Dick asked me to assess the potential of that area and see if building a tram to that peak was feasible—he wanted to discuss it with the Forest Service for future expansion. I had time to go look at it one day, and told that pilot that I would like him to take me up to look at White Pine Peak. It was a beautiful, sunny day and he was happy to go flying.

We took off and went up past Hidden Peak where the crew was finishing the top terminal, then flew west toward White Pine Peak. We were several thousand feet above ground level, but even so, as we crossed the ridge between Hidden Peak and White Pine Peak, there was a strong updraft and a sudden, very strong vibration in the helicopter. I had never felt anything like it before, and wondered what was going on. I looked over at the pilot, getting ready to ask him what was happening, but the look on his face told me that I should not. He had gone pale and was obviously fully concentrating on flying the ship. He never said one word and neither did I, even though we were now dropping rapidly. We were still moving forward and dropping into a large bowl and it quickly became obvious that we were going to crash. I could see the bottom of the bowl—which had been logged a couple of years before and was littered with downed, broken snags, large stumps, and boulders. It did not look like a good place to crash, and we were rapidly approaching what would become the scene of the accident. The pilot still seemed to have some measure of control and was obviously working hard to point us in the direction of one of the less cluttered areas in which to crash. When we were still a few hundred feet above the bottom of the bowl, he managed to use our forward momentum to clear the north edge of that bowl and, dropping fast, point us toward the bottom of the next drainage, which was Little Cottonwood Creek and the highway between Sandy and Snowbird. It was hard to tell whether we could make it to the road or not—we were dropping rapidly—and my only thought was, "Thank God I didn't bring the kids...."

We made it over the creek and crashed hard onto the road. The doors both popped off and all the windows blew out—there were parts all over the road. We both got out quickly and were standing on the highway shaking. The entire tail rotor was gone. Earlier, when I had I boarded, I had put a heavy, hand-knit wool sweater in the basket on the outside of the helicopter—where they carried skis in the winter—and when we hit the updraft, the sweater had blown out of the basket and into the tail rotor. The tail rotor had stopped turning, the driveline sheared, and the tail rotor and gearbox had fallen off. The pilot had done an amazing job of autorotating; keeping the main rotor turning and the helicopter flying—dropping like a stone, but still flying. He later told me he knew of only two other pilots who had survived losing a tail rotor. Now he knew three.

Of all my close calls with death, this one was the most frightening, by far. It was probably all over in less than a minute, but during the whole time we were scanning the ground, we were figuring that we were looking at where we were going to crash and probably die.

The crane and steel truck at Tower 4, which is nearly complete in this photo.

We had two cranes—a small Grove rough terrain crane that we used mostly on the terminals and a larger crane that I rented to build the towers. After building the towers at Squaw Valley using the Garaventa "needle" system—Karl Garaventa had been reluctant to spend the money to rent a crane—I thought we could achieve greater efficiency using a crane. The needle worked well in the hands of a capable, experienced operator, and if access for a crane was impossible, it was the only alternative, but the Snowbird project demanded efficiency and I knew we could work a lot faster with a crane. Toni ran the crane for the crew building the towers and did a great job.

Between long hours, working seven days a week, snow and cold temperatures, not to mention the difficult, dangerous and arduous work, I was pushing the crew hard. It was not unexpected—I had known from the start that this would be the case and I also knew that if I took good care of them, they would deliver on every expectation. The accommodations at the Gold Miner's Daughter were excellent and we had three girls from Switzerland who prepared three hot meals a day for the guys. We flew hot lunches in insulated containers up to the tower sites and top terminal every day with the helicopter. Toni had constructed a little shed with a table and benches so the crew could sit inside and have lunch out of the weather. Eating a good meal at lunch time served several purposes: It was the familiar, European way of doing things; it helped the crew maintain their energy and stamina for hard work in the afternoon, especially in miserable weather; and it showed that we cared for the crew, which was great for morale. I bought a yellow Ford station wagon for the three Swiss cooks to use to go into Salt Lake City and buy groceries. They were going through a lot of food and cooking pretty much constantly—we were pushing them as hard as the crew. My wife, Hedi, helped in the kitchen as well—everyone ate very well that summer.

The secret weapon, however, was schnapps! Packed in the shipping containers with the parts, the Garaventa crew had included special barrels marked "Cable Cleaner" which, although it probably could have been used as cable cleaner, was high-test Swiss schnapps, distilled from apples and pears—Swiss moonshine. One of the Swiss crew had a still in his barn at home and had run off a few hundred gallons for the Garaventa crew to bring to the United States. The crew seemed to have a special knack for knowing which containers concealed the schnapps, because when a new batch of parts arrived, they would always unpack that container first. The customs inspectors never caught on to this ruse—I guess they never imagined that anyone would drink cable cleaner. The crew would have a few rounds of coffee schnapps every night after dinner and frequently Dick Bass would stop by and partake along with the Swiss guys, which enhanced his reputation as a regular guy with the crew, and he seemed to have a genuinely good time as well.

The helicopter really enhanced the efficiency of the operation, even though it was not a heavy-lift machine capable of flying parts or concrete to the towers. It provided us with a few tense moments as well. One day, the guys working at the top terminal called and said that I needed to come there and look at something—there was a part that did not fit correctly or that needed to be modified slightly. The helicopter was available, and flying up would shorten the overall time required by quite a bit, so I went and found the pilot and told him where I needed to go. He was reluctant. The weather was cloudy and variable, although it was clear along the path we needed to take. We could just fly up to the top, look at the problem, come right back down.

"Do I need to get a Russian pilot?" I asked. "A good pilot would have no problem getting me up there and back…."

The Snowbird crew putting on some evening entertainment. There may have been schnapps involved in this production.... Left to right: Ernst Gisler, Toni Burkhart, Franz Voneu, Hardy Herger, Art Brogli.

NEAR-DEATH EXPERIENCE #9
Snowbird Dozer

Pulling the track cables on the Snowbird tram was a challenging and time-sensitive aspect of the project. The towers and top terminal were finished, and we needed to pull the track ropes because the subcontractor building the lower terminal could not close in the building until the track ropes were pulled through it and tensioned. The weather was threatening—it had already been -30 degrees at Tower 4 with a bitter wind out of the bowl, and it was clear that we had to keep the project moving along without delay. We had a large winch that Garaventa had sent from Switzerland with which to pull the ropes over the towers to the top terminal, but midway through the job, a critical part on the winch had broken. It would have to be manufactured, and was going to take a week to arrive from Switzerland. We did not have that kind of time: We had to keep pulling the ropes. I figured that we would be able to pull them with one of the large dozers, and we set up a couple of deflection sheaves to allow me to pull the track ropes into position while driving the dozer down the Regulator Johnson run just east of the tram line. We got everything set up and I started pulling, and it went well, at first. The slope I was driving down was very steep. Part way down, a section of willows matted down under the tracks of the dozer. The dozer started to slide on them. The tension of the cable attached to the back kept it straight, but the brakes had little effect—the Cat was sliding on the flattened saplings. This was okay until I came across a large boulder and the Cat went up onto the boulder and stopped, high-centered on the rock. The tracks were off the ground, and even with the blade dropped all the way, I could not reach the ground to try to free the machine. I was stuck. Because the pulling cable was attached to the back of the machine, we could not move it backward, and it would be impossible to get another machine below it in a location that would allow us to use it to pull the Cat forward. The only solution I could come up with was to get rid of the boulder under the machine.

I got on the radio and called Hardy, who had a little six-wheeled utility vehicle. I told him to get a couple of cases of dynamite out of the magazine, as well as some blasting caps, the blasting machine, and a long reel of wire, and come up to where I was stuck with the Cat. When Hardy got there, we set to work packing dynamite around the boulder, into any cracks we could find, and then placing the blasting caps and connecting the leads from the caps to the wire.

I said, "Okay, so roll the wire out to the tree over there, connect the ends to the terminals on the blasting machine, get behind the tree, and when I tell you to, push the plunger down."

What?" Hardy said. "I thought you were going to do it. Where are you going to be?"

"I'm going to be on the Cat," I said. "I have to be on it because when we blow up the rock, it's going to take off down the hill. If I'm not on it, it could flip over and then we'll be in a worse pickle than we are now."

"Well, I'm not going to blow up the rock with you sitting on the dozer, Hans," Hardy said. "You'll get killed!" He was getting very excited and walking back and forth in agitation. "No way, I'm not going to do that!"

This went on for quite a while, Hardy walking around in circles, waving his hands and exclaiming about what a crazy idea it was and that he wanted no part of it.

"If you won't do it," I said, "I'll just get on the radio and have someone else come up, Hardy. We have to get the Cat off the rock, and this is the only way to do it, so just go over there and push the plunger!" I thought he was going to go crazy, but I rolled out the wire and connected the blasting machine, then got him to hide behind the tree, still very worked up and nervous about the whole thing. I got back on the Cat, fired it up, put it in gear at idle and yelled, "Push the plunger!" There was a short delay, during which I am sure Hardy was praying, hoping that he was doing the right thing, then the dynamite went off with a terrific boom. Rock flew everywhere, and the Cat lurched forward and to the right, so far that I thought it was going to flip over. There was no cab, so if it started to go, I would have to jump off to avoid getting crushed, but it settled back onto both tracks, slid down a little more on the willows and then continued down the run as if nothing had happened.

We finished pulling the track cables without further drama, and Hardy did not ruin our friendship by blowing me up. It was a story that he loved to tell, even years later.

Werner Auer, in recalling that day said that he just stood there in disbelief and commented, "Hans, you're the craziest German I've ever seen."

Walt McConnell in *The Snowbird Tram, One of the World's Great Tramways*

"Okay, let's go", he said, "I can't have you hiring any Russians—you'd get killed."

We climbed in the helicopter, flew up to the top and I went to look at the problem, which was more complicated than I had anticipated. After a few minutes, I peeked outside—the weather was closing in and we really could not afford to have the helicopter stranded at the top of the hill. There was still a promising looking clear spot toward the south. Maybe we could head that direction and circle back to the west and back up the canyon. I went back to the ship.

"I think we'd better get out of here," I said. "We can't afford to have you stuck up here."

"You're reading my mind," said the pilot, "I'm going to follow that blue sky and try to skirt around the front." We took off and headed toward the patch of blue, which was south of us—taking us farther away from the base of Snowbird every minute. We kept looking for an opportunity to head east or west and loop back toward Snowbird, but there were no breaks. We kept going south, dodging the weather and finally had to give up and land… at the Provo airport.

We were fine, but back at the job site, someone called the top terminal on the radio looking for me: "Hey, is Hans up there?"

"No—he should be down there."

"No, he's not down here."

"Is the helicopter down there?"

"I don't see it."

The top terminal with Sandy, Utah and the South Valley in the distance.

"Well, he left here in the helicopter about a half hour ago."

"Oh." Long silence

So, for about twenty minutes, the helicopter and I were "missing"—creating a minor panic—until I called the office looking for a ride back from the Provo Airport. Unfortunately, it was not to be the last dramatic moment involving the helicopter.

While work on the tram was progressing on the mountain, we were also building three chairlifts—Wilbere, Gad 1, and Gad 2—lower on the mountain. I had built roads to the tower locations the previous summer and fall, and I had an excavation contractor dig the tower footing holes according to the specifications from Doppelmayr and a concrete contractor who formed, set the anchor bolts and rebar, then poured the concrete. Werner Auer was working at the fabrication yard in Salt Lake City every day, and it was a tough assignment. The difference in working conditions between the mountain and Salt Lake City was dramatic: Werner worked many days in temperatures above 100 degrees fabricating the lift towers, crossarms, and bases, and would come back up the canyon in the evening just as temperatures in the city were cooling down. We probably should have put him on a night shift. We had a trucking company bring the completed towers up the canyon to be installed by the Swiss crew, who worked on the chairlifts on Sunday. Each week one of our challenges was to have the work for Sunday lined out so that we could make the most efficient use of the labor on the chairlifts when we had it. It was amazing to see how much we could get done every week with just one day of concentrated work on the three lifts. I built a work tram—a track rope supported by a few towers with a platform moved by a small winch at the top—along the line of the Wilbere chair to make it easier to move tools and equipment along the line. That lift would be in a prime viewshed from the hotel, and Dick and Ted wanted to minimize the number of roads we built to the towers, so the work tram expedited our work with minimal lasting impact. The top and bottom terminals of each of the chairlifts were assembled and erected as the parts arrived from Austria.

The design of the tower saddles—the curved supports for the track ropes—used a larger than normal radius so that the

The saddles were large and heavy and a good bit longer than the truck that transported them to the towers.

JOE ZOLINE

While working on the Snowbird project in 1970, I got a call from a man in Los Angeles named Joe Zoline: he wanted me to evaluate some land that he owned in Colorado for potential development as a ski area. I did not really have time and told him that, but he was the kind of guy who wouldn't take no for an answer, and it was clear that he was determined to get someone in the ski industry to have a look at the property.

"It's easy," he said. "Just park at the Salt Lake City airport, rent a car, drive down to Southwest Colorado and look around. Then drive down to Albuquerque and drop off the rental car. I will send a plane to bring you to L.A. to fill me in. Then you fly back to Salt Lake. It's a real quick project, and I'll make it worth your while."

I agreed—the fee he offered was generous for a day or two of work and it would just be a verbal report, no need to do a big write up.

I rented a car and drove over to Grand Junction, Colorado, then south for a couple of hours, passing through a few western slope farming towns along the way. Farther south, the road narrowed, and I passed through a handful of what I suppose had been mining towns, now long abandoned and with only a few houses occupied. Clearly the mining economy had dried up long before. I drove down the main street of the little town where Zoline's land was located: It showed more signs of life than the surrounding area because it was the county seat—the county courthouse was right on the main street—and because there was a mining operation at the east end of town that was still in operation, providing some jobs for the residents. The downtown area, while only a couple of blocks long, had a lot of interesting buildings, but only a few businesses were in operation—it was a very sleepy looking place. The mountains around it were tall, steep and magnificent however, it was quite a dramatic setting: more like a town in the Alps than in the Southwestern U.S.

I drove up the highway a little where I could get onto a road that would let me explore the area above the little plateau to the south of the town. I had a topo map with an estimated outline of Zoline's parcel, which had been a large sheep ranch. The slope angles and aspect were very favorable, and there was a mix of forested terrain and peaks above tree line that looked very appealing. Satisfied that the topography and configuration of the mountain would support skiing, I drove south to Albuquerque, dropped the rental car and located Zoline's pilot, who flew me to Los Angeles. A car waiting at the airport drove me to a country club—I do not know which one, but by the look of it, it was the country club for millionaires and billionaires. Joe Zoline was waiting for me in a private dining room. He was a successful businessman and attorney and looked the part: expensive suit, gold watch and jewelry. I told him I thought his mountain had great potential. The escarpment between the plateau and the town was steep enough to be expert skiing, but it was north facing and would have excellent snow quality and great glade skiing, while the plateau had a generally southwestern exposure and moderate slope angles that would provide fine beginner and intermediate skiing as well as sunny open expanses with great views. The areas above tree line—and there looked to be some dramatic terrain within the area that he owned— had excellent potential for expert skiing, but would present an obvious avalanche control challenge.

"However," I said, "it's in 'no-man's land.'" It was not close to a city of any size, and there's no population base, lodging, or a way to readily get there. I told him I did not know how he could possibly make a success out of a place that was so remote, no matter how terrific the mountain might be. "I'm going to build an airport and fly skiers in from L.A. in 747s," he said, as if the planes were just sitting there waiting to be used. "You know all those skiers who drive up to Mammoth every weekend from L.A?" he said. "They could get on a plane, fly to Colorado, and be asleep in their hotel in less time than it takes to drive to Mammoth after work."

I had to admire his confidence. Mr. Zoline's former sheep ranch turned out to be a rather good ski resort even though the sleepy little town had a funny name: Telluride.

tram cabins would be able to cross the towers without slowing from full speed. The saddles were the single largest and heaviest components of the towers and were a long and heavy load to transport to the towers. To accommodate the extraordinary length of the saddles, we built special roads to the bases of the towers that were backfilled and restored once the saddles were installed. The saddles could be hoisted into position using the lifting frames on the tops of the towers, or set into place using the crane, and once they were in place, the towers—except for the electronics—were complete and ready the installation of cable.

As the towers were completed, the crew would dedicate each one to someone special who was then expected to climb the tower to see the wood plaque inscribed with their name. Tower 4 was called "Wilma" after Ted Johnson's wife, and Tower 2 was called "Hedi," after my wife at the time—both of whom gamely climbed the towers to see their plaque. Art Brogli would go up the tower with his accordion to serenade the honoree as they climbed—it was quite a party and was accompanied with a picnic dinner and, of course, plenty of schnapps.

Preparing to hoist the saddle for Tower 4.

The top terminal was constructed and equipped and the lower terminal—although installation of the drive equipment had to be coordinated with the Cannon Construction schedule—was nearing completion. We had hiked hemp rope down the line with which we could pull strong, small diameter winch pilot cables that would allow us to pull the track ropes into place. The track rope had to be pulled through the lower terminal building and as we were pulling one of the track ropes, I noticed that the Cannon Construction guys had a concrete pump set up behind the building, near the line we were pulling. I told them they needed to move it because once we had pulled the track rope, there would be no way to slack the line. They did not take my warning seriously, because as we finished pulling the rope and it came under tension at the lower terminal, it lifted the concrete pump right off the ground so that it was hanging on the track rope. As might be expected, this created great excitement among the

Cannon guys, who wanted us to slacken the track rope and let the pump down. I told them that was impossible, and they ended up having to rent a crane to rig the pump and lift it clear of the track rope and back to the ground. They took our warnings with more seriousness after that.

The cabins arrived, having endured an ocean voyage and a truck journey over Donner Summit which was, naturally, delayed by snow. The cabins were crated and someone at the port had decided that it would be a good idea to truck them on their sides, rather than upright. This caused damage to the doors on one cabin. The crew was able to repair the door onsite, however.

With the cabins onsite, the carriages were placed on the track ropes, the hangers installed, and the cabins attached to the

Lifting Cabin 2 into place below the hanger.

hangers. The tram was really starting to shape up and, even with the miserable weather, it seemed likely that we could make the deadline. As snow started to pile up on the slopes, I thought it would be a little bit of a reward for the crew to ski down after work, if it was still light out. We did this once—I led a handful of the Swiss guys down from the top—and after watching them ski, I decided that we had better finish the job before allowing any of them to ski again. If they kept skiing, soon we would not have enough people to complete the project: they were a lot braver than they were skilled.

The project wrapped up with a big celebration and a grand opening. The end of our work was the beginning of a new resort, and it was an exciting and glamorous time. Dick and Ted invited every important person in Utah and every politician who had had even a small part in getting Snowbird off the ground. There were speeches and tributes to all of them and a lot of self-congratulation. The one omission was the Swiss crew, who had worked incredibly hard for seven-day weeks for months and months in miserable weather with a great attitude, and they had finished the tram and three chairlifts on time to make the opening. Not a word about them, which was a serious and painful oversight.

Since Hedi, Markus, Kathrin and I were living in the little cabin just up the road, I stayed for most of the winter to babysit the tram and the new lifts, making sure that they were running well and that the lift operators and lift maintenance crew felt confident about their work. Markus was in first grade at the elementary school in Alta—the school bus stopped every morning for him on the highway. One snowy morning Hedi walked the kids up the path to the highway to wait for the bus. They waited and waited—no bus. They finally returned to the house and Hedi called the school to ask what was going on. It turned out that the highway was closed waiting for avalanche control work to be finished and the bus could not get through. Hedi realized that all that time she and the children had been standing on the side of the road waiting, they were right in the crosshairs of one of the most dangerous avalanche paths in Little Cottonwood Canyon. Someone had forgotten to call and let her know to stay in the cabin. I think the school may have learned some new Swiss swear words by the time Hedi finished with them.

Dick Bass was right—it was a perfect place for a tram!

16

Grouse Mountain, Vancouver, B.C.

In 1973, I had a call from Doppelmayr about a project in Vancouver, British Columbia. Grouse Mountain ski resort was expanding and planning to build two fixed-grip double chairlifts. The resort had been in operation since the 1930s and was conveniently located at the north edge of the city of Vancouver. I flew to Vancouver to look at the project, arriving in the evening. The general manager of the resort, Mr. Stokes, picked me up at the airport. I thought he would just drop me off at a hotel and pick me up in the morning to go look at the site and talk business, but he invited me to his house for dinner, which was a very friendly and generous offer—Canadian hospitality!

We had a nice dinner with his wife and daughter, and then we talked about the project and the plans for the resort. I was thinking I had better get to the hotel so I could get checked in, and mentioned that to Stokes.

"Oh, you don't have to do that," he said. "You can stay with us!"

Well, even more Canadian hospitality!

We talked some more about the project and it was getting pretty late. Finally, Stokes said, "I guess we'd better turn in. Now, my daughter's nineteen, so I can't really expect you to sleep with her, so I'll have my wife sleep with her, and you can sleep with me." To say I was surprised would not even begin to describe my shock at this idea, but it was so weird and unexpected I had no idea what to say or how to politely extricate myself from the situation without offending my host (and a potential client).

I just had to write it off to Canadian hospitality.

Grouse Mountain had a small tram, built in 1966 by a company called Voest which had built the original tramway at Jackson Hole in 1964. It was a forty-five-passenger tram and was very much an old-school design in that it had a single-track rope (two are much more common for passenger tramways). The haul rope had been damaged and although the resort had ordered a new rope from Fatzer in Switzerland, delivery of the new rope was going to take months, and they desperately needed the lift soon. The damage was too far from the socket to allow them to simply shorten the haul rope, so they wanted to splice a replacement section into the haul rope, which is simply never done. It is against all the codes in Europe, and the U.S. and Canadian codes don't address it, because they're much less focused on tramways than on chairlifts, and the writers of the codes never thought to include it, because it just doesn't happen. The damage was just uphill of one of the cabins. It was a particularly difficult location, because as the cabin approached the terminals, there was vibration in the haul rope which increased in frequency as the distance between the cabin and the sheaves in the terminal saddle decreased. That variable frequency vibration could have a lot of effects on a splice, which relies entirely on friction and tension on the rope to keep it intact and safe. A vibration is always problematic, because it makes things move and it may cause them to move in relation to one another and eventually come apart. Vibration that varies in frequency is particularly problematic because while a single frequency may not be trouble-some, when you run through a whole spectrum of frequency, you will probably hit one or more that creates an issue.

Chairlift ropes are large loops—generally a length of wire rope with a single splice. When the rope stretches, the splice is taken apart, the rope shortened and then re-spliced. On a tramway, there are generally separate upper and lower haul ropes: rather than being a spliced loop of rope, they are just long pieces that attach to the carriages that roll along the track ropes and support the cabins. The upper haul rope attaches to the upper end of the carriage on each cabin and runs through the upper terminal where the haul rope may be tensioned and the lower haul rope attaches to the lower end of the carriages and runs through the lower terminal, where the drive may be located. The ends of the haul rope are attached to the carriages using "sockets," steel fixtures which secure the ends of the haul rope in a housing that, correctly assembled, is stronger than the rope itself. When the haul rope on a tram needs to be shortened, you cut off the socket, shorten the rope, and make a new socket.

I knew that no one would splice the haul rope for them, because the splicer would be sticking his neck out a mile if something went wrong. At the same time, I was certain that a good splice would be perfectly safe and would allow the tram—and the rest of the moun-tain—to operate until the new haul rope arrived and could be installed. They had enough extra wire rope to provide the piece that we would need, so I told them I would do the splice and mark it well. They would have to inspect it daily without fail prior to operation of the tram. They were only too willing to agree, so we spliced in the replacement section of rope, and made a new socket on the downhill end. It performed flawlessly until the new rope arrived and was installed.

The chairlift construction project in North Vancouver was a unique experience. I have never been in a place that was so wet so much of the time, and if I am never in a place that wet again, that will be fine. It rained almost all day, every day. We had to wear rain gear constantly and were often soaking wet inside the rain gear. We would go back to our rented cabin at lunchtime every day and change out of the soaking wet clothes and into dry clothes. Once we went back to work and put on our rain gear, our dry clothes would stay dry for about a half hour.

The trees were all full of moss and there were blueberry bushes everywhere and they were loaded with berries. Thanks to this abundant food supply, there were bears all over the place, all the time. In the middle of the day, there would be bears stuffing themselves with blueberries. Hardy was with me on the project and he needed a vehicle so he could carry the electrical parts and go from tower to tower, so I got him a Jeep. It was an open-topped Jeep with no doors—an old CJ5—and it had no brakes. I told Hardy that it had no brakes thinking that he would take it somewhere in town and have the brakes repaired.

He said, "I can drive it without brakes; no problem!" (He loved to say that: "No problem!")

I said, "Hardy, are you sure about that?"

Oh, yeah—he was sure. It had a manual transmission and low gears and if you were cautious and went slowly in a low gear, it worked out fine. He drove the Jeep all summer, and was proud that he could drive the Jeep all over the place without brakes. Late in the job, Hardy had pretty much wrapped up his work, and he gave the Jeep to one of the other guys who needed a vehicle. I'm sure Hardy told him that the Jeep had no brakes and maybe the guy thought Hardy was kidding or was exaggerating about how bad the brakes were, but at the end of the job Hardy and I were on one of the towers doing something and we heard a noise and looked up in time to see the Jeep coming down the hill, driverless, picking up speed as it came down the mountain and then hitting a road cut and getting airborne, crashing to the ground and flipping over and over, until it was just a wadded mess.

There was an engineer from Doppelmayr who came to the job site in Vancouver a couple of times—once he flew into Vancouver from somewhere in the Far East or Australia, and he called and said that he had just gotten into town and was at the hotel. He said he had not been able to sleep on the plane and was going to get some rest. I figured he would come by the job site the next day, but he never showed up. The following day, there he was. I asked where he had been and he said, "At the hotel…." He had checked into the hotel and had slept for twenty or twenty-four hours. I had never heard of anyone who could do that before.

As the job was winding down in North Vancouver, Hardy and I were going to drive back to Nevada in one of the pickups, where I would leave it and come back with the Kenworth tractor-trailer rig to start demobilizing. I told one of the guys on the crew to gather up any tools or parts we would not need again and load them in the bed of the pickup so that we

Lucky for us, Hardy and I never got to see 'The Rock'!

we would not be driving it back empty. He put a good-sized load together and Hardy and I left the next morning, driving south through Vancouver and Surrey, then going through U.S. Customs at the border and into Washington.

We stopped to get some coffee in Bellingham, and when I got out of the truck, I glanced at the load in the back just to make sure that everything was tied down and stable. It was then I saw something that I had not noticed before, and fortunately for us, neither had the U.S. Customs officer who checked our ID and asked a few questions at the border: Right on the top of the load in the back were two cases of dynamite.

I said to Hardy, "I didn't notice that dynamite. It's a good thing the Immigration guy didn't notice it either or we'd be going to The Rock."

"Rock?" Hardy asked. "What rock?"

"Alcatraz," I replied.

"Oh boy, oh boy…."

17

Pacific Crest Trail— Ebbetts Pass, California

I n 1974, looking to take a break from the deadlines and hassles of lift construction, I came across a solicitation to bid for a Forest Service project—to build a section of the Pacific Crest Trail (PCT) near Ebbetts Pass, California, which is about forty-five miles south of Lake Tahoe. The project was to build a small parking area, a bathroom (pit toilet), and five miles of trail from California State Route 4 to Noble Lake. I worked up a bid, which was accepted, and bought a trail-building machine from a company in Oregon—a small backhoe mounted on very narrow crawler tracks. This was long before anyone was

Highway 4 north of Ebbett Pass shows the rugged and beautiful terrain of the eastern Sierra Nevada.

building a mini-excavator, and the backhoe arm pivoted on the body of the machine, rather than rotating with the cab, but it was a useful little machine for working on a very narrow space, like a trail. I also found a two-wheel-drive motorcycle, called a Rokon Trailbreaker, that would allow me to carry cargo into the worksite along a trail or even on relatively steep terrain.

The east end of Ebbetts Pass is south of Markleeville, California, and the road reaching it, California State Route 4, is old, narrow, and very winding—more of a pioneer-era wagon road that has been paved than anything resembling a modern highway. The road is so steep and twisting in places that it is very rarely used by large trucks, which need to use both lanes to navigate the corners; not always possible even on a lightly traveled road like State Route 4. A tractor-trailer with a load of ice cream made the mistake of using Ebbetts Pass while I was working on the project. He started out in a gear too high to provide effective engine braking for the descent, then wore through his brakes. Gaining speed toward a hairpin curve, the driver realized he could not slow down and would not make the turn. He jumped at the last second and the truck plunged into the canyon, destroying the trailer and scattering ice cream everywhere. The Forest Service required the company to clean up the ice cream, which was quite a project.

View of the meadow adjacent to the parking area and bathroom I built as part of the Pacific Crest Trail project. The parking area provides day-hikers on the PCT a place to leave their car without parking on the narrow highway.

The terrain through which the Pacific Crest Trail segment was to pass was a mix of forested areas, meadows, and traverses across slopes and rock outcroppings—beautiful country, surrounded by mountain peaks topping out above tree line. At the highway, the elevation was about 8,700 feet, and the trail dropped down to just below 8,300 feet and then climbed to almost 8,900 at Noble Lake. There were a few small creek crossings along the way—most seasonal, but Noble Creek ran all year in a typical year.

In the forested areas and meadows, the trail-building machine worked well, clearing vegetation and allowing minor cut and fill and grading using the small blade on the front of the tracks and the backhoe. Traversing a slope required more cut and fill using the backhoe and, although the machine was slow and awkward to operate compared to a more modern machine, it did a good job and was much faster than doing the same work with pick and shovel. There were areas where I had to drill and blast rock to create a wide enough pathway at the allowed gradient. I had a Pionjar; a Swedish-made rock drill powered by a small, two-stroke gasoline engine that, while a miserable tool to operate, did a reasonably good job of drilling holes for the explosives. The drilling got to be enough of a chore that I hired one of the Squaw Valley ski patrollers—Barry Dow—to come down and help me drill for a week or two through the section requiring the most blasting.

For those four months, I worked by myself quite a bit, although my son Markus came down from Squaw Valley and worked with me on weekends and when school was out. We could start early in the morning to avoid the hottest part of the day and work into the evening. We camped where we were working and moved our campsite every few days as we worked our way south toward Noble Lake. There was an existing trail into Noble Lake from State Route 4, but it intersected the highway west of the PCT alignment. I found that using this trail worked well for resupplying my camp as I got farther south. One week, I brought in a couple of fifty-pound cases of dynamite on the motorcycle using that existing trail. Part of it traversed a section of slope that was very steep below the trail. This, of course, was where the top-heavy load on the motorcycle got the best of me. The Rokon tipped over and tumbled off the trail and down the slope, the cases of dynamite rolling and bouncing down the hill as well, although fortunately the boxes stayed closed. I hiked down and carried the dynamite back up, somewhat farther down the trail. It took quite a while to traverse the motorcycle across the slope to a place where I could get it back onto the trail and repack the load. Fortunately, the Rokon was tough as nails and was undamaged by the off-trail excursion—it was a good thing because that happened more than once.

The Pacific Crest Trail (PCT) project, while a lot of hard work, was a very pleasant and relaxed period in my life. That it is such a popular section of the PCT—a well-used "out and back" hike to Noble Lake—is especially gratifying, and it makes me proud that my first trail construction project has been such a lasting success.

Smithers, British Columbia

Just after Thanksgiving in 1974, I got a call from Doppelmayr in Kelowna, British Columbia asking for help. One of their chairlifts in a little town called Smithers had caught fire and had badly damaged the drive terminal and a section of the haul rope. Thanksgiving is always a busy time in the lift construction business—everyone is racing the weather to finish installation work and load test the new lifts—you are literally working seven days a week, twelve (or more) hours a day. Doppelmayr had no one to repair the lift in Smithers, and the town was desperate to get the lift ready to operate, because it was their only chairlift and without it, there would be no skiing that winter. I flew to Vancouver and then arranged a ride in a private plane to Smithers, a logging and mining town about 425 air miles north of Vancouver.

The lift was intact other than the burned drive terminal. The gearbox and bullwheel could be reused, but all the other components in the drive had been burned beyond repair, and the wire rope was damaged where it had been subjected to radiant heat from the fire. It was repairable and everyone in town seemed to be anxious to have it fixed by Christmas, which was going to be hard to accomplish.

Hardy Herger flew up to Vancouver and I tasked him with finding the components and building a drive that I could have trucked to Smithers and simply plug in. There would need to be some structural modifications—a couple of new footings—to match up with the equipment that Doppelmayr had in inventory, so I dug and formed new footings. The only problem was that the air temperature was thirty below zero—the concrete would freeze as soon as it was poured and have no strength. I built a framework of lumber around the terminal, covered that with plastic sheeting, and put several propane-fired space heaters inside to bring up the temperature.

The concrete batch plant operator said, "Oh, no. We can't make any concrete when it's this cold…."

I told him that in order to have the lift ready by Christmas, they would have to figure something out. Evidently, they did, because they delivered a couple of loads of perfectly good concrete for me.

Every place I went in town, people knew who I was, and they'd say, "Oh—you're the guy who is going to have our lift fixed for Christmas! Dinner is on us…." It was the same at the lumber yard, the hardware store, the five restaurants in town: "Your money's no good here—you're going to get our lift going for Christmas." It was all very nice, but clearly, the pressure was on.

Working in Vancouver, Hardy assembled and wired the motor room. He had it set up so that I would need to connect about ten plugs then hit the start button—exactly what I needed. I sent a truck down from Smithers to pick it up. It bolted right up to

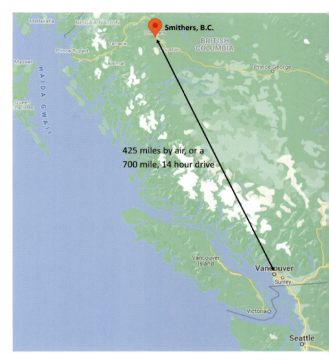

Smithers was a very nice little town, but it was a long, long way from a source of lift parts.

the support structure, and I got the gearbox and bullwheel mounted and figured out how long the replacement section of cable had to be. We did two splices to insert the replacement section of haul rope, put the cable back on the bullwheel, hung the chairs. The lift was ready to run on the day before Christmas.

While I was in Smithers, I had a call from a company that had a gondola in Prince Rupert, Canada. "Can you come take a look at the top terminal?" the manager asked. "It has a clicking noise that I can't figure out."

I got a flight to Prince Rupert, and as we came in to land, we came in low over the ocean and touched down just as soon as pavement appeared. Right away, the pilot started braking hard and everything in the plane vibrated and rattled like crazy until we had finally slowed enough to turn onto a taxiway. I noticed we were right at the far end of the runway, looking, once again, at the ocean.

The gondola owner met me, and we drove a short distance to the bottom terminal. We rode up to the top and watched and listened while the gondola ran—sure enough: "Click… click… click." I listened to the bullwheel bearing to rule it out as a source of the sound, but it was quiet. I could see movement in the haul rope against the rubber bullwheel liner as it went around toward the downline—it should have been motionless in relation to the liner—and the friction between the rope and the liner seemed to be the source of the sound.

We went back to the bottom and I took a piece of plastic flagging and poked the end of it into the cable, then went back to the top. When the flagging got to the top, it had wrapped around the haul cable seventeen times—the cable was twisting on the up-line and the clicking noise was the built-up tension in the cable releasing as it reached the bullwheel at the top station. What had probably happened was when the haul cable was installed, the crew had unspooled it in a different manner than the way in which it had been wound onto the spool when it was manufactured. They introduced twist into the loop of cable, then spliced it, trapping the rotational energy in the loop. The only solution would be to take the splice apart and allow the cable to relax and release the twist, so that it was in a state of rotational equilibrium all the way around. The rubber liner in the bullwheel would last a lot longer that way, too.

Once we opened the splice, allowed the twist to come out of the upline, and re-spliced it, the clicking sound went away—job done.

The road to Smithers, just a 700 mile drive from Vancouver. I'm sure a lot more of it is paved today.

19

1970s Squaw Valley

The 1970s brought significant and lasting change to Squaw Valley, in many ways establishing the course for the resort for the next thirty years or more. After investing almost $8 million in facilities for the Olympics (the equivalent of $71 million in 2020), the State of California had for years been looking for a way to offload the State's assets in the Valley—property and buildings that should have been something of a cash cow for the State, but instead actually cost the State hundreds of thousands of dollars annually to operate and maintain. At one time, the State put out a solicitation for bids for Squaw Valley property—over 1,200 acres of land, the Siberia and Red Dog lifts, Olympic Village, Hofbrau, and movie theatre. They received only one offer, for $25,000. Alex never seemed to have any interest in acquiring real estate and with the State of California claiming to lose $300,000 annually on the Squaw Valley assets, it is little wonder he never made a play to acquire the property, but it turned out that he would get what was most important to him—the land and lifts—for nothing.

In 1974, an Australian company called Mainline purchased the state's holdings for about $25 million and entered a joint venture with Alex to do a major development in the valley. Mainline had the capital to transform the ski area into a destination resort—Alex's dream from the beginning—and after acquiring the State of California assets in the valley, it signed over the skiable land and ownership of the remaining lifts built for the Olympics and still owned by the State (Siberia and Red Dog) to Alex. This finally gave Alex ownership of the upper mountain, except for a couple of small corners of National Forest that were within the ski area boundaries. Mainline lasted about a year and a half before going bankrupt, but the land transfer to Alex was by then final, permanent, and safe from any action by Mainline's creditors. This more than doubled Alex's land ownership and opened the door to development of Squaw Valley as we know it today. Mainline's departure also opened the door for the U. S. Olympic Committee to establish an Olympic Training Center in the Olympic Village and Blyth Arena.

The Mainline transaction was by no means Alex's only financial intrigue. The contract for the tram equipment and installation—a total of $928,000 (not including the construction of the lower terminal, which was a contract with Campbell Construction)—had been financed by Garaventa, with twenty percent payments due each year from 1969 to 1973. The rate of exchange for the Swiss franc to the dollar had been pegged by international agreement at 4.375 Swiss francs to the dollar since 1949, but for the purposes of the contract, Alex and Garaventa had agreed to an exchange rate of 4.315 francs/dollar. In 1971, the Swiss National Bank decided to unlock the rate of exchange and allow the free market to determine the rate. Thanks to Switzerland's strong and very stable economy, the franc strengthened considerably against the dollar in the following years. Even though the contract signed in 1967 specified all the prices for the tram equipment, transcontinental shipping, duty fees, and installation in dollars—and had called out a rate of exchange to be used for the purposes of the contract—Alex decided that it would be to his advantage to leverage the value of the strengthening franc and pay the remaining balances based on that. So, while in 1968, it took 437,500 francs to equal $100,000, by 1973 you only needed 300,000 francs and Alex reduced his payments accordingly. The Swiss freaked out—a deal was a deal and Cushing had agreed to a fixed rate of exchange, not one that floated with the market. The argument was eventually settled for a figure somewhat lower than what Garaventa wanted.

"It is a standard joke around Squaw Valley that Cushing really does not have too much of an idea what is going on around the place from day to day. Ask him if a certain lift is operating or where the best place is to have lunch or if the lodge is full for the weekend and he is likely to say, 'I don't know'. He keeps a staff of button-down Ivy Leaguers for such details and as one of them said recently, 'Alec can't be bothered about what's going on right now. He's thinking about three years from now."

"… a writer asked Cushing when his lifts would be integrated with those of Alpine Meadows. 'I don't know', Cushing said; 'I'd like to do it as soon as possible, but they seem to be a little hesitant. The last time we talked about it, I got so enthusiastic that I think they thought there must be some hitch to the idea.'

'Well, Alec,' the writer replied, 'at least you're getting to know yourself.'

That broke up the room, and no one laughed harder than Cushing, who thrives on contention and is inwardly pleased by the thought that he is known as Cushing the Impossible—an epithet that can be read several ways."

Alfred Wright – *What Goes Up Must Ski Down*, Sports Illustrated, February 9, 1970

Exhibition following the 1975 conversion.

KT-22 following the 1975 upgrade. It had an odd offset counterweight design that provided a good loading pathway, but never worked all that well.

In the mid-1970s, I did contract work for Squaw Valley—we refreshed the aging KT-22 and Exhibition lifts with new Riblet equipment and did a number of grading projects to improve the skiing in key areas around the mountain. The KT-22 lift had originally been built by Heron Ski Lifts in 1956 and by 1975, KT was showing its age. The Riblet upgrade provided twenty years of outstanding service until it was replaced by the detachable Doppelmayr KT-22 Express in 1995. Exhibition had originally been a Hjorth chairlift and we converted it to a kind of Frankenlift with a Riblet drive and return terminal, Doppelmayr line machinery and grips and Ski Lift International (SLI) chairs. Exhibition, too, had a long service life following the retrofit. At one point, Alex was pitched by a fellow who represented a company that made plastic products—he had sold a few ski resorts in the East on the idea of putting a "bubble" on their chairlifts and the resort clients had been pleased with the protection the bubble, a protective cap that lowered over the passengers in the seats, offered in the frigid northeast. Alex said that it sounded interesting, and hired the company to install bubbles on the Squaw Peak chairlift. They installed them, but we quickly determined that while the bubbles might have worked well on the East Coast, they performed very poorly in the wind at Squaw Valley. On some days, we couldn't run the tram or gondola because of high winds, and prior to that season, we had at least been able to operate the Squaw Peak chairlift to get skiers up to the mid-mountain level. The bubbles changed all that—when open, they acted like sails and the wind blew the empty chairs wildly. Loaded chairs with the bubble flipped down were much more stable in the wind, but we rapidly determined that the bubbles were a disaster, and they were removed and returned to the manufacturer. I'm sure Alex never paid them a dime.

Assembling the top terminal of the Solitude triple chairlift.

I did several grading and widening projects for Alex. They were very casual deals given the fact that we had faced each other across a courtroom only a few years before. We would discuss what needed to be done, I would write up a proposal with a price, and he would sign it—simple. The run from the top of KT to the Saddle finally got widened so that skiers would have a run that was wide enough to be skied safely. We created skiable "bypass" runs on each side of Mogul Hill: A tremendous amount of drilling, blasting, and dozer work created the Bellevue run on the skier's right under the Seven Sisters, and a run was created on the left that tied into the top of Sunnyside, including "Klammer's Corner." In addition, I did a lot of dozer work on Tower 20 Traverse and the run now known as "Burkhart's" leading to the bottom of the Headwall lift.

Alex was always wanting to expand the lift inventory. In 1976, I built a pair of new Doppelmayr chairlifts for him—a double chairlift called Newport and a triple (the first triple chair at the resort) on Solitude, just north of Shirley Lake. These were the first Doppelmayr lifts at Squaw Valley and, for a long time afterward, the only ones. The crew included John Moors—a funny and hard-working guy from New Hampshire (although he pronounced it "New Hampsha", of course) and Don Cole, who was a dedicated and energetic worker also, despite being a lawyer. Hardy and my brother Toni pitched in as well.

The Solitude lift was one of the first projects on which the resort and Alex received some pushback from the community, some of whom felt that Alex had little regard for their opinions about growth and the operation of the ski area. In this they were correct. Most of the problem had to do with the fact that the bottom terminal of the lift was adjacent to Shirley Lake, a very popular day-hiking destination for locals and visitors alike, a lot of whom would hike up Shirley Canyon, have a picnic at the lake and then hike up to High Camp and get a free tram ride back to the bottom. They felt that the lake belonged to them—even though the lake and virtually all the hike was on land that Cushing owned—and that having a ski lift within sight of the lake somehow ruined the experience of enjoying their picnic lunch before hiking to High Camp for the ride down. The lift never ran in the summer and in the winter, it was impossible to see the lake, because it was frozen and covered with snow, so the uses seemed utterly compatible—it was just the visual impact of the lift that Alex wanted to build on his land, next to his lake, that annoyed a few of the locals. In any event, the lift was built, and some members of the community had a new grievance to add to their growing list of Cushing's misdeeds. It would not be the last. This controversy aside, the mid-to-late-70s were generally a particularly good time at Squaw Valley. Although there were two serious drought years in 1975-1976 and 1976-77, business at the resort was booming, skiing was popular, and a new generation—arguably the first generation that had grown up from child-hood as skiers—was expanding the sport into new territory.

At Squaw Valley, there were two distinct subcultures within the local skier demo-graphic—the freestyle crowd and the speed skiers. The freestyle group included some very skilled and studiously stylish mogul skiers. Mogul skiing was kind of a big thing because there were lots of big moguls. Slope grooming was still in its infancy and what limited grooming could be done was utilized where it would be most appreciated on beginner and intermediate runs, leaving the more challenging terrain a mogul skier's paradise. The free-style/bump skier crowd had a distinctive, almost cult-like choice of equipment and apparel, at least at Squaw Valley. If someone was wearing neoprene ski pants and skiing on "The Ski" with Spademan bindings and Scott boots, they were a freestyler, no doubt about it.

The other unique group were the speed skiers. While the freestyle group was somewhat natty in appearance, the speed skiers—whose unofficial leader was Steve McKinney—tended

By the 1970's, Squaw Valley had developed a reputation for indifferent, if not outright rude customer service. Alex's answer was to hire a group of pretty young women, whom he dubbed "Sno-Hostesses." His comments promoting the Sno-Hostess program in his season pass letters were vintage Alex:

"These girls will have less hostility per inch than any girls on record."

"I have given myself the special assignment of choosing these girls."

"Sno-Hostesses—where else has sex been introduced to the great outdoors?"

"For years we tried everything we could think of to reverse our reputation for being churlish, and with some degree of success. Then we hit it with our Sno-Hostesses—wow! Nothing speeds up the hospitality process like a spectacular girl. Our Sno-Hostesses—you loved them! They will be around for a long time. Life can be beautiful after all."

The upper terminal of the Mainline chairlift being plowed out with a Hydromaster after being buried by an avalanche.

It's obviously not a powder day, but here's a look at the lift lines on Exhibition and KT-22 from the 1970's—these would have been considered pretty long lines!

toward a distinctly grungy appearance. A lot of them spent their summers big-wall climbing and living in the venerable and notorious Camp 4 at Yosemite and skiing at Squaw Valley in the winter. If someone was wearing Navy surplus wool pants and a down parka held together with duct tape, and was skiing on 223cm downhill skis with Salomon "green spring" bindings, chances were good they were a disciple of Dick Dorworth and Steve McKinney. Although the speed skiers gave us a lot of trouble from a management perspective, Steve McKinney was an intelligent and thoughtful man. It is ironic that despite the huge risks he took as a competitor—he was the first human to go faster than 200 kilometers per hour on skis—he lost his life to a drunk driver who struck his parked car.

Although Squaw Valley was on an upward path—better access to its fantastic terrain than ever and a reputation for being home to the most exciting and extreme skiers—a single Saturday in April 1978 would present the greatest challenge it had ever faced.

20

The Squaw Valley Tram Accident

On Saturday, April 15, 1978, I had spent the day at the yard in Verdi and drove back to Squaw Valley in the late afternoon, because it was windy and starting to rain in Verdi, and I thought I should go home before driving conditions on Interstate 80 started to be affected by the storm. When I got to the entrance to Squaw Valley, it was almost dark and there was a Placer County Sheriff's Department vehicle blocking the road. The deputy came over to my truck and asked if I was a resident. I said I was, and asked what was going on. "We're only allowing residents into the valley," he said. "Didn't you hear? The tram fell down." My first reaction was, "No, the tram didn't 'fall down'—that's not possible." But I thanked him and drove up to the west end of the valley instead of going home—I had to see what was going on.

It was snowing and windy and hard to see, but I could see Cabin 1 stopped midway between the lower terminal and Tower 1. I could see that the slack carriers on the Cabin 2 side were hanging from only one of the track ropes, not both. Rope #4—the track rope farthest to the north—seemed to be on the ground at the base of Tower 1. Things were not right.

I went to the Tram Building and rushed up to the third floor, where the control room is located. The crew had hoisted the Cabin 1 rescue cabin—which is normally stored lying flat below the cabin when it is docked—upright and was preparing to attach the rescue rope that moves it along the track ropes. They were getting ready to go rescue whatever passengers were in Cabin 1.

"What's going on?" I asked.

"Something went wrong as Cabin 2 was coming into Tower 2 on the trip down," someone replied, "As far as we can tell, the track rope came off the tower and is on the floor of the cabin with people trapped under it. There are ski patrollers in the cabin evacuating the uninjured passengers and trying to lift the track rope. Jimmy Mott is there, along with (Jimmy) King and some lift maintenance guys."

Cabin 2 just uphill of Tower 2 following the accident. Track rope #4 is still on the floor of the cabin.

"How are they evacuating the cabin?" I asked. The evacuation system consisted of a small, hydraulically braked winch with a drum of thin but strong cable that allowed the operator to lower passengers to the ground through a hatch in the floor of the cabin. If the track rope was on the floor, the compartment where the winch was stored might be inaccessible and there had to be a great deal of damage to the roof of the cabin, which is where the evacuation winch had to mount.

To my question, the person responded, "They have a small pulley rigged to the hanger and they're manually lowering them one at a time using equipment from the lift evacuation cache at Siberia. The communications aren't particularly good, but that's what we've been able to make out." It was a long way to the ground from Tower 2—over 100 feet—and in the wind and snow, it would be a very unpleasant trip.

"How many people are hurt?" I asked.

"Nobody is really sure. There are some that are dead and some that they are going to lower using a Stokes litter, but the numbers are not clear. They're getting them to the ground, then hiking out to where the grooming machines and Sprytes can drive them over to Gold Coast and down the gondola."

"How many were in the cabin?" I asked.

"Danny said about sixty." Danny was Dan Gutowski, the conductor.

I wondered what the hell had happened but forced that thought out of my mind to focus on the situation at hand.

"Do you really think it's a good idea to run the rescue cabin up to Cabin 1?" I asked. "How certain are you that the rescue rope is undamaged and on the sheaves?" Everyone stopped—the rescue cabins were very much a last resort: They were simple steel cages that could carry only a few passengers at a time, and were propelled very, very slowly along the track ropes with a small cable independent of the main haul rope. They had no track rope brake and no protection from the weather. The rescued passengers would have to climb out the window of the tram cabin and into the rescue basket. The rescue cabins were effective enough, but there were no redundancies for safety. We would be completely reliant on the rescue rope—if it were damaged or severed, we'd have another disaster on our hands very rapidly.

"You're right—the rescue rope may be derailed or damaged," someone said. "We'd better tell the Cabin 1 operator that he needs to get the evacuation winch set up and start lowering people. We can see if there's any way to get ski patrol on the ground under the cabin with a radio and lighting to coordinate; otherwise, one of us had better start hiking up there."

You discover the true character of people and communities when there is a crisis, and the tram accident revealed the caring, tough, resilient character of the community of Olympic Valley and the individuals involved as nothing before. The rescue of the passengers in Cabin 2 was an extraordinary and heroic effort, and it was undertaken in the teeth of a howling blizzard, much of it in the dark, in desperately dangerous conditions. Ski patrolman Chris Phillips along with Jon Krauss and Jeff Dowling from the lift maintenance department climbed 140-foot-tall Tower 2, then Phillips and Krauss walked the haul rope to the cabin wearing ski boots, clambering onto the carriage and down the ladder on the hanger so they could provide first aid to the passengers and set up a lowering system. Ski Patrol Director Jim Mott was hoisted up to the cabin so that he could manage the situation in the cabin and provide radio communication. Dr. Charlie Kellermyer loaded up a backpack with medical equipment at the clinic at the bottom of the mountain and went to the scene, where he, too, was hoisted up to the cabin to treat passengers. Virtually everyone on the mountain pitched in—vehicle mechanics, groomers, members of the race team, ski instructors, and locals with backgrounds in climbing and mountain rescue. Although most of the people in the cabin were dressed for skiing, a significant number were part of a birthday party for local plumbing contractor Dale Cox, and they were wearing street clothes and party shoes. Once passengers were lowered from the cabin, the job had only just begun, because they then had to be carried or climb and hike several hundred yards through deep snow to the closest access point for over-the-snow vehicles. Rescuers built a path in the snow, fixed ropes for handrails, and carried or escorted the traumatized passengers to the vehicles, which then drove them, traversing the slopes, to the Gold Coast Lodge, where they could warm up, get into dry clothes, and have a hot drink before being transported to the base area. It was a remarkable, selfless operation that went long into the night. Jim Mott was the last one to leave Cabin 2 and he touched the ground at 1:30 a.m.

The next day, my son Markus and I skied up to Tower 2 on Nordic skis. Cabin 2 was a hundred feet or so uphill of Tower 2 and, just as reported, the outer track rope had smashed through the roof of the cabin and was sitting on the floor. The inner track rope had derailed into the center of the saddle and was sitting on the sheaves for the haul rope. The roof and one wall of the cabin was virtually destroyed, but the structural parts had fared amazingly

I'm sure Dr. Karl Bittner—the head of the Austrian Tramway Safety Board and a distinguished engineering professor—had no idea why Alex compared him to Red Adair, the famous oil well firefighter, but it made for a great headline in the Santa Cruz Sentinel.

well and kept a terrible situation from being even worse. Nevertheless, it was a grim sight.

Alex called a press conference and vowed that he would launch an investigation and find out what had gone wrong and how to correct it, or the tram would be torn down. He asked me who he should hire to conduct the investigation, and I told him that Dr. Karl Bittner from the University of Graz was highly respected as Austria's chief aerial tramway inspector. Alex agreed to bring Dr. Bittner over to investigate. Alex being Alex, he started to refer to Dr. Bittner as the "Red Adair of tramways"—a reference to the famous oil-well firefighter played by John Wayne in the movie "The Hellfighters," which is probably how Alex came to know about Mr. Adair.

"The following modifications will be made before the cable car is placed in operation again:

The profile of the saddle will be modified, special rope clamps will be installed on all saddles to hold the track ropes in place, and cable catchers will be installed to prevent the cable from ever coming completely off the tower, which is what caused the disastrous accident. In addition, all cables are being replaced.

All field work on the tram is being done by local Squaw Valley contractor, Hans Burkhart. I can think of no other local contractor more qualified to accomplish this task."

Janek Kunczynski, interviewed in 1978

The Garaventa people were, of course, deeply concerned with what had happened and why, but they wanted nothing to do with rebuilding the tram. We contacted other tramway manufacturers like Von Roll and Leitner and they all said the same thing—they were leery of creating liability for their companies if they accepted the project. If the tram was going to be rebuilt to run again, the responsibility was going to be on my shoulders.

I worked with the Garaventa engineers and Dr. Bittner as they investigated every aspect of the accident, including the wind speed and direction from every sensing location that we could find, carefully measuring the location of Cabin 2 and calculating how much swing and deflection would have been generated by wind gusts of various strengths from different directions. Dr. Bittner stayed for several weeks—literally stayed at my house—and worked through every possible scenario, then went home and issued a report. It was inconclusive, as was the Garaventa report. Basically, they both said, "We don't know what happened." I disagree with that—I think it is obvious what happened and how it happened, and it is also obvious what needed to be done to prevent similar situations in the future.

The key to preventing such a catastrophe was retaining the track rope in the saddle, so one of the engineers at Lift Engineering in Carson City designed a series of clamps that would keep the track rope positioned in the saddle without interfering with the track rope brakes. We also designed and installed a set of rope catchers that would bolt to the outside of the saddle supports and prevent a track rope from sliding down the outside of the structure in the unlikely event that the rope came out of the saddle. To satisfy the State of California, the designs had to be approved by a California-licensed engineer, and Jan Kunczynski from Lift Engineering was extremely help-ful providing drawings that were acceptable to the State and fabricating the parts at his plant in Carson City.

Although the investigations could not conclusively identify a proximate cause or specific failure, the tram had to be rebuilt and returned to operation. A new cabin was ordered from CWA, new track ropes for the Cabin 2 side and new haul ropes were ordered from Fatzer. There was a tremen-dous amount of work to be done—work that was demanding and technical and totally unanticipated. In addition to the obvious—replacing the track ropes on the towers, moving the cabins to the terminals,

Lifting the track rope out of the cabin for inspection and replacement on Tower 2.

John Moors and State of California lift inspector Al Beaton check the track rope as it is lowered onto the saddle on Tower 2.

and then removing and replacing the potentially damaged ropes, we needed to inspect everything: towers, saddles, counterweights —everything that could have been affected by the uncoordinated and sudden movement during the accident. It was an opportunity to upgrade the control and communications system—significant improvements had been brought to the market since the original system was designed—and the State of California was demanding better monitoring of wind speed and direction at the towers and terminals, information that could be transmitted through the haul rope in a newer system.

We started by lifting track rope #4—the one that was on the floor of the cabin and on the ground over the breakover by Tower 1—most of the way toward the saddles. By doing this, the longitudinal displacement of the two track ropes was reduced, which helped equalize the tension of the counterweight between the two track ropes. We reinstalled the #3 rope on the saddle after doing a careful cleaning and inspecting for damage of any kind. It had stayed in the saddle structure and looked fine. We cleaned and inspected track rope #4 before replacing it in the saddle—it was scuffed in a few places but would be safe to use until the replacement ropes arrived from Switzerland. Once the track ropes had been returned to their normal positions, we could check the towers for any misalignment caused by the sudden change in pressure from the track ropes –fortunately, the towers and terminal saddles were exactly where they belonged.

With the track ropes and haul rope replaced in their normal locations, and correct alignment verified, we could finally move the cabins to the terminals. We moved very slowly, watching everything with great care to make sure that nothing hung up and that there were no surprises. Cabin 2 moved downhill over Tower 2, then Cabin 1 was stopped at Tower 1 so that we could get into the cabin and retrieve the evacuation cable, which had been dangling from the cabin. We slowly moved Cabin 2 over Tower 1 and started toward the lower terminal, where a small crowd gathered, curious and drawn by the activity. When Cabin 2 reached the lower terminal, we removed it from the hanger, put it on a truck, tarped it and hauled it away. The hanger and carriage could now be removed for inspection and repair, and the work to replace the track rope and haul rope could start. Cabin 1 was also removed and refurbished—new windows and a paint job inside and out. The new Gfeller control system was installed and tested, a big improvement over the original control system.

CWA did an amazing job of building a new cabin—a subtle upgrade from the original cabin design—and very quickly shipping it to us from Switzerland. At the same time, Fatzer was manufacturing new track and haul ropes. Once the new ropes were received, we removed the old track ropes (much more difficult and dangerous than installing new ones, which is demanding and very technical work) pulled the new ropes into place, poured sockets, and tensioned the system. The new cable retention clamps were installed on the bronze saddles on the towers, and the newly approved and manufactured rope catchers from Lift Engineering were installed on the outside of the saddle structures. When the cabin was delivered, it was lifted into place and attached to the newly rebuilt carriage. The new control system was installed and tested, and the tram was once again ready to run on January 6, 1979—less than a year after the accident.

The reception from Squaw Valley's skiers was unremarkable. The people who had ridden the tram before the accident continued to, and those who had preferred the gondola tended to stay with it. People frequently asked about the tram accident, which, although the question may not

Werner Auer walking the cable back to Tower 1.

The arrival of the damaged cabin at the bottom terminal attracted a curious audience.

The new cable catcher installed on the Tower 1 saddle.

have been intended to make other passengers nervous, often had that effect. The best response was from Pete Heuga, who had been literally the first employee at Squaw Valley—running a rope-tow in 1949—and now worked on the tram at almost eighty years of age. When some wise guy would say to Pete, "Hey—isn't this the one that fell??" Pete would always reply, "I don't know: It's my first day…."

After building the tram in 1968 with the Garaventa crew and then rebuilding it again in 1978 with Squaw Valley employees, the 1978 accident is something I have given a great deal of thought through the years, and after reading through all the files, memos, reports, depositions—the reams and reams of material generated for the lawsuits—and incorporating my personal observations, the following is my conclusion:

Shortly before 3:30 p.m., the lift operator at the top of the Shirley Lake lift reported a sudden increase in gusty winds and problems with chair swing. Also at 3:30 p.m., Cabin 2 left the upper terminal of the tram at High Camp with sixty-three passengers on board. Immediately, as passengers later recalled, the cabin was slammed with gusting winds from the southwest, and the cabin tilted abruptly. The tram was operating at five meters per second, the slowest of the maximum speed settings for the system, which were ten meters per second, seven meters per second, five meters per second. This slower speed was a choice made due to the gusty wind and because the tram "controller" (the person in the lower terminal control room) had left the building to go to an appointment at the medical clinic a few hundred feet away in another building. The conductors in the cabins had full control to start, stop, slow, or reverse the system using controls in the cabins up to the preset five meters per second maximum speed. Cabin 2 conductor Dan Gutowski recalled the passengers appearing fearful as the gusty winds caused the cabin to swing wildly.

As the cabin approached Tower 2, with minimal visibility due to the swirling snow, Gutowski was probably concerned about the cabin slamming hard into the stout tubular steel tower guide that surrounds the structure of the tower and would certainly have been worried that he would not be able to slow and stop the cabin rapidly enough to avoid an impact once he became able to see the tower through the blizzard. With the howling wind propelling the cabin into increasingly dramatic swings and the passengers' fearful cries growing louder, Gutowski's decision to make an emergency stop before reaching Tower 2 is entirely logical. The sudden stop even from a five meters per second travel speed produced a dramatic downward motion in the cabin—some passengers reported that they felt that they were falling. After the significant downward motion due to the stop, the system rebounded upward just as a large gust of wind—directed and intensified by the ridge to the south-west of Tower 2—produced a surge of lift and pressure on the side of the cabin. (The gust was estimated at seventy-four to eighty miles per hour.) As the now-tilted cabin rose, it exerted leverage on the track ropes, which passed through a narrow gap between the track rope brakes. This changed the fleet angle between the carriage and the saddles at Tower 2.

Cabin 1 approaches Tower 1 as the first rays of sunrise light up the mountain peaks.

Combined with the downhill movement of the track rope over the saddle as the track ropes moved upward, this caused both track ropes to begin peeling out of the saddle profiles. This motion continued as the gust diminished. As wind load on the cabin was reduced, the peeling action of the track ropes out of the saddles continued, and rope #4 dropped clear of the saddle, sliding down the hanger above the cabin and slicing through the roof of Cabin 2— with devastating consequences.

Knowing the Squaw Valley tram as well as I do, I am convinced that the accident was the result of a specific set of conditions, all of which contributed to the outcome. If any of the conditions had been absent—it would have resulted in an uneventful arrival at the lower terminal for Cabin 2. The topography, wind direction, and wind speed combined to produce wind load on the cabin in a specific horizontal direction, as well as uplift. All of the factors had to be exactly right in order to produce the displacement of the track rope from the saddle and to allow it to continue to deflect to the outside: the location of the cabin with respect to Tower 2 when the gust hit it; the weight of the load in the cabin; the speed of the cabin prior to the gust; the cabin's deceleration as it approached the tower, which caused loading on the track rope and then a rebound as the counterweight adjusted; and the change in tension on the haul rope as the system suddenly stopped and the counterweight adjusted. Modify even one factor even slightly, and the outcome would have been totally different. This accident was unlike any other, and the fact that the tram has now operated for over 40 years since the accident would seem to indicate that the causes were identified and correctly addressed. It was a tragic situation, and one that will never be forgotten.

Squaw Valley: 1979 to 1983

The inevitable result of the successful reconstruction and reopening of the Squaw Valley tram was that Alex wanted me to come back to work for him and run the operations of the resort. During this period, Alex was all but invisible. He had married a woman named Elizabeth "Libby" Woodward Pratt who hated coming to Squaw Valley, and they spent most of their time in New York and Newport, Rhode Island. John Buchman, a non-skier, was at a distinct disadvantage when it came to understanding what was happening on the mountain or how advances in the industry could be leveraged to improve the guest experience. Although the department heads were very competent and hardworking people, there was a management and leadership void in the daily operations—a lot of departments doing their own thing quite well without anyone in charge who knew what was going on. Alex convinced me to become the general manager and to oversee operations.

In 1978, while we were busy rebuilding the tram, Lift Engineering had replaced the Squaw Peak double chair with the resort's second triple chair, Super Squaw. Always ahead of his time, Jan Kunczynski was interested in microprocessor-controlled lift operations, and Lift Engineering tried to incorporate some of this new technology into the design of the Super Squaw lift. Jan had promised the lift would be ready to operate on November 1, 1978, but the balky electronics created a long delay—it would not be ready until Black Friday: November 25.

To further complicate things, a fire in the motor room on November 3 knocked the Siberia lift out of commission. Alex had promised that the rebuilt aerial tramway would be operating on December 17, a ridiculously optimistic date, given that after the accident on April 15th, we could not touch anything for more than two months while the investigation was conducted. Then we would be waiting for new track and haul ropes as well as a new cabin and hanger to be somehow pushed to the front of the manufacturing schedule

The Olympic Lady lower terminal destroyed by a very wet avalanche in 1980.

at Fatzer and CWA and shipped over from Switzerland. We were ready late in the day of December 22, but the State of California inspectors were only allowed to work until noon that day, because it was the Thursday before Christmas, and then they had two weeks off for the holiday. By the time the tram was back online, the Christmas holiday was over. The start of the 1978-79 ski season was an unholy mess, and did little to build confidence among our clientele.

The following season—1979 to 1980— was much better. There was good snow early, and we had a good Christmas holiday, but in January things really went crazy. We had heavy snow for a few days followed by a very warm, very wet storm system that stretched from Hawaii to the Sierra Nevada. Heavy rain on top of a deep snowpack caused a large, wet avalanche that ran right through the lower terminal of the Olympic Lady lift, causing so much damage that the lift was out of commission for the rest of the season. The volume of rain and melting snowpack combined to overwhelm a minor creek bed in the middle of the gondola line, undermining a tower that tipped into some trees, derailing the lift. Fortunately, this happened at night while the gondola was parked and we were able to realign the tower, secure it in place with guylines, and station an operator there to monitor it every day for the rest of the season. It was repaired permanently the following summer.

Squaw Valley continued to embrace new technology, and slope grooming was an area where rapid advancement in technology provided a vastly improved experience for skiers. In the late 1960's we had experimented with a Prinoth machine that was hinged lengthwise and was capable only of track-packing the snow. It was so disorienting to operate that after a few hours you could hardly walk when you got out of the machine. We had used an early Tucker Sno-Cat as transportation for lift maintenance, but while it drove well in the snow, the notion of grooming the slopes was still years in the future.

By the 1970's, the state of the art was a rather anemic gasoline-powered Thiokol Model 2100 "Packmaster" with a compactor bar or a roller. In the 1980's we invested heavily in Thiokol's new 3700 Hydromasters with diesel engines and hydrostatic drives because they could push a full blade of snow while smoothing the filled slope with a compactor bar or a hydraulically powered tiller. The Hydros could also out-climb the Packmasters and groom uphill on modest slopes. Within a few years, the arrival of PistenBully grooming machines moved us another giant step ahead. The PistenBully machines had reliable, quiet Mercedes-Benz diesel engines, excellent visibility, and operator-friendly cabs with cassette players! The PistenBully machines also allowed a less experienced operator to deliver a better skiing surface. It could out-climb the older machines and could groom uphill on even more difficult terrain than the Hydromasters. The moguls had met their match.

The season of 1981-82 was the first of a pair of back-to-back monster winters. It snowed early and often, with a gigantic storm in the first week of January and a much larger one that arrived at the end of March. While the January storm was inconvenient, the March event was a killer, literally. On the afternoon of March 31, an avalanche that started on the ridge between Squaw Valley and Alpine Meadows swept toward the base area and parking lot of Alpine Meadows ski resort, destroying the bottom terminal of a lift and killing seven people, including Bernie Kingery, the mountain's ski patrol director. There was a simultaneous avalanche in Squaw Valley that started on the ridge to the north of the valley and ran across Sandy Way, damaging a house beyond repair and burying the road. It was quickly determined that there

The hinged Prinoth groomer never caught on and by the early 1980's Squaw's grooming fleet was all Thiokol.about 1980.

was one minor injury on Sandy Way, but that the Alpine Meadows event was a disaster, and they needed our help. We sent snow removal equipment, several snowcats, and a dozen or more ski patrollers to Alpine Meadows to help search for survivors. Several were rescued alive in the immediate aftermath of the avalanche, and several of the dead were located, as well. There were still missing Alpine Meadows staff members, so the search continued for several days—a process complicated by the fact that it was still snowing, and the avalanche

Alpine Meadows base area following the 1982 avalanche.

debris was loaded with the shattered remains of the building and lift terminal that the slide had destroyed. Finally, on April 5—five days following the avalanche—searchers discovered Anna Conrad, a young Alpine Meadows lift operator, alive in a collapsed section of the employee locker room. It was the first rescue of a live victim by an avalanche dog in the United States, and anyone who lived in the North Tahoe area at the time can tell you where they were when they heard the news that Anna Conrad had been found alive—it was that dramatic a moment.

At the Central Sierra Snow Lab on Donner Summit, a total of fifteen-and-a-half feet of snow was received between March 27 and April 8—the record for that location, which has been recording snowfall since 1879.

Alex had announced in his June 15, 1980 season pass letter that he and John Buchman had retired from active management of the ski resort and that he had promoted me to president and general manager, noting that we had worked together for almost twenty years. Although made a vague reference to his accusations of theft and the 1971 lawsuit that he had lost, he said a lot of nice things about me. He said that I was a perfectionist and needed "a long leash" which he promised he was providing, and said that my hands "will guide the destiny of Squaw Valley USA for the foreseeable future." With this mandate, I instituted some changes that I thought would make a real impact in the areas in which we needed improvement the most, and that would have the most direct impact on improving the guest experience. I realized that I could not do everything myself, so I brought ski patrol director Jimmy Mott into the administrative office in the Tram Building as assistant general manager. Jimmy knew the operation of the mountain extremely well and wanted to continue to do avalanche control, which was fine with me. He picked Mark Mueller to become the patrol director. Mark had great leadership skills, a friendly but no-nonsense personality, and the support of his crew. He was a great choice for the position and did an excellent job.

Alex had believed that the role of the resort operator was strictly uphill transportation, and had given other companies concessionaire agreements to provide the many auxiliary services that a ski resort offers—food and beverage, ski rentals, retail sales, etc. While this was a simple, reasonably profitable and low-risk model of operating, to the guest it was all "Squaw Valley," and the resort had little to no control over the quality of the services provided. Those services, I knew, were also significant profit centers for other resorts, so I decided to gradually bring those operations "in-house" to be operated as departments of the company. This was not universally popular, especially with Joe Marillac, who had run the ski rental operation in the base area for many years, as well as operating a successful real estate business. Joe did not speak to me for a long time after I did not renew his concession for the ski rental operation. A company called Mountain Host had operated as the exclusive food and beverage concessionaire in the base area and at the mid-mountain lodges for many years—and done a good job—but I thought we could provide a different level of service if we focused on one location, so I took back the food and beverage operation at High Camp. Gold Coast—more centrally located in the lift network—was by far the busier of the two mid-mountain locations and was very profitable with an efficient, fast-food orientation. High Camp was set up for sit-down dining and a more leisurely experience and Mountain Host was probably not sorry to let us try to make it profitable—they would do fine operating Gold Coast and the restaurants and bars in Olympic House. One of the secret weapons of this era in the management of the resort was my secretary, Kay Jones. Kay was in her fifties and was totally professional and efficient, she would have been right at home in a

THE KING IS DEAD, LONG LIVE THE KING!

Our new leader, Hans Burkhart, is a courageous, tough, vigorous man of forty-four who commands respect and inspires confidence. He and I have worked, played and occasionally fought together for nearly twenty years. Over this not inconsiderable period of time I have learned at least two things about him. First, if you don't want to do something in the best way possible, Hans is not your man. Second, if you are not willing to give him his head to work out problems as he sees fit, don't get Hans.

Alex Cushing in the Squaw Valley Season Pass Letter—June 15, 1980

Fortune 500 corporate office and no one expected to find someone with her presence in a ski resort setting. She had terrific skills and was an efficient and ruthless gatekeeper: She made sure that no one wasted my time with something that she could handle. Guests would come into office the complaining that grease from a lift had ruined their expensive outfit, and Kay would either send them on their way with a smile on their face or with their tail between their legs if they were trying to pull a fast one. Cars that were left overnight in the parking lots on nights that we had to plow were towed to an impound area by the snow removal crew—the owners invariably turned up in front of Kay's desk in search of their vehicle. If they were humble and apologetic about leaving their car in the lot (which had very prominent signage prohibiting overnight parking), they could pay a $25 fee for the tow and drive away. If they were rude and argumentative, the towing charge could be much, much higher. Kay kept everyone in line, up to and including John Buchman, and she made my job a lot easier than it might have been without her.

I drew up an employment agreement that would have given me a five-year contract as president of the resort and—in accordance with Alex's stated wish that Squaw Valley would "never be sold"—would have provided continuity of management if he died. I knew that his wife and daughters had no interest in the ski industry, and since I had Alex's confidence to manage the operation, an agreement seemed like it would provide him with peace of mind that we would continue his work even if he was unable to. He never signed it.

With all the responsibilities of running Squaw Valley, one of the few places I found peace and relaxation was in the cab of my Kenworth truck. That might seem odd, but focusing on uncomplicated tasks like loading the trailer, tying down the load, and then driving the semi allowed me to consider a problem or a complex situation with no distractions, and I did some of my best thinking while driving the truck. In early 1982, I had hauled some loads with the Kenworth and the wet and snowy roads had left it filthy, so I took it to a truck wash in Sparks, Nevada. I dropped it off and went to do some errands, and when I came back about forty-five minutes later, I did not see the truck. I went into the office and asked where it was.

"I don't know," said the owner. "It should be done by now."

We went outside and looked for the truck.

He asked one of the kids who worked there, "Hey—where's Chris?" No one knew where Chris or my truck was.

It turned out that Chris had decided to take the truck for a little joyride. He had left the truck wash and gotten on Interstate 80 headed west, at first not attracting any attention, but when he blew through the agricultural inspection station in Truckee at eighty miles per hour, the "bug station" employees took exception and called the California Highway Patrol, who wasted no time in pursuing the Kenworth. Chris was kind of a bigmouth, as it turned out, and he was chattering away on the CB radio telling the other truckers to get out of his way, he was going to drive the rig all the way to Mexico, etc. The CHP was on his tail and the big rig drivers were driving side by side in an attempt to block him, but he swerved into the median to get around them. More CHP units joined the chase as they headed down the west side of Donner Summit toward Sacramento. The CHP did not want to let him get into Sacramento, since he was driving so erratically and aggressively, so as they got toward Newcastle, California they put two officers in one car, isolated the Kenworth from the other traffic, and the cop in the right-hand seat of the car shot out the left front tire of the Kenworth with a shotgun. The tire went flat but stayed on the rim and Chris was able to keep driving for a while, but before long he had to pull over and was taken into custody. I had to go down to Roseville, get a new Michelin radial tire installed on the rig, and bring it back. It was still clean, but the front of the step into the cab on the driver's side had the imprint of the first load of buckshot that the CHP had fired at the tire and missed. It is still there to this day.

When asked how he got started in Public Relations, Bill said "I just fell into it. There wasn't really any marketing department until 1979 when it was formed by Hans Burkhart under the direction of Roger Haran."

Interview with Bill Boardman, *The Voice of Squaw Valley*

SAN FRANCISCO CABLE CARS

In early 1981, I had a call from an engineering company in San Francisco—Chin and Hensolt—that had been commissioned by the San Francisco Municipal Transportation Authority (which everyone in San Francisco referred to as simply "Muni") to conduct a study of the San Francisco cable cars. The intent of the work was to determine if the system—which has been in operation since the 1870s—could be modified to utilize modern components and updated mechanical concepts. The operation of the system was simple: a loop of wire rope cable was constantly in motion at a speed of nine-and-a-half miles per hour in a groove below street level between the tracks of the cable cars. When the gripman in the car moved the large lever in the car, a grip gradually closed on the cable, propelling the car forward until it was travelling at the same speed as the cable. To slow down or stop, the gripman released the grip and engaged brakes that would slow, stop, and hold the cable car even on the steepest hills in the system (which were very steep). The cable was 1¼ inches in diameter, at least it was that big at the beginning of its service life. Unlike wire rope used in ski lift applications, which had a service life of a decade or more, the service life of wire rope cable in the San Francisco cable car system was measured in weeks—generally less than two months—during which it might be shortened once and then replaced when the outer wires had become so worn down, brittle, and broken that it was no longer safe to use.

If you were to design a system to intentionally destroy wire rope, it would be difficult to imagine a more effective method than the San Francisco cable car system. The pull curve pulleys that guide the wire rope around curves had metal on metal. With the wire rope and the grips were a metal-on-metal clamp capable of exerting a force of 30,000 pounds per square inch, and the wire rope—which ran constantly—simply burned through the jaws of the grip (called the "die") as the gripman gradually increased the clamping force. The amount of friction and heat this exerted on the wire rope was hard to imagine. The dies were to be replaced every three days.

Given the primitive system, it was no surprise that the wire rope was considered disposable by the Muni, although it certainly increased operating costs to have to install a new rope every seven weeks or so and to have to shorten and re-splice the rope sometimes twice through that span due to stretch. When this amazing situation was explained to me, I was interested in learning more about it and contributing to the study—I had never seen wire rope damaged so thoroughly in such a short time, and I was certain that there must be ways to improve the performance of the system so that the rope would have a significantly lengthened service life.

I was invited to watch the Muni splicing crew shorten the loop of rope on the Powell-Mason line. The work was conducted overnight, after the line had shut down for the day. The loop of rope for the Powell-Mason line needed to be shortened because of a stretch that was two-and-a-half times the length that would normally be expected. There were also multiple broken wires in strands of rope at the splice. It was an impressive operation, and the crew was fast and efficient—they were splicing a cable car line just about every week, so they had plenty of practice. Unlike a ski lift splicing operation, where you make the splice right under the lift line on whatever terrain happens to be there, this operation was done indoors in the powerhouse for the system—ideal conditions!

The work started at 12:30 a.m. and was finished by 5:10 a.m. According to international standards, a splice should be a minimum of 1200 times the rope diameter or 120 feet for 1¼-inch rope, but the Muni practice was to make a ninety-six-foot-long splice. Because a splice requires replacing the flexible, fiber core of the rope with a straightened strand of the rope in six different places, the flexibility of the rope in those sections is considerably reduced, leading to greater bending stress (not that much of a factor in a ski lift application, but a significant issue in the cable car application) and broken wires. Along with the heat and friction caused by the grip and the metal-on-metal scuffing of the pull curve pulleys, the system was just an ideal environment for the destruction of wire rope. Along with the other experts consulting on the project, I made several suggestions for reducing damage to the rope, lengthening the service life, and reducing costs, but when the system was shut down for major repairs and improvements from 1982 to 1984, few, if any of those ideas were implemented—the hundred-year-old technology was just too familiar and reliable enough.

22

1980s Mountaineering and Competition

In the early 1980s, with a steady job at Squaw Valley, I had the opportunity to indulge in a couple of my favorite recreational activities, mountaineering and Nordic ski racing. With the opportunity to take vacation time (and the necessity to do so since Squaw Valley had a "use it or lose it" policy) I took trips to see family in Germany and do some scouting on the state of the European ski industry, as well as enjoy some ski mountaineering or compete in a race.

In May of 1981, I had the opportunity to climb Mont Blanc, the highest peak in the Alps at 4,808 meters (15,774 feet). I climbed it with my nephew, Stephan, who was a teenager and an experienced skier and racer. Stephan had done some mountaineering, but not a great deal. We left Oberammergau and drove through Switzerland to Chamonix—about 600 kilometers. The weather in Chamonix was stormy, which worked in our favor, because, although demanding and dangerous (ten to twenty people die each year attempting the climb), it is a popular climb and can be crowded. Despite the bad weather, we took the tram to Plan de L'Aiguille and skied from there up to the Refuge Grands Mulets to spend the night. Normally crowded, the hut was almost empty—there were two Swiss guys who were outfitted like professional climbers. They said they were heading to Mount McKinley next, so we concluded that they were sponsored professionals. We had a good night. The hut is normally wall to wall people but with almost no one else there, we could get a decent night's sleep, even though the hut was at 3,050 meters (10,000 feet) elevation.

I woke up in the dark to hear the Swiss guys leaving, and quickly woke Stephan so we could follow their tracks—I figured they would know where they were going and the best route to take. The weather had cleared, and it became a fantastic morning for climbing, but close to the summit, Stephan started to really struggle, and I was afraid that we would have to abandon our attempt and descend, but he pressed on at a slower pace, and we made the summit, where the Swiss guys were enjoying the panorama and taking pictures. The ski

My nephew Stephan and I at the summit of Mont Blanc. We followed the tracks of a pair of Swiss professional climbers, who arrived at the summit ahead of us—always handy to have someone to take your picture at the top!

down to Chamonix was wonderful—new snow and a long, long run in which to enjoy it. The good weather had brought out the fair-weather climbers and the mountain was once again crowded—our timing had been perfect.

Later that year—on a different trip to Germany—I was able to climb the Matterhorn, which I did by myself. Unlike Mont Blanc, which is a long, moderate ski ascent, the Matterhorn is a *climb*. Zermatt is at about 1,600 meters elevation, and the tram network takes you to the trailhead above tree line at the Schwarzsee. The first day's hike is about four kilometers and gains only about 700 meters in elevation, bringing you to the Hörnli Hut at the base of the peak of the Matterhorn. It is a well-developed trail that gets a lot of use, and the views are spectacular in every direction. From the Hörnli Hut, the route becomes a lot more challenging and technical, following Hörnli Ridge to the summit. There were a couple of Austrian guys at the hut who were planning to summit the following day. They looked well equipped, very fit and seemed knowledgeable about the climb.

By the time I got started in the dark the next morning, the Austrians were gone, but about ten centimeters of snow had fallen overnight, giving me the advantage of being able to follow their tracks from the hut to the base of the Hörnli Ridge where the climbing begins. This section is tricky in the dark, which is when nearly everyone encounters it. If you go too far to the left, you get lost, but the Austrians must have either been there before or were good navigators, because they never faltered on the way to the base of the ridge. I caught up

At the base of the Hornli Ridge with the peak of the Matterhorn in the background.

The Austrian climbers on the Matterhorn.

to them an hour or so later. They were roped together, which gave them a greater measure of safety, but required them to maintain a slower pace than I could maintain climbing alone. There are a lot of sections of the climb which have a significant and serious exposure to long drops. A fall would be deadly, but being roped to other people is not necessarily a winning strategy, as the first party to conquer the Matterhorn proved. On their descent, one of the group fell, knocking another over and, because they were roped together, two other members of the party were dragged to their deaths with the first two. The only reason that any were spared was because the rope broke. Fortunately, my climb had none of this drama. I passed the two Austrians and continued up as the day grew lighter.

The Hörnli Ridge route was the first route climbed to the summit of the Matterhorn, because it is a straightforward line to the top. The climb up the ridge is in rock at first and then transitions to snow and ice as you approach the summit. I climbed in crampons with an ice axe once I reached the snow, and the climbing was both easier and more solid underfoot than on the rock section farther down. I reached the summit and realized that since I was the only one there, it was going to be hard to get a picture, so I took off my Squaw Valley jacket, draped it over the ice axe standing in the snow, and snapped a couple of pictures at the summit, then headed down. I passed the Austrians again and continued down to the Hörnli Hut, expecting that they would be along, but they never arrived. There is a small intermediate shelter—the Solvay Hut—midway between the Hörnli Hut and the summit, and they must have decided to spend the night there rather than continuing to descend.

In 1982, I took Jimmy Mott, then assistant general manager at Squaw Valley, to France to meet up with my brother Toni to ski the Haute Route. Connecting the towns of Chamonix and Zermatt, the Haute Route is a legendary ski mountaineering tour through some of the most beautiful and rugged Alpine terrain on earth. A tram ride out of Argentiere got us to the start of the tour, the first day and a half were in France, before crossing into Switzerland. The skiing was a mix of skinning uphill followed by hiking/climbing steeper sections and a lot

One of several crosses on the Matterhorn—a reminder that it is a challenge that occasionally proves deadly.

of moderate downhill sections. We had good snow and generally fine weather, though at one point we were in a fog so thick that we were nearly immobilized. I thought I had a fairly good idea where we were on a topographic map (this was well before GPS units were available) and sent Mott one direction and Toni the other to see if the location I thought we were in matched the topography.

"If we are where I think we are, you should be able to go about 100 yards that way and you'll be in a little saddle with a drop-off ahead of you," I told Jimmy.

He skied off and came back a few minutes later to report that he had, indeed, found a little saddle just as I'd described.

"Then we continue this way," I said, "and we'll be to the right side of a pretty large outcropping—we pass it and drop down in the valley." The topo map did not let us down— we were headed in the right direction.

An attraction of the Haute Route is the ability to spend each night at the huts strategically located along the way, so that skiers can carry a minimum of weight—some extra clothing, lunch, snacks, water, gear, and not much else—it is the ultimate in lightweight touring. The huts vary in the quality of accommodation, but you get a hot dinner and breakfast included in the nightly fee and the huts are in some of the most spectacular locations in

I was alone on the summit of the Matterhorn with no one to take a picture of me, so I draped my Squaw Valley Ski Corp jacket over my ice axe and took a picture of that.

Below: One of the 'huts' on the Haute Route.

With Jimmy Mott on the Haute Route.

Below: The Haute Route offers great skiing, but there are impressive and dangerous crevasses that may or may not be visible, depending on the conditions.

the world. To the great delight of the tired and thirsty skier at the end of the day, they have beer and wine, but one thing they did not have in 1982 was a telephone. That was important to us because just before we left on the trip to Europe, Jimmy's girlfriend of some years had broken up with him and he was heartbroken. He had been calling her every day trying to get back into her good graces, but once we started skiing the Haute Route, he was incommunicado. He was eternally hopeful, however, and as we approached each hut, he would ask, "Hans—do you think they have a phone?" They never did. Although our time away from modern technology was probably not to blame, Jimmy was never able to reignite the spark with his ex. It was a great trip, nevertheless, with beautiful scenery and great skiing.

I had entered an annual event in Oberammergau—the King Ludwig Race, a popular twenty and forty kilometer Nordic ski race from Ettal to Oberammergau—and skied well enough in that event to qualify for a "citizen racer" spot in the Swedish "Vasaloppet," which has the dual distinctions of being the world's oldest cross-country ski race (first held in 1922) and having the largest number of participants. In 1982, there were about 14,000 racers. For a long time, the Vasaloppet was also the longest cross-country ski race in the world at ninety kilometers (fifty-six miles), but as ski technique has advanced, a few longer races have been established. The route is historical in origin. In 1520, a young Swedish nobleman, Gustav Vasa, after unsuccessfully attempting to organize a rebellion against Christian II, the oppressive king of the Kalmar Union (Sweden, Denmark and Norway), fled on skis to escape the king's troops. The race commemorates Gustav's flight from Mora to Salen, Sweden. Gustav's efforts to organize a rebellion were eventually successful and he defeated King Christian, dissolving the Kalmar Union. Sweden became an independent country and Gustav was crowned king. The race is run in reverse, from Salen to Mora.

As you might imagine, organizing a race with 14,000 competitors is quite a project, and the Swedes take it very seriously and scientifically, dividing the field into groups based on previous race results with the fastest, most experienced racers at the front in the first group—literally Olympic and World Cup level competitors. I was in the second group with other citizen racers who had qualified to start toward the front by virtue of their performance in other races.

Everyone starts at once, with the first group sprinting out of the start for all they are worth and subsequent groups starting as soon as room opens in front of them. To say that it is chaotic would be an understatement—one skier will fall and create a huge, chain-reaction pileup of tangled skiers which affects the field behind them as they try to veer to the left or right to find an opening through the confusion, which causes others to fall. I was positioned to the right side within my group and stayed as far to the right as I could as the race started. I was able to avoid any pileups as we headed through the critical first kilometer and started up a long, steep climb between the second and fifth kilometers. The hill tends to string the

Competing well in the 1982 King Ludwig Race in Oberammergau gave me the opportunity for an advantageous starting location in the legendary Vasaloppet in Sweden that year.

field out, which helps to prevent additional pileups and gives everyone the chance to focus on their skiing rather than avoiding other racers and trying to stay upright. There are aid stations about every eleven or twelve kilometers along the course that serve "blabarssoppa" (blueberry soup), sports drinks and Vasaloppet buns to the racers—at the fifty-mile mark, you can get a cup of coffee!

The 1982 race ran at a very typical pace for the era: The winner finished in four hours, twenty-eight minutes, and fifty seconds, but the following year, the winner broke the four-hour barrier for the first time in history, finishing in 3:58. I did not win the race, but I skied well, had fun and finished 505th, which put me in the top 4 percent of finishers.

I had the opportunity to get together with Fritz Frey when we raced the American Birkebeiner in Wisconsin. In the years following our lift construction work at Alpine Meadows, Fritz had a long and rewarding career with the ski schools at Banff, Alberta and Mammoth Mountain, California. He had moved to Ketchum, Idaho and met me in Wisconsin for the race. We both skied well, and it was great sharing the experience with an old friend.

Although the early 80's were a good period for me professionally and I achieved some personal goals in mountaineering and competition, my marriage to Hedi ended in divorce. The different expectations we had for our relationship led us to the conclusion that we would be happier apart than together.

Blyth Arena

The centerpiece of the 1960 Olympics, Blyth Arena dominated the west end of the valley with its unique profile and massive size. The arena had seating for over 8,000 people and a unique design with an open south side that faced the speed skating oval, the ski jump hill, slalom courses on Red Dog, the Tower of Nations, and the Olympic Flame where medal ceremonies took place. The rear bleachers were built on wheels, so that they could be rolled open to create a huge, three-sided ceremonial area for the opening and closing ceremonies of the Winter Games. Once rolled closed at the conclusion of the Games, the grandstands never moved again.

Ice skating at the arena was a popular activity on bad weather days in the winter, and during the summer there were figure skating and hockey camps that augmented public skating sessions, local figure skating club, junior hockey programs, and broomball games. During the period that the U.S. Olympic Committee operated a training center in Squaw Valley, Blyth Arena hosted the U.S. Figure Skating Team, the gold-medal winning 1980 Olympic Hockey Team, and even training by competitors in luge and bobsled. After several years of operation, the Olympic Committee decided to consolidate operations in Colorado Springs and Lake Placid, vacating the facilities in Squaw Valley, which were empty during the winter of 1981-82.

In 1982, Congress authorized the sale of the Olympic Village and Blyth Arena as separate parcels. It seemed clear that the Olympic Village would become some sort of condominium operation, but I was convinced that Blyth Arena was a particularly important acquisition for Squaw Valley

The vast clear span roof of Blyth Arena afforded every spectator an unobstructed view, but would prove to be its undoing.

Ski Corporation—if for no other reason than it was right in the middle of our parking lot. Alex was not enthusiastic—the arena was not interesting to him at all, and he did not see the value in spending needed cash to acquire the building, even with 5.3 acres of prime real estate—he always referred to Blyth as "the white elephant." After a lot of discussion over a long period of time, I was finally able to persuade him that we HAD to do our best to acquire the arena, and he agreed to let me bid on it… to a limit.

We knew that Phil Carville—who had acquired the Olympic Village in the first auction—would be bidding. He had financing available from Ken Kidwell at Eureka Federal Savings and Loan, but we did not think he was really interested in owning Blyth—he just did not want Alex to have it. I discussed the situation with Paul Minasian, one of the attorneys for the Ski Corporation, and suggested that we find another bidder, so that we could avoid a head-to-head bidding war with Carville. We knew that he would be trying to either outbid Alex or make it a very costly acquisition for him. Paul suggested Scott Brooke, an attorney in South Lake Tahoe who had been a Squaw Valley professional ski patrolman for a few years before going to law school. I called Scott to ask if he would be willing to act as the third bidder and he agreed.

The auction started with Phil Carville and I bidding against each other in $50,000 increments until the price got to $700,000 on Carville's bid, when I announced that I had reached the limit that I was authorized to spend. I said I could maybe go to $725,000, but that was it. At this point, Scott Brooke speaks up and bids $750,000. Phil Carville asked to take a break and during the break asked me who the other guy (Brooke) was. I said I did not know. The auction resumed with Carville believing that Alex was out of the picture, so he announced that he, too, was done, leaving Alex Cushing the new owner of Blyth Arena, thanks to Scott Brooke.

With the acquisition of Blyth Arena, we had not only secured control of a very key piece of real estate in the base area of the resort, but we had the opportunity to provide our guests with a recreational alternative on bad weather days, something to do in the evening during ski season and a unique summer attraction in the valley. The building—at this point twenty-three years old—had been operated by concessionaires ever since the Olympics. Since they did not own the building, they had little incentive to do any but the most urgent maintenance and repair and the Forest Service—the building's owner—had taken little interest in investing in improvements or upgrades. As a result, the building had been slowly deteriorating ever since the Olympics. It was functional, but it looked worn. Furthermore, when the Olympic Training Center left, all the equipment needed to operate a skating operation went with them. Fortunately, we had a couple of people who had the experience and enthusiasm to get the arena open and operating again. Peter Onorato grew up in Squaw Valley and had worked at Blyth on and off ever since he was about twelve years old and Pete Bansen had worked at the Colorado College ice rink while a student there, then came to Squaw Valley to be the assistant manager of Blyth while it was operated by the Olympic Training Center. Bansen had then come to work for the Ski Corporation as a tram operator and heavy equipment operator and had done a good job as the snow removal foreman during the epic winter of 1981-82.

Pete Bansen and Peter Onorato set to work as manager and assistant manager of Blyth Arena and started scouring the West for a used Zamboni ice-surfacing machine, rental skate inventory, skate sharpener, and all the other equipment we would need to get a skating operation ready for the winter. They got the ice-making system working and coaxed the old boilers into life. There was a lot of excitement in the community to have the ice rink open again. Once Blyth opened, the public skating sessions were well attended, broomball teams were organized—there was even a morning "Tiny Tots" session for children too young to be in school and their mothers. Blyth was an instant success. "The Petes" had figured out that they could reduce the high cost of operating the ice-making equipment by shutting off the refrigeration compressors overnight when outside temperatures were cold, and restarting them early in the morning, so the operation was making a small profit.

The winter of 1982-83 was the second winter in a row with extraordinary snowfall. The roof of Blyth Arena had been designed and constructed with a sophisticated snow removal system that allowed a building with over an acre of roof and no internal supports to survive in the harsh climate of the Sierra. The roof was supported from outside, with steel pylons at the base of the roof on the east and west sides anchoring wire rope cables that suspended huge interior box beams by attaching to them at two points along their lengths. It was an elegant and extremely strong system, and provided every seat in the building with an unob-structed view. It did not have unlimited snow load, but the designers had engineered a system that reliably caused snow to slide off the roof when the load reached a certain level. The surface of the roof was galvanized sheet metal, and the lowest section of the roof on each side had a large heat exchanger and blower system using heat generated as a byproduct of the refrigeration process. When the lower section of the roof was heated, a film of water would form between the roof surface and the snow, reducing the friction holding the snow in place on the roof. That section would then slide off (into semi-circular pits provided to contain and melt it), taking the snow above it as well. It was an effective system for manag-ing the amount of snow that accumulated on the roof

At some point in the early 1970s, a group that rented the building each fall for a huge church gathering had complained to the Forest Service (which managed the upkeep of the building for the federal government) that the roof leaked where the support cables were attached to the interior beams. The drips annoyed their members, who were dressed in their "Sunday best." The Forest Service had a roofing contractor look at the problem and the

Grooming foreman Steve Brehler and I watch as Casey Train in the PB170 grooming machine prepares to climb onto the roof of Blyth Arena.

Watching the Pisten-Bully groomers make the first few passes.

contractor suggested coating the entire room with a layer of tar and gravel. No one at the Forest Service understood the snow removal system well enough to realize that following this recommendation would incapacitate the snow removal system, so they approved the proposal, effectively dooming the building. There were several drought years in the mid-1970s when the inability to remove snow was not an issue and during the huge snow year of 1981-82, the Forest Service had brought in a firefighting hand crew from the California Department of Corrections to hand shovel the roof. Now that the building was in the hands of a private owner, that option was off the table, so in the winter of 1982-83, we had to come up with another means of removing snow from the roof.

One thing that Squaw Valley had in abundance was snow grooming equipment and skilled operators, so we did some calculations and determined that the overall weight and ground pressure of a grooming machine was well within the allowable load on the roof, so we decided to plow the roof using a couple of Pisten Bully grooming machines. We built a ramp of snow to the edge of the west side of the roof, and operators Casey Train and Steve Brehler gingerly drove their cats onto the roof. Initially, we thought we would tether the machines together, to prevent one from falling off the roof in the event the snow beneath it started to slide, but it quickly became apparent that this was unnecessary. The lightweight machines removed hundreds of tons of snow in a couple of days and could hardly be heard plowing away overhead from inside the building.

The plowing operation took place in January 1983. Through February and March of that winter there were continued heavy snows with strong winds, but the depth on the roof of Blyth never reached the loading that we had seen in January—at least not on the west side of the roof. The east side—downwind of the ridge in the prevailing southwest wind pattern—was always loaded more heavily than the west side because the ridge of the roof tended to cause snow to load up there during a storm, and even when it was not snowing, a strong wind would scour snow from the west side and dump it onto the east side. That repeated loading

Blyth Arena after the collapse was a dismal sight.

pattern had been occurring since the building was constructed, year in, year out. In March of 1983, however, it proved to be the building's undoing.

On March 28, Blyth Manager Pete Bansen came to work early—about 6:15 a.m.—to turn on the refrigeration system and deposit money from the previous day's operation at the cash office. When he returned to the arena, he glanced up at the roof and noticed an odd bow in a group of conduits running along one of the large beams. The conduits carried power to the lights that hung from the ceiling, and they should have been parallel, but some were farther from the beam than others. He walked up the bleachers at the east end of the arena and sighted along the bottom of the beam with the bowed conduits, comparing how it looked to others. That beam seemed to be deflecting a lot more than the others, and what Bansen was seeing was the first stage of the catastrophic failure of the beam due to metal fatigue that would result in the collapse of the center section of the roof several hours later. As the beam sagged, it gradually exerted increasing pressure on the support cables, which initially failed slowly—Bansen could hear individual wires breaking in the support cables throughout the morning—and later rapidly, when one of the sockets attaching a cable to a beam broke, causing the box beam to rip in half, dropping tens of tons of beams, roof decking, and snow onto the bleachers and the ice surface below. Fortunately, Bansen's observation had prompted him to close the building and lock everyone out. He saved lives in the process.

It would have been virtually impossible to get approval to rebuild Blyth in the same configuration, especially since a building with a roof of similar design had collapsed in Oklahoma City, and the costs to rebuild would have been prohibitive, so the building was demolished in the summer of 1983, ending a twenty-five-year lifespan that witnessed one of the most dramatic moments in Olympic history and sadly removing yet another landmark of Squaw Valley's heritage.

First Look at
Mt. Bachelor, Oregon

I first talked to Bill Healy in the winter of 1981-82. Bill was the CEO of Mt. Bachelor, in Bend, Oregon—a modest-sized town roughly in the middle of the state, on the east side of the Cascade Range. Mt. Bachelor was a successful regional ski resort. It had good snow and a long season and a very loyal customer base in Bend and even as far away as Portland. I had never been to central Oregon, and really had no awareness of the resort, but Bill sounded like a nice guy and I agreed to look at his project.

Mt. Bachelor is a huge, cone-shaped, extinct volcano, and the ski operations were distributed along the east and northeast slopes. The mountain was completely within the Deschutes National Forest and the ski operations had originally been an endeavor of the Bend Skyliners Mountaineering Club. As with so many of the founders of ski resorts in the United States, Bill had been a ski trooper with the Tenth Mountain Division in World War II. Bill's family owned a furniture store in Portland, which he had moved to Bend in the 1950s.

Working with a handful of other Skyliners members, Bill secured a special use permit to develop a ski area on Bachelor Butte, about twenty miles west of the town of Bend. After raising $100,000 by selling $25 shares, the ski area opened in 1958 with a long Poma lift, two rope tows, and a 1,500-square-foot day lodge. Lift tickets were $3; season passes, $50. The resort steadily added lifts and lodge space—always a modest but successful operation through the 1960s and 1970s. One element was always glaringly absent, however: skiing from the top of the mountain. The location of the resort, at the very eastern edge of the Cascade Range, tends to wring moisture out of flows off the Pacific before the moist air mass moves into the arid high desert of eastern Oregon. Because of this, Mt. Bachelor has a serious rime ice problem: anything exposed to the wind toward the top of the mountain can accumulate a dramatic amount of ice during a storm—even overnight. A fixed grip chairlift would be inoperable much of the time due to ice buildup, and would likely even be damaged while parked from the weight of ice building up on the carriers and cables. Bill had heard about the new detachable chairlifts being built in Europe, and he believed that a detachable chair could allow Mt. Bachelor to provide skiing to the top of the mountain, because the chairs could be moved onto indoor storage rails at the end of the day, preventing them from becoming weighed down with rime ice overnight if a storm moved in. That would increase their lift-served acreage significantly, lengthen the season, and provide a much more favorable guest experience.

In the summer of 1982, a short Doppelmayr detachable quad chairlift was built in Breckenridge, Colorado. The intent was to see if novice skiers would accept and benefit from the slow loading and unloading speeds afforded by the detachable—the lift moved skiers a few hundred yards from a condominium project to a base area. The condominiums could then be marketed to Breckenridge skiers as "ski-in, ski-out" which greatly enhanced their marketability. There were no other detachable chairlifts in the United States or Canada, and only a few in Europe.

Bill Healy wanted a lift to the top of his mountain, and the technology of the detachable chairlift seemed to address the ice problem, but none of the lift companies would touch the project. There was no road to the top of the mountain, the ski resort received hundreds of inches of snowfall annually, and the logistics of building a lift there seemed overwhelming: there were so many variables that the installation costs would be impossible to forecast with any accuracy. Furthermore, the lift would be built on National Forest land and an environmental group called "1,000 Friends of Oregon," while not antagonistic to the concept of the lift, were staunchly opposed to the construction of a road to the top terminal.

I went to Mt. Bachelor in 1982 and met Bill, who struck me as smart and determined with a great sense of humor. I liked him right away. Bill was afflicted with Lou Gehrig's Disease—ALS—and used a small motorized scooter to get around. He speech was affected also, but that just meant that you had to listen carefully when he spoke. If you did, it was no problem. I met Bill at one of the day lodges at the base area of the mountain. Bill told me that he would get me a snowcat so I could go up the mountain and look at the project, but I had brought my one year old daughter Anika with me and I told him that I would do it another time.

"Just leave her with me," he said, "I'll keep an eye on her—we'll be fine!"

Bill called the mountain manager, Jerry Blann, who came over and met us. "Hans needs to go to the top—can you give him a ride up to take a look?"

Jerry replied, "It's a terrible day—the wind is blowing, and visibility is lousy…."

Bill said, "No better time to see what the weather at Mt. Bachelor has to offer! Get someone to take him up." He was not going to take "no" for an answer, and he seemed genuinely happy to babysit, so I left Anika with Bill while I went to see his mountain.

Jerry was right—it was a miserable day—windy and snowing, visibility near zero. We drove to the top with a snowcat, mostly following the line where the new lift was proposed and trying to stay in the fall line. The profile was straightforward—a consistent, moderate slope angle from the site of the lower terminal to the top, about 1,700 feet of vertical, much of it above tree line. The top terminal site—what I could judge of it under the conditions—was large enough and relatively flat. It seemed like an ideal application for a detachable, and I thought that, rather than just moving the carriers from the haul rope to storage rails every night and parking the lift, we could install a low horsepower auxiliary drive motor that could keep the line machinery turning enough to prevent the sheaves from becoming embedded in ice and unable to turn. The loading and unloading areas would be in enclosed buildings, but if we could keep the equipment on the towers from freezing overnight, the lift would be ready to operate right away in the morning, as quickly as the operators could fill the line with chairs. It was just a matter of figuring out how to build the lift and two build-

Mt. Bachelor is perfectly situated to collect amazing amounts of rime ice on any surface exposed to the weather.

ings, one of which would be accessible only over the snow (while it lasted).

I went back to the day lodge and found Bill and Anika having a perfectly great time. He had given her some financial reports and memos and she was carefully tearing all the papers into little pieces as Bill looked on approvingly: "I got a free shredding service," he said.

Bill asked me what I thought about the project and whether it was feasible. I kidded him about the terrible weather: "You really want to put a lift up there?"

He laughed.

"There are a lot of potential problems," I said, "but it absolutely *can* be done. It would be the first installation of a detachable chair in North America that would show what a detachable can do. All the focus in the industry has been the ease of loading and unloading and the benefits of the higher line speed and shorter ride time, but this would allow ski industry people to see the benefit of the technology in a harsh

Bill Healy and his mountain—
Mt. Bachelor, Oregon.
Illustration by Dave Adamson.

environment where icing has prohibited the use of a fixed grip chairlift. It's not going to be cheap, though. We can move as much material as possible over the snow, but there's going to be a LOT of helicopter time, and we can't use a small helicopter—it's got to be a heavy-lift."

"A Skycrane?" asked Bill. "You know Erickson Air Crane is just over in Medford…."

"Probably some time with a Skycrane," I replied. "But the cost per hour doesn't really work unless you have loads that can't be broken down enough to be handled with a smaller ship. I think a Bell 214 or a Sikorsky S-61 is a better choice—the hourly cost is a lot lower and the load capacity is more appropriate for what we'll be needing to fly."

"So… you're interested?" asked Healy.

"Definitely," I said. "There are some things I need to work out, but I am definitely interested." "That's good," replied Bill, "because no one else seems to be capable or willing to build it."

I already knew that. Lift Engineering, Riblet and Miner-Denver had evaluated the project and were convinced that the logistics of building the lift were so risky that they would likely lose money on the job. One told me, "You're wasting your time—it can't be built." It presented challenges but compared to some of my other projects it seemed far from impossible. It would be an installation that, for the first time, would demonstrate the capabilities of a detachable chairlift in North America—technology that was rapidly taking hold in Europe but had been explored only tentatively here. It was an interesting opportunity. Too, I had a good feeling about Bill Healy—and not just because he was a good babysitter.

Janek Kunczynski

Janek Kunczynski (pronounced "Yah-neck Kun-chin-ski") emigrated to the United States as a young engineer from his native Poland in 1962, working at first for Poma, the large French lift manufacturer. In 1963, Jan and Bernie Pomagalski built four lifts at Squaw Valley as part of a major expansion: Gold Coast, Cornice I, Cornice II, and Little KT. The total cost for the four lifts was less than $200,000—a bargain even at the time—the equivalent amount in 2020 would be less than $1.7 million. Bernie Pomagalski went to South America that winter and was killed when he fell from a lift tower. Jan continued to install Poma lifts for several years before joining forces with the Miner-Denver company—two lifts that opened important new terrain at Squaw Valley were Miner-Denver equipment installed by Jan: Emigrant and Shirley Lake.

Spending time in Squaw Valley had other benefits—Janek dated several of Alex Cushing's daughters. The oldest, Justine, was first, but Alex packed her off on a year-long, around-the-world trip, ostensibly to expose her to great art, but more likely to keep her away from Jan. Not to be denied, Janek dated and eventually married Alex's middle daughter, Lily.

Lift installation work for other companies paid the bills, but Jan had ideas of his own and was anxious to design and build his own lifts. Dave McCoy was developing Mammoth Mountain at the time and was looking for a lift manufacturer who had the ability to supply lifts reliably and economically. With McCoy's financial support, Jan was able to set up a manufacturing facility in Carson City, Nevada and open his own company, Lift Engineering and Manufacturing. Janek's fixed-grip chairlifts were badged as "Yan" lifts and were simple, durable, and fast and easy to build. He used a direct-embedment tower footing where the base of the tower tube was set on a small pad of concrete in the bottom of the hole for the footing, surrounded by a minimal rebar cage, and then encased in concrete with little to no forming or other time-consuming or costly labor. Using this method, a small crew could field-fabricate towers, dig holes and—in a matter of a couple of days—have all the towers standing and poured by using a heavy-lift helicopter on a weekend break from a logging contract. It was a fast, economical, and very efficient way to construct a chairlift. Yan lifts also had simple, sturdy, and well-designed motor rooms and operator booths—everything constructed from readily available, inexpensive steel tubing and plate steel. The line machinery and carriers were equally simple and durable. Yan lifts quickly became a popular option among ski area operators as the original American manufacturers like Heron and Miner-Denver faded into obscurity. Jan was also more than willing to retrofit his line machinery and drives on existing installations by other companies, increasing the installed base of Lift Engineering product across the country. It did not hurt that he was a charming and enthusiastic salesman for his product and company, always looking for ways to incorporate new ideas and more efficient designs.

As successful as his company and lift designs were, Janek's ambitions were always several steps ahead. He bought his own Bell 214 heavy-lift helicopter and built a tower installation machine out of a Caterpillar crawler tractor with a built-in crane and on-board air compressor and welding machines. As the market changed, his lifts transitioned from doubles to triples and he started working on even more ambitious designs. When Alex Cushing started to talk about replacing the twenty-year-old, four passenger PHB gondola at Squaw Valley, Janek cranked up the sales pitch. He had never built a gondola, but what better place to build his first than at a resort that was practically in his own back yard—and for his father-in-law? When Alex told me that he was seriously considering allowing Janek to build the new gondola, I told him that it was a terrible idea. Alex asked why. I told him that no matter how enthusiastic about the idea Janek was, there was no escaping the fact that the lift would be a prototype and the first year would be a disaster as they ironed out the myriad problems with the equipment that would inevitably arise. Alex asked about the second year. I told him that Janek was a smart guy and that he would figure things out and correct the inevitable problems and that the second year of operation would be better. When Alex told the story, he would always conclude with the punchline, "But Hans was wrong—the second year was even worse than the first…."

It seemed particularly risky to me to install a prototype lift in a location that was literally the primary artery of the skiing operation for most of our customers, and especially at a challenging time in the industry and for our image. Squaw Valley was still on the rebound from the tram accident and I had worked hard to realign our business operations to try to establish a reputation for providing a quality experience for our customers. Squaw's image had always been about great terrain for skiers who knew what they were doing, but customer service had never been close to good—since 1949, virtually every article in the national press about Squaw Valley had smirked about Alex's disdain for interacting with guests and the uneven customer service that could be expected at the resort. It was a point of pride among long-time Squaw Valley skiers that you had to be tough to ski the mountain: it was not a place for weenies. At a time when the ski industry was concerned about declining interest and an aging population of skiers, it seemed to me that delivering a more consistent and welcoming customer service experience would help solidify our position in the market. To do that, you had to—at the very least—have a reliable, efficient lift network. Innovation and creativity were great, but for our customers nothing was more important than reliable, consistent operations. My philosophy and operational and management style were just beginning to pay off for Squaw Valley—Alex had said that he and John Buchman were retiring from the operation and while their "retirement" was less than complete, Alex, anyway, had been taking a smaller role in management decisions. Alex's eagerness to replace the PHB gondola with a prototype from Lift Engineering was a clear message that the authority I had been given to effectively manage the operation had distinct limitations.

I would have been delighted to build a state-of-the-art, reliable, efficient Doppelmayr gondola, but Alex's willingness to risk installing an untested prototype assembled from parts sourced from various vendors was a looming threat to the success that the company had achieved at rebuilding our reputation following the tram accident. We had moved the needle significantly on improving guest experience at Squaw Valley—articles in the national ski magazines had noted a marked improvement in Squaw Valley's guest experience, but this did not seem to matter to Alex. He had never accepted the employment agreement that I had proposed, and now seemed willing to significantly compromise my ability to run the resort and continue the leadership and positive changes that I had implemented. It put me in an exceedingly difficult position.

As 1983 began, it was apparent that Janek was lobbying Alex hard to allow him to build the replacement gondola. He had an enormous potential advantage over every other lift manufacturer, because he could practically sell the lift at cost as well as offer to finance it on extremely attractive terms, which would have been music to Alex's ears while providing Jan with a conveniently located example of his new product. The amazing part was that he was not doing that—Lift Engineering's price was higher than what Doppelmayr was quoting, and the interest rate Jan proposed was higher as well—the only explanation was that Jan was leveraging his position as Alex's son-in-law to get the job.

In a November 5, 1982 memo to Alex summarizing the proposals, I compared the prices, financing rates and experience of the three companies:

Lift Engineering:	$3,650,520 plus tax	Financed at 11.5 percent for five years
Doppelmayr:	$3,410,000 plus tax	Financed at 8.5 percent for five years
Agudio:	$2,971,040 plus tax	Financed at 12.4 percent for seven years

The Italian company Agudio had the most experience, I noted, with installation of eleven six-passenger gondolas in the past three years. Doppelmayr had completed four installations over the previous two years. Lift Engineering had no experience building a gondola, and I noted that the system they proposed was pieced together from different manufacturers. "The total package is a prototype and experimental," I said. "We are not exactly looking forward to it." That was something of an understatement.

Before long, it became clear that Janek would have his way and would get to build the lift. I told Alex that I had no interest in watching that work go forward and that I had a project that would require part of my time in Oregon. In his giddy state about building a new gondola, he agreed to allow me to work half-time at Squaw Valley while I built the detachable chairlift for Doppelmayr at Mt. Bachelor.

Mt. Bachelor— Bend, Oregon

After making a quick trip to Mt. Bachelor from Squaw Valley in late April, we assembled the crew and started work on the project on May 15. There was a great deal of snow—the winter had been as bountiful in Oregon as in Tahoe—and while this put us behind schedule in some respects, it was advantageous in others. Since there was no road to the site of the top terminal and we would not be able to build one, we needed to develop alternate modes of transportation for materials and people. The first few weeks of the project were devoted to building infrastructure for the project. We had a core crew of three people, Don Cole and John Moors, who had worked on the installation of the Newport and Solitude lifts at Squaw Valley, and Pete Bansen, who had worked at Squaw Valley and, most recently, managed Blyth Arena until the roof collapse. All three had good skills for this project: Moors, in addition to being a skilled heavy equipment operator, was an excellent carpenter. Bansen could operate equipment, blast, and had spent several years on the tram at Squaw Valley. Don Cole was an attorney who had fallen out of love with practicing law and wanted to get his hands dirty again—he was a great worker, too, for a lawyer!

In the months prior to the start of work at the mountain, John Moors built a portable building that could be broken down into 4-foot by 8-foot panels for

The D4 dozer parked at the job site gave us a preview of the conditions we could expect in the months to come.

transport and then bolted together to make a fully enclosed 400-square-foot shelter. It would allow the crew at the top a dry space to store their tools and get out of the weather for a while if it were snowing. After clearing the snow from the top terminal site with a dozer, we hauled the portable building pieces to the top using a snowcat from Mt. Bachelor and a trailer on skis. The weather in late May was warm and sunny during the day, and it became difficult to pull the trailer to the top over the soft, wet spring snow, so we started work at 4 a.m. when cool overnight temperatures firmed

The skis welded to the outriggers on the Grove crane looked odd, but they worked well at keeping it from tipping when driven over the snow.

up the snow and the snowcat had good traction. During the day, it was sometimes possible to firm up the snow enough to get the snowcat moving by salting the route ahead of the machine with bags of rock salt, which would temporarily harden the snow enough to allow the cat to get started, after which it would frequently be able to maintain traction enough to keep moving. Once the portable building was assembled, we tied it down with cables to keep it from being blown away by the wind.

We moved a small Grove rough-terrain crane to the top so that it would be available to install the return terminal machinery as well as erect the building that would enclose the equipment. This did not go exactly as planned—we started by trying to drive the all-wheel drive crane to the top over the snow, but even chained up all the way around, it sank in the snow and threatened to tip over. We could pull it with the D6, but the tipping problem remained an issue, so we tried fabricating a pair of giant steel skis that we welded to the front outriggers. Although the large surface area of the skis kept the crane from tipping, there was no way they would slide on the snow when deployed. We finally removed the boom, which greatly lightened the crane and lowered the center of gravity dramatically, and then, with the crane alternately driving on its own and being pulled by a Caterpillar D6 bulldozer, moved it to the site of the top terminal. The following day we dragged the boom to the top over the snow behind the D6. We had a small John Deere crawler backhoe for digging the building footings at the top terminal and then digging a trench down the mountain for the chairlift communications line. The backhoe also had to be dismantled to get the top over the snow by removing the backhoe attachment, walking the crawler to the top over the snow (with some help from the D6), and then chaining the backhoe attachment to the blade of the D6, walking the Cat to the top, and then reattaching the backhoe attachment

The backhoe attachment perched on the dozer blade, ready to be transported to the top.

to the crawler tractor. Once the backhoe was at the top terminal site, we were able to install the boom on the crane by lifting it into place with the front-end loader bucket on the backhoe. With the addition of a diesel generator and an air compressor, the top terminal site was fully equipped and ready for work to begin—every challenge could be met if we were smart enough to adapt and improvise.

I had decided that we could use a work tram to move materials to the top terminal as I had in Banff and Snowbird, so we spent about a week building a simple ropeway that paralleled the lift line and was about 75 feet north of it. We had to remove snow down to the dirt, dig a small hole to stabilize the foot of each tower, then start building the tower out of triangular sections of "needle," which were tied off with guy lines to trees or stakes. The towers were generally about thirty-feet tall and leaned toward the lift line. From the top of the tower, we hung a saddle for the track rope. When the towers were all in place, we pulled a track rope (an old piece of wire rope from a chairlift) into place over the saddles using a large winch that had enough cable to reach the bottom. We tied the track rope off at the top to some large rocks, then tensioned it from the bottom using some trees and a couple of large rocks downhill and north of the lower terminal. Some of the Mt. Bachelor employees were openly skeptical of the work tram concept, and would come by and tell our crew, "This is never going to work—you guys are wasting your time." But we persisted. Once the track rope was installed, aligned by adjusting the tower angles, and tensioned, we built a cargo platform about six feet long and four feet wide out of steel tubing and plywood, hung it from a carriage, attached the haul rope from the winch—and we were in business. The work tram was instrumental in moving parts and material, although we did not allow people to ride it.

At the beginning of June, there was still an enormous amount of snow on the planned line of the lift, so I hired a dirt contractor in Bend—Robinson Construction—to plow the line so that we could make some progress on the tower footings. Robinson brought in two large Terex bulldozers and a couple of operators, and they started plowing snow out of the lift line—sometimes cutting through twenty feet of compacted snow before finding the dirt. We would load a couple of fifty-five-gallon drums of diesel fuel on the work tram every evening, run the fuel up to where the dozers were working, and fuel them on site, saving

Don Cole unloading a drum of fuel at the top terminal of the work tram.

significant time and fuel over walking them to the bottom each day to be fueled.

Containers started arriving from Doppelmayr, and we unloaded and sorted the parts in the parking lots, separating the drive and return terminal machinery, tower equipment, chairs, and grips. Loads of tower tube started arriving also and the crew was able to start fabricating towers. The crew was now larger with the addition of Tom Healy (Bill's son), Peter Wild (Hardy's brother-in-law from Switzerland), and several guys from Bend, including Mike Joy and Dave Irons. Jimmy King and Jon Krauss came up from Squaw Valley to do some of the welding, and we hired a great welder from Bend—Dewey Cummins—a pleasant and unflappable guy and an excellent welder. Dewey was a little superstitious, however. He might send all his tools up the work tram but he insisted on carrying his welding hood with him in the snowcat—I do not think he trusted the work tram completely.

The weather at Mt. Bachelor was anything but cooperative. Although the east side of the Cascades is the "dry" side, it rained a good bit in June, and we had snow at least once every month we were there. The crew was very adept at overcoming weather-related challenges. Early in the project when we were building towers in the parking lot, one of the welders was getting soaked welding ladder rungs onto towers. The crew improvised a rolling canopy out of lumber and plastic sheeting wide enough to protect the area that he was working on from the rain and supported by the truck towing the welding machine. The mountain was a constant challenge even if it was not raining or snowing. The lower terminal of the lift was just below tree line and while the ground on that part of the mountain had actual soil, the landscape above tree line had sparse vegetation and was nothing but gradations of volcanic lava, from fine dust to rock outcroppings made of lava. The lava rock tended to break down into round chunks, which might as well have been ball bearings. You could dig in it readily enough, but the material removed from the hole did not stack well and about half of it would ravel back into the hole. We dug a trench to bury the communications line for the lift and install some additional conduit for the ski resort, and as we dug the trench it would just backfill itself automatically. The volcanic dust was powder-fine, and nothing was more effective at creating a choking, impenetrable cloud of dust than the rotor wash from the helicopter. It would take a long time to settle again, usually just in time for the helicopter to arrive with the next load. Since we had not been allowed to build a road to the top terminal, we used a Tucker Sno-Cat to transport the crew for as long as the snow lasted, but when it was gone, the crew working at the top terminal had no choice but to walk up, which took about forty minutes.

I had hired a subcontractor to build the lower and upper terminal buildings. It was a company from Eugene, Oregon and they had two divisions: R.A. Chambers Construction (which was union) and Nusteel (which was non-union). Nusteel was doing our project. The union/non-union designation was an artifice because the same people worked for both

The Grove crane at the top terminal site on July 4th, 1983.

companies—they used R.A Chambers Construction when they needed to be union and Nusteel when they did not. We had cleared the snow out of the area for the lower terminal, and the Nusteel guys started digging and forming footings for the building, and poured concrete while there was still snow surrounding the excavation. Once the foundations were in place, we started receiving loads of structural steel for the lower terminal, and Nusteel's concrete guys moved to the top terminal to repeat the process there. Pouring concrete at the top would require a helicopter, however, and we brought in Jim Crawford to handle that work and to fly structural steel to the top terminal. Crawford learned to fly helicopters in the U.S. Army during the Vietnam War and had earned a solid reputation in ski lift circles as a highly skilled heavy-lift pilot when he worked for Columbia Helicopters. He was just getting his own company, Timberline Air Service, off the ground with a Bell 214B-1 helicopter that had been newly assembled in Southern California from three wrecks. Bell developed the 214 in 1970 as a hot-rodded version of the tough and versatile Vietnam-era UH-1 "Huey" helicopter, with a long body and a much larger engine giving it the ability to fly an external load of about 6,000 pounds. The narrow ship gave the pilot excellent visibility of the sling load, and it was a great platform for projects like ours at a relatively reasonable hourly rate. Jim and his crew chief/co-pilot, Neal Stanley, spent so much time on the project it was like they were part of our crew.

Pouring concrete with a helicopter is a simple enough process once you develop a good system. We used two buckets so that one was always in the air and the other was behind the concrete truck, full and waiting to be picked up. The pilot flew a full bucket to the waiting crew at the site, carefully bringing it into position, then hovered while the ground crew positioned the outlet port on the bottom of the bucket over the intended destination for the concrete, and pulled the handle to dispense concrete into the form. The pilot then lifted the bucket away, returning to the bottom where the crew member filling the buckets helped him to fly the empty bucket into position behind the concrete truck, removed the sling on the empty bucket from the hook on the end of the helicopter's cable, attached the sling for the full bucket, and signaled the pilot that it was ready to go. The crew generally had radio communication with the pilot, but while the helicopter was directly overhead, the noise of the ship generally required the use of hand signals to guide the pilot. The pilot would generally radio back to the person filling the buckets the weight of that load and whether he would like more or less in the next load, because as the helicopter burned fuel, it could accommodate a heavier external load. Concrete is of a consistent weight per cubic yard, so knowing how much a bucket weighed was helpful in knowing how full to fill the next bucket, but the speed and accuracy with which the bucket was filled was up to the concrete truck driver, who controlled the flow of mud into the bucket. Under pressure, some performed better than others.

It was our responsibility to get the materials for the buildings to the building sites, then Nusteel's job to construct the building. The lower terminal of the lift was some distance up the mountain from the parking lot and Sunrise Day Lodge where our operation was based. Loads of structural steel arrived every day from the fabrication shop and had to be unloaded at the parking lot, then hauled to the lower terminal site by truck or flown to the top terminal. We were able to use one of Mt. Bachelor's trucks to haul structural steel to the lower terminals—it was a military surplus, all-wheel-drive truck with a Continental gas engine and somewhat iffy brakes. We welded a couple of I-beams across the steel bed so that we could haul long structural columns by laying them along the side of the cab on the right side of the truck, allowing the column to extend well out in front and behind the truck, then chain them down securely and drive them to the lower terminal. It was a unique experience driving this truck up the narrow, winding dirt road to the lower terminal with a column or two sticking out ten feet ahead and behind of the truck and a couple of feet off the passenger's side door: It made you think ahead. Structural steel for the upper terminal was flown to the top in stacks with individual pieces separated by wood blocks or boards called "stickers." The loads were generally easy work for the helicopter, because odd shapes in the stack would make a load bulky before it got very heavy. The advantage was that the pilot could hover with the light load easily and put it wherever the crew at the top needed it with power to spare. Generally, though, we did our best to make every load carried by the helicopter as close to his maximum as we could. The Nusteel crew wanted to have a Bobcat (a small, skid-steer loader) taken to the top to speed up the backfilling process inside the perimeter of the foundation. We rigged the Bobcat to be flown, and weighed it and it was light—an easy load for the 214. We reasoned that it would need fuel while it was up on the top, so we put a fifty-five-gallon drum of diesel fuel in the bucket and strapped another one on top of the canopy. It was still light, but was a much more efficient load with the addition of the accessories. The Nusteel crew learned a lesson about helicopters the hard way early in the job. They were pouring concrete for a footing at the top terminal, and when the helicopter came back to the bottom for another load of concrete, Jim Crawford said on the radio, "Well, those guys are not very happy with me…." We asked him why and he said, "When I came in with that load, I blew their porta potty over the edge and down the hill. Fairly sure there was nobody in it…." From then on, the porta potty was tied down with a cable.

A couple of months into the job, for reasons that were never clear to us, the R.A. Chambers union members decided to set up a picket line at the entrance to the ski resort. Now, these were, in many cases, the same guys who had happily worked on the top and bottom terminal buildings as Nusteel employees, but every day a dozen or so would show up and walk back and forth with picket signs across the entrance to the Sunrise Lodge parking lot. It had no effect: The Nusteel employees drove right through, as did the structural steel

The top terminal structure nearing completion.

deliveries and the concrete trucks—no one was phased in the slightest. One day, as mysteriously as the picket line had appeared, it vanished.

As part of the labor action, one of the subcontractor employees called Oregon OSHA and told them that the crane at the top of the mountain was unsafe. It was true that one of the outriggers had a bad seal and would bleed off while you were working, but if you kept an eye on it and reset it every few minutes, it was fine. An OSHA inspector turned up one day and said that they had had a complaint about the crane and that he needed to look at it. At that time, we were hauling the crew working on top up to the site in a snowcat and we explained that the snowcat had already gone up and would not be down until the end of the day. He showed up the next day and the snowcat had just left; too bad. Same thing the next day. We took the hydraulic cylinder out of the outrigger one afternoon, had it rebuilt, flew it back up and reinstalled it, good as new. The next day the OSHA guy showed up with new hiking boots and a daypack and announced he was going to hike up and look at that crane, because every day when he arrived the snowcat has "just left…." We said, "Hey, there's no need to go to all that trouble—the snowcat is still here. Hop in—we'll give you a ride!" He looked totally confused, but he accepted the ride, checked the crane—which worked perfectly—and hiked back down.

Pete Bansen, John Moors and Don Cole—the core crew at Mt. Bachelor.

Although the Mt. Bachelor corporate offices were twenty miles away—on the west side of downtown Bend—Bill Healy would come up to the jobsite a couple of times a week. He could not walk, but he would drive around and watch our progress and visit with the crew from inside his car. He was always keenly interested in what was going on and how we were doing, and it was easy to see how excited he was about this lift that would finally reach to the top of his mountain. It was a pleasure to work for someone who had every excuse to stay in the office but made it a point to be knowledgeable about day-to-day activity on the project, and who took such pride in the progress that was being made.

We finished digging the tower holes and poured a concrete base pad in each hole with an angle-iron guide to align the tower. The towers had all been fabricated, sand blasted, painted, and then equipped with line machinery. It was time to fly the towers and pour concrete—after which the lift would really start looking like a lift. Many of the towers were too heavy to be flown with the Bell 214 helicopter: We would need a Sikorsky S-64, better known as a "Skycrane" to place the towers one day and pour concrete around them the next. The Siller brothers were millionaire rice farmers in California who also owned forest land that they logged. They had several helicopters that they used in logging and contracted helicopter construction work, mostly the Sikorsky S-61 model, which has similar capacity to a 214, but they had recently acquired an S-64 and were eager for work. I talked to them and negotiated a "by the tower" rate rather than an hourly rate: I was a little skeptical about their efficiency setting lift towers, which is a difficult and technical task. We scheduled to fly towers on a Saturday—not unusual for a helicopter working on logging jobs because the loggers frequently have weekends off and the helicopter can go produce extra revenue on the weekend. The Siller's S-64 and their fuel truck were waiting at the day lodge when we arrived in the morning, pre-flighted and ready to go. They were going to fly the towers with a 100-foot line, which is a customary length for logging. An S-64 is purpose-designed for heavy lift operations and has a rear-facing seat and controls for a second pilot who can look directly at the load and "fly the hook" when the ship is in position to precisely place the load. The 100-foot line would reduce the noise and rotor wash on the ground and allow the crew to communicate better between themselves and with the pilot, if needed. One of the guys from Siller Brothers was even going to work with the ground crew and could give the pilot directions on the radio. It seemed like they were well organized and capable.

We started at the top—Tower 23—which was a medium-sized tower, not a load that was going to give the Skycrane any weight issues even with a full load of fuel. Pete Bansen hooked it up down in the parking lot and sent it up the hill. There were guy cables pre-rigged to the crossarm and tied to the ladder with flagging. The pilot would set the base of the tower on the concrete base pad in the bottom of the hole; notches on the bottom of the tower would straddle the angle-iron set in the concrete, indexing it precisely on the center-line of the lift. The crew could grab the guy cables, pulling them free of the flimsy flagging, and connect the free ends of the cables to winches that had been anchored in advance to trees, stakes, or rocks uphill and downhill of the tower. The crew would take up the slack in the cables by tightening the winches, and, once the tower was securely tied off, the pilot would remotely release the slings attaching the tower to his electric hook and fly down for the next tower. The crew would then hurry down to the next hole and repeat the process. It was a fast, noisy, stressful, and potentially dangerous operation, but done correctly it worked extremely well.

This was all on my mind as I watched the Skycrane approaching with the first tower dangling from the long line. The pilot brought it into the site very smoothly, approaching the hole with the tower at the right level for the crew to guide it, not moving too quickly, then lowering it into the hole. One of the guys jumped down into the hole to guide the base onto the angle iron and aligned the notch on the uphill side of the tower base with the angle iron as the pilot lowered it. So far so, good. The crew had the guy lines pulled off and were heading for the winches. This tower needed to lean ten degrees downhill, and as the pilot allowed it to lean downhill, it spun around. There were more sheaves on the upline than the downline and the heavy side of the crossarm wanted to go downhill as soon as the pilot started to lean the tower. We had him set it on the angle iron again and repeated the lean move with the same effect. Some head-scratching ensued as the Skycrane hovered holding the tower upright. Finally, I told the pilot to take it back to the parking lot so we could regroup and figure things out. He flew it back to the parking lot and Pete reorganized the guy lines, untangling them and retying them to the ladder for another attempt. I had him wire a 2-by-4 to the bottom rung of the ladder, thinking that we could have two guys stabilize the tower against rotating while the pilot leaned it. The Skycrane picked up the tower again and brought it our direction, flew it smoothly into the hole and I had a guy grab each end of the 2-by-4 and guide it on to the angle iron, but as the pilot let the top end lean downhill, the tower still twisted, overwhelming the ability of two strong men to hold it in place. This was a problem. Once again, we sent the tower back to the parking lot. In the end, while the Siller Brothers' pilot was clearly very skilled, the technology of the long line did not translate well to setting towers, at least not those that were anything but plumb.

The following week we were able to get an Erickson Air Crane S-64 to the jobsite. Erickson used a completely different method for setting towers—multiple points of attachment to the helicopter and short cables. This minimized the tendency of the rigging to twist and allowed the pilot to very accurately place the tower base and then lean the tower while controlling any rotation. The downside was that the huge helicopter was right on top of you while working, and the noise and rotor wash were punishing. In the parking lot when the Erickson ship picked up the towers, Pete had to keep his head on a swivel to avoid the heavy wood stickers on which the towers had been supported that were blowing across the asphalt like matchsticks. Overall, it was a very satisfactory and professional operation, and we had all the towers standing within a few hours.

Pouring concrete with the Erickson S-64 Skycrane.

We poured concrete the next day—Sunday—after warning the concrete company that we were going to need a lot of concrete fast and could not tolerate any delay. They brought in all their drivers and even had some concrete trucks come in from a company in another town. The concrete buckets that Erickson used were several times the size of the buckets we had been using with the 214, and they would empty a concrete truck in a hurry. We moved the staging area for the bucket loading operation up the hill to near the lower terminal to shorten the turn length for the helicopter and dug a hole where we would fill the buckets. They were so much taller than the other buckets that the chute on the back of the concrete truck was almost horizontal—placing the bucket at a lower level allowed the chute to be inclined more steeply and assured a more rapid flow of concrete into the bucket and quicker fills. The concrete pouring operation went as smoothly as the tower placement had, with no delays in arrival of concrete trucks, no mechanical issues—everyone worked well together, and it was efficient and low-stress.

With towers standing, suddenly the project started looking a lot more like a lift. The lower terminal was nearing completion. We could start assembling chairs and hanging them on the storage rail located to the side of the loading area. There was a large ramp on the outside of the building where skiers would enter the building then turn left and load the lift. The top terminal was much smaller—no storage rails—and it was a short distance from where you unloaded from the lift to the door leading outside. The buildings were both steel frames with concrete "tilt-up" panels bolted to the framing—typical industrial building construction and well-suited to the harsh environment of the mountain. The large barn doors at the upper terminal were covered with rubber so that the lift operator could whack them with a hammer to knock off any accumulated ice.

We pulled the haul rope to the top terminal with the winch, then down the downline with the D6. Once the rope was tensioned and spliced, we had a working lift. Hardy completed work on the tower wiring for the derail system, and we were able to test run with the main electric motor, the diesel auxiliary engine, and the "creeper" drive—the low horsepower motor that drove the haul rope slowly overnight when ice was predicted. Everything worked as expected.

As the first storms of the winter season rolled into the Pacific Northwest, Mt. Bachelor collected a few feet of snow and with it our first real test of the ability of the lift to cope with ice. Unfortunately, the creeper drive proved to be a little too slow to keep the sheaves from icing up. Ice started to accumulate, the electric motor shut off, and the towers on the upper half of the lift turned into giant popsicles. We knocked the ice off and got it running and ordered a larger, slightly faster creeper drive motor. The problem never reoccurred. The top terminal building looked like a giant, square igloo: Every square inch of the outside of the building was covered with rime ice several inches thick. It was a remarkable sight.

We load tested the lift just after Thanksgiving, using sandbags and kegs from the beer distributor in Bend—easy to load and unload and the kegs sat nicely on the chairs. The load test went smoothly, and we were ready to open on November 6, a little ahead of schedule. Mt. Bachelor now had skiing from the top and local skiers were thrilled with the high-speed ride up the mountain and the new terrain that the Summit Express made accessible to them.

As the upper terminal building neared completion, we had taken down the work tram and flown the big winch back to the base area along with the Bobcat. John Moors disassembled the portable building, stacked the panels, and banded them together to be flown down. Jim Crawford with Timberline Air Service brought his Bell 214 helicopter back to move some materials around for us, and the crew hooked the portable building panels on to the helicopter's cargo hook to bring them down on a backhaul. It was heavier than anyone thought, and Jim had a difficult time getting it into the air and flying—but Jim was determined and eventually got the load off the ground. On the way down the mountain, he hit a downdraft and had to choose between releasing the hook which would drop the building panel package or crashing the helicopter. He dropped the building, which landed on the

The top terminal of the Summit resembled a giant igloo by November, 1983.

slope just below the top terminal, significantly the worse for wear. We repackaged the debris into two lighter loads that the 214 was able to handle without a problem.

The only thing left at the top was the small Grove rough-terrain crane. The crane was parked out of the way to the north of the top terminal, and as the snow deepened, the Grove simply disappeared under the snow until it was completely buried. When the spring came and a lot of the depth of snow at the top had melted, I went up and dug the crane out, got it started, and drove it down the mountain over the snow. It was tricky, because I had to keep it pointed down the fall line and it wanted to get sideways and tip over. It also had an odd, bouncing motion as the tires sank into the snow and then climbing out of the hole they had just made, only to sink in again. Word had gotten around while I was digging the crane out that "a crazy guy is going to drive a crane down the mountain over the snow," so by the time I got to the lower terminal of the lift, there was quite a crowd to cheer me on; but the tough little crane—which had hibernated all winter under the snow—deserved most of the credit.

Every project has doubters, and the Summit lift was no exception. There were old-time Mt. Bachelor skiers who thought that Bill Healy was hopelessly optimistic about how much the Summit lift would run because of the extreme weather at the top of the mountain. Bill's optimism and his knowledge of the mountain were validated. The Summit lift extended Mt. Bachelor's already long season, and in the first year of operation, there were only five days on which Summit could not operate.

Two Gondolas in Three Years

eanwhile, back at Squaw Valley, Janek Kunczynski's Lift Engineering crew was tasked with not only building the new lift, but also dramatically altering and enlarging the top terminal to accommodate a six-passenger gondola with indoor cabin storage. As part of the package, Janek had agreed to build the structure of a new and much larger mid-mountain lodge at Gold Coast. It would mimic the design of his drive terminals and operator booths—all black steel tubing and mirrored glass—ultra-modern. The gondola, itself, was a showcase for Jan's ideas and industrial design—he was using everything he had learned building fixed-grip chairlifts and developing more efficient, less expensive manufacturing processes. Tube towers supported large, heavy crossarms

The Lift Engineering gondola with Siberia Ridge and Emigrant in the distance.

and line machinery. Jan had designed a new cast aluminum sheave that looked for all the world like the wheel cover on a dragster. The cabin was an innovative, injection-molded plastic design with wrap-around windows, and the conveyors that moved the cabins through the terminals used v-belts and a series of pulleys of graduated sizes driven by the haul rope to proportionately increase and decrease cabin speed depending on the location of the cabin in the terminal. A lot of it was very clever and aesthetically pleasing, but operationally it was a disaster. The lift would stop, sometimes for long periods of time, before the operators could figure out what was wrong and restart it. The windows in the cabins—which had a simple, three-sided cut in a sheet of polycarbonate that "warped" open—were far less than adequate for providing ventilation, and the black plastic cabins heated up to unbearable temperatures in the California sun. Because the terminal conveyors were driven by the haul rope, when the lift stalled, any cabins in the terminals were essentially locked in position. The only way to move them was to take a knife and cut all the v-belts, which would then allow the conveyor wheels to turn freely and the operators to move the cabins. The inaugural year was a disaster, and the howls of outrage from stranded skiers could be heard—literally—in Alex's home (the "Blue House") which was directly below the line.

February 5, 1984 memorandum from Jim Mott to Janek Kunczynski detailing issues with the Lift Engineering Gondola (partial list):

1. *Bullwheel flange must be installed.*
2. *The fact that the carriage does not move presents problems.*
4. *Hold-down towers need to have cable catchers and guards installed.*
6. *Accelerator/decelerator problems are extensive. Appears to be an engineering application problem as opposed to performance of the equipment.*
9. *Grip problems must be fixed. The safety of the grip must be scrutinized and it must be proven that this grip and its components are compatible with all other components of the Gondola.*
10. *All of the preliminary safety orders issued by the State must be finalized.*
11. *Cabins are getting damaged due to acceleration/ deceleration problems.*
12. *There seems to be a major grip problem that needs to be solved.*
13. *Cable catchers are not yet installed on all towers. Bring it up to Code.*
15. *There is no top bullwheel retaining device to retain the bullwheel if a failure occurs in the shaft or bearings. Required by Code.*
19. *The flooring at the top terminal is not level and has holes in it. This should be repaired and leveled for the safety of our customers.*
22 *The cabins, being black, heat up easily and do not have sufficient ventilation. Additionally, the windows scratch much too easily.*

Alex called me in the summer of 1984, and we talked about the various problems with the gondola, most of which, it seemed to me, could be corrected easily. "Don't worry," I remember telling him. "Jan will fix it."

John Moors and Mike Joy drilling rock for the Siberia breakover towers.

reached the top terminal of the chairlift, Poma's order had gone from one lift to two.

Construction of the new gondola and the detachable chairlift—which replaced the tremendously popular Siberia chairlift—was split into separate crews, because the work and complexity of each project was significant. The project got off to a tragic start—a Bell 214 heavy-lift helicopter was being used to dismantle the Yandola, and as it lifted and flew with a section of Tower 4, it lost power, causing the ship to crash and burn just uphill of Betty's Bridge at the bottom of the mountain. The tower section it had jettisoned narrowly missed the ground crew, but the pilot and co-pilot were killed. The accident was a horrifying reminder that this is a dangerous business, but the NTSB investigation found that a failed engine part had caused the crash, unrelated to the work being performed.

I was not excited about building the Poma lifts. The drawings, specifications, and engineering calculations were all in French, and the French had that superior attitude—you could not tell them anything. The Siberia lift was Poma's first detachable in the United States, and between their snobby attitude and the fact that I had built a detachable Doppelmayr chairlift two years before, I found them annoying. I put together a crew to build the Siberia detachable—Don Cole, John Moors and Mike Joy, who had worked with me at Mt. Bachelor, along with my son, Markus, and his friend Rob Sproehnle. I had a contract with Poma to build the gondola, the Siberia Express detachable, and a detachable chairlift on Shirley Lake the following summer, but as the projects progressed there were increasing issues with Poma that created all kinds of problems for me. The Poma engineers had consistently underestimated the quantity of concrete required for the tower footings, and we had poured nearly double the amount of concrete (at over $100 per cubic yard) that I had based the contract price on. Poma had sent over a young engineer to oversee the project for them, and he was causing headaches with the construction crew—for example ordering them to remove a particular group of bolts one day and replace them the next.

The footings for the breakover towers at the top of Siberia were massive.

There were Squaw Valley vehicle mechanics "moonlighting" on the gondola project on weekends and Squaw Valley lift maintenance mechanics thrashing to remove the Yan drive equipment from the upper terminal, as well as Poma technicians working to install and tune the drive components— so the gondola project was complicated.

The beauty of the Siberia project was that there had been a lift on that line since 1958, and the main access road at Squaw Valley went right past the lower terminal. You could drive to all the towers and the top terminal as well. It was a very straightforward project, for the most part, but it required some complex calculation. The top terminal was located on a narrow ridge with little room beyond it for skiers to unload, so the top terminal had to be squeezed as much as possible toward the front of the ridge. This would be okay in most installations, but there was a tremendous amount of pressure on the tower array: the line approached the top terminal with a long span over a steep bowl, so the breakover towers before the top terminal were complicated, heavy, and interconnected because they needed to support the haul rope as it transitioned a dramatic change in direction carrying a lot of weight. The Poma engineers had designed an elaborate connecting brace between the towers and a long arc of sheaves with walkways connected to the top terminal. This assembly had to be set using a crane perched at the very edge of a bowl that dropped nearly straight down

The crane is at full extension as we assembled the breakover towers at the top of Siberia—very sketchy.

Grooming Siberia Bowl with a Pisten-Bully winch cat.

for about 300 vertical feet. Between the weight of the angled towers and the challenge of placing the long, heavy sheave assemblies, it was a technically difficult and very dangerous situation for the crane operator—me.

Hoping to improve the situation, we built a little road that traversed across the bowl slightly below the ridge to try to get the crane a little closer to the foundation for the towers—anything to gain a little advantage over gravity. The side of the road toward the ridge was cut into the slope—and was therefore solid—but the outer edge of the road was all "fill" and could only be compacted a certain amount, which was a distinct disadvantage when placing the crane's outriggers there, because the fill under the outriggers tended to squash down, leading to a less-than-confident feeling when looking down at a very long, nearly vertical slope. If the outrigger sank into the fill as the crane was moving a maximum-load piece, there would be no way to set the load down, and there was a very real possibility that the load, crane and operator could go tumbling down the bowl. Finally, there was no way of delaying the inevitable any longer, and I placed the angled tower assembly and the line machinery without incident—despite the considerable anxiety that the situation had produced.

The gondola project, too, progressed according to plan. Both the gondola and the Siberia chairlift were going to be such tremendous upgrades to the level of service experienced by the customer that it was exciting to anticipate the rave reviews that would accompany their unveiling. It was satisfying to build two lifts with such significant operational return on investment for the resort, even if the lifts were French.

28

Late '80s

With the completion of Squaw Valley's Poma gondola and Siberia Express lift—during a demanding and stressful summer and fall—I went back to Bend for the winter with the hope that my next project would not involve reading blueprints written in French. I had been involved in trucking for long enough to have become familiar with the equipment market for power units and trailers and to understand what a trucker was looking for—what made their job easier, allowed the operator who would be loading and unloading a trailer to perform that work with efficiency and minimal wear and tear, and to enhance durability without too much weight. Truckers tend to be obsessed with weight because that is how they get paid. Weight limits are rigorously enforced, and the lighter a truck and trailer combination can be, the greater payload it can haul, resulting in a larger payment for the trucker.

After researching the availability of trailers in the Pacific Northwest, I found a great piece of industrial property with several buildings in the north end of Bend, and set up a trailer manufacturing operation. We assembled and sold Lufkin lightweight flatbed trailers. I picked up the trailer decks in Texas, and hauled them to Bend. We installed the suspension, axles, and running gear, and then plumbed the air brakes and installed wiring, lights, and reflective striping. I sourced all the parts and could assemble a trailer to order in just a couple of weeks. I hired a truck driver to make the 4,200-mile round-trip haul to Texas and back, and he could make a trip

We could haul four trailer decks at a time from Texas to Bend for assembly and sale.

This view of Telluride was unchanged from my first visit there in 1971, but in the intervening fifteen years, virtually everything else about the place had changed dramatically.

each week if needed. It was a solid, profitable, reasonably predictable business. Bend was growing by leaps and bounds and competition for good employees was intense, but we managed to do very well.

In the fall of 1986, I had another call from Doppelmayr asking for help. They were installing a chairlift at Telluride and the project was way behind schedule. The Sunshine Express lift would be the world's longest detachable chairlift, if it ever got done. Doppelmayr's contract called for the lift to be ready to open on a specific day, and it imposed a huge penalty for each additional day required to complete the project. I drove out to Telluride and looked at the job. The crew was too small, and they were only working eight-hour days. The towers were standing, but the line machinery had not been installed. There was snow on the ground, but they had no snowmobiles, which greatly impeded their ability to do the work. There was still a lot of work to be done on the drive and return terminals, and the chairs had not yet been assembled. It was a disorganized mess. In terms of motivation, they needed someone to give them a dose of "old-time religion."

I tried to hire some workers in Telluride, but I was unable to find anyone there who wanted a job. There were a lot of scruffy looking hippies hanging around in town who looked like they could use the money, but they all seemed to have trust funds that paid their expenses. I hired some guys from Eagle, Colorado—over 200 miles away—and they came down to Telluride and assembled chairs for a week.

Since the lift was gigantic—almost exactly two miles long and with thirty-eight towers—it was monumentally inefficient for the crew to have to walk to the towers over the snow, so I drove up to Montrose, Colorado—the closest town of any size to Telluride—and rented six or eight snowmobiles for a month. I hired some guys to add to the crew, and we ran two eight-hour shifts every day. Just to make sure things ran smoothly, I worked both shifts. Once we had an adequate number of people, over-the-snow transportation, and effective leadership, the crew rose to the challenge of getting the project done on time and the efficiency and pace of work quickened. We got the line machinery and communications line installed, pulled the haul rope, and spliced. The drive and return terminals were completed, and we hung the chairs and were ready to load test the lift in time for the deadline.

Once I finished the Telluride chairlift, I had a contract to construct a 300,000-gallon water tank for Squaw Valley Mutual Water Company back in Lake Tahoe. The Mutual Water Company was one of two water purveyors in the valley, and provided water to about half of the residential customers in the community—about 260 homes. The company had been in business since the 50s, and for many years, a small redwood tank had been adequate to meet the demand, but with increasing full-time residency in the homes served by the company, more storage capacity was required.

I hired Billy Dutton, a local concrete contractor, to assist with the project. Billy surveyed the site and laid out the grading while I was in Telluride, and I levelled the site when I returned from Colorado; then Billy poured the base for the tank. Fortunately, it was a late winter, and we were able to keep working right through December and January. I hired a welder from Reno who welded the steel sheets together after I placed them with the crane. Although it was a slow process, the weather held and allowed us to finish the tank by February and install a supply line between the new tank and the existing underground water main.

Alex and Nancy

In the summer of 1982, on one of his infrequent visits to Squaw Valley, Alex called my office in the Tram Building and said he wanted to go for a hike down Shirley Canyon. This was an unusual request: We had never hiked the canyon before, and it made me wonder what was up. There had been some community comment about preserving the canyon and I figured it must be related to that. For Squaw Valley residents, hiking in Shirley Canyon was a regular thing—it was kind of the "great outdoors" experience so close to your backyard that you did not even have to get in the car. Kids in Squaw grew up exploring the canyon and knew it like the backs of their hands. Was it possible the Alex had never hiked it?

We met at the lower terminal of the tram at the appointed time. Alex was wearing hiking clothing and had a young woman in tow who was probably in her late thirties. (Alex was almost seventy.) She got on the tram with us and all he said to me was, "This is Nancy." When we reached the top terminal, she walked outside ahead of us, and I had an opportunity to ask who she was. He replied that her name was Nancy Wendt, and she was from New York—that was it. We walked outside and set off across what the Squaw Valley staff always referred to as the "New Area"—the large, gentle meadow served by the Bailey's Beach and Links lifts. ("New" because it had been developed in 1968….) It was carpeted with bold yellow "Mule's Ear" flowers, which were in bloom under a cloudless sky. It was a beautiful day in the Sierra Nevada. Nancy seemed to like the landscape and the vistas from the top, and she was a better hiker than Alex, who was always chatty and easily distracted, stopping to talk about this idea or that as he noticed a lift that needed paint or a sign that was not quite level. We walked down the road and under the Shirley Lake lift, then past Solitude, which Alex was quick to point out was a lift I had built: "Nan, this is another that Burkhart built for us." (In his Boston dialect, "Burkhart" always came out "*Burkhot*." Nancy did not seem impressed—she never said a word to either of us as we walked. Alex, however, talked the whole way down. I walked in front and the two of them followed me, because I had the distinct impression that Alex had no idea where he was going. I do not think he had ever walked down the canyon before and, because there was no clear, singular trail, had I not been there, he would have had no idea how to get back to the valley.

Toward the bottom of the canyon, there was a point that overlooked the valley. We stopped there, and Alex said as much to Nancy as to me, "Now, this is how stupid I am: At one time, I could have bought all of this for $75,000!" He indicated pretty much everything we could see from the overlook. This was about the time that the federal government was selling off the Olympic Village, Blyth Arena and five-plus acres of the parking lot, and I had been adamant that he loosen the purse strings and buy Blyth and the adjoining land, because otherwise our ability to provide parking for our guests would be at the mercy of whomever bought it.

By the 1980s, Squaw had had plenty of experience with uneven management and the resulting operational dysfunction, bad press, and adverse financial impact. Now the resort was in the midst of a rebuilding process. The lifts were safe and customer service was improving, but there was work to be done to bring Squaw to parity with the best resorts in the business. Although Alex had announced that he and John Buchman were "retiring" in a 1981 season-pass letter, his decision in 1983 to allow Jan Kunczynski to build the new gondola made it clear that my authority to make critical decisions for the company was limited, and that he was not about to let go. He was conflicted. He knew that it would be better for the operation of the company to allow someone else to run it, but he could not bear to let go—a classic "founder syndrome" situation.

His decision to give in to Janek's sales pitch to build a Lift Engineering gondola—and the abysmal customer service impression that two years of unreliable, unsatisfactory operation of that lift had created—was a giant step backward for the resort's credibility and prestige. When I left in the summer of 1983, Alex brought in Tom Richardson, a fellow easterner and ski industry professional who had worked his way up through the ranks at Aspen and had been president of Aspen Skiing Corporation from 1979 until 1982. Richardson took over as general manager, but only stayed for a few months. Alex then looked within the company for leadership, naming Jimmy Mott—whom I had promoted from ski patrol director to assistant general manager—to the general manager position, which put Mott in charge of day-to-day operation while Alex held the title of President and Chairman of the Board. After Jimmy had spent a year as G.M., Alex gave him the title of President. Jimmy was loyal to Alex and a hard worker, but while his leadership of the ski patrol had been effective—essentially supervising a small group of peers—his skill set did not translate as well to running a corporation with hundreds of employees. Even though he had given it his best shot, the results had been inconsistent.

With Nancy's arrival on the scene—and her keen interest in the company—the seat of power at Squaw Valley was, more than ever, Alex's Blue House. People have suggested that Nancy was a "gold-digger," interested only in Alex's money. (This belief was evident even within his own family....) While she certainly seemed to be interested in cementing a position for herself financially, there was more to it than that. Although Alex could be frosty, abrupt and downright rude, he could be equally charming, charismatic and a captivating character, and I think Nancy found his personality very appealing. He had never been afraid to speak his mind and let the chips fall where they might, a rare quality in an increasingly politically correct world. I think Nancy admired that about him. He seemed to be crazy about her, even if her feelings for him might have been more calculated.

After Alex's wife Libby died in 1986, Nancy became very visible and involved in Alex's life and the operation of Squaw Valley. They were inseparable. Alex liked to tell a story about how she challenged whether he had really done the best that he could with Squaw Valley, and as a result of her comment, he decided—after years of being what he described as an "absentee landlord"—that his vision for the resort had yet to be fulfilled. In Nancy, he found what his relationship with Libby had lacked—a partner who was interested in the ski resort and wanted to help him run it and succeed—and perhaps be a successor to him. Alex's daughters had never shown the slightest interest in Squaw Valley, but Alex had said to me many times that he had set up the corporation so that its ownership would stay with the family and that "it could never be sold," so there was a vacuum within the family that needed to be filled in order for his commitment to family ownership to succeed.

While her interest in the business and developing the resort enriched their relationship, Alex always wanted her to focus her attention on the legal demands of the company, while she seemed to be more interested in operations. Unfortunately, her personality and temperament were much better suited to sparring with other attorneys than to leading a company largely composed of free-spirited young California skiers. Although she tried to project a more casual, informal personality, her eastern prep-school upbringing always came through and made people feel that they were being judged and found wanting in either their intelligence or devotion to the company. She made people uncomfortable and at times, seemed to enjoy it.

Squaw Valley was at that time a company with a core group of year-round, highly skilled, experienced, blue collar employees, many of whom had been with the company for decades—lift mechanics, vehicle mechanics, electricians and equipment operators—and a smaller group of administrative office workers in accounting, marketing, and human resources. In addition to the year-round core, we needed hundreds of enthusiastic, personable, entry-level seasonal employees each year. For all of them, the general manager, not Alex, was the face of "management:" Alex knew the names and faces of no more than six or eight of his employees—the ones with whom he interacted most frequently. You could work at the company for decades without ever having met or spoken to "the Chairman" and you could have been a manager for decades and Alex would honestly have no idea who you were.

My management style had been to build a group of managers for each operational area—lift operations, lift maintenance, vehicle operations, grooming, ski patrol, ticketing—and each business enterprise area—ski school, food and beverage, race services, and race team—and allow those managers to run their departments with a minimum of interference. I did not like being micromanaged, and I believed that other competent people felt the same way. At one time I had told Alex, "The biggest favor you can do me is to get on a slow boat to China." If something were not working in one of those departments, I would meet with the manager and we would figure out a solution, but there were not a lot of meetings. By the time someone had become a manager, I had confidence that they knew how to do their job without a lot of input from me.

Nancy entered the picture with no history with any of the managers, no experience in the ski industry except as a consumer (and that was limited), but with a strong drive for success and a devotion to Alex and his desire to fulfill his life's work. She was determined to prove her capabilities and her value to Alex as they together brought his vision for Squaw Valley to fruition. It was inevitable that she would make mistakes and rub people the wrong way.

Nancy was in a difficult situation because Alex and his daughters owned a controlling interest in the stock of the company and Nancy owned none, so if something happened to Alex, she could have been completely shut out. In the early 1980s, Alex had made clear that he wanted to turn over operational authority to me, and had said on many occasions that I was "the only one he trusted" to give him advice on the operation and future development of the company. This created an uncomfortable tension between Nancy and me, because while I had a long history with Alex and a depth of knowledge and understanding of the ski industry and resort operations, she wanted to carve out a niche for herself at Squaw Valley that would provide her with authority and financial security. I had no problem with her ambition to find a way to deal herself in for a piece of the Cushing fortune, but she always treated me like one of "the help," rather than recognizing that my work and dedication to building Squaw Valley complemented Alex's: every visionary must have someone who knows how to get their hands dirty. She had a distain for the people who worked at Squaw Valley—and I suppose that included me. She said once that, "employees are a necessary evil."

I came back in 1985 to build the Poma gondola and detachable Siberia Express, but I was not on the Squaw Valley payroll again until 1988. Alex and Nancy had married in 1987, and she was positioned not only as Alex's wife, but as General Counsel of Squaw Valley Ski Corporation, which gave her the opportunity to influence virtually any part of the operation that caught her eye. Nancy's most significant achievement was the acquisition of much of the land that the federal government had auctioned off in the early 1980s. Phil Carville had purchased the Olympic Village property, then demolished two of the original

Alex's renewed interest in the company in the 1980's also provided him with the opportunity to be the face of Squaw Valley in television commercials—a role that he seemed to relish.

dormitories and converted the other two into condominiums which were then sold as time-shares—the Olympic Village Inn. The parcel that Carville had bought was significantly larger than what he needed for the time-share project and Nancy engineered the purchase of virtually all the property except for the buildings housing the time-share condos and the common area owned collectively by the owners of the condos. She created a new corporation for the ownership of that real estate, which was called the Squaw Valley Preserve. This gave Squaw Valley a handful of new buildings, as well as control over a significant amount of parking and valley-floor real estate that could conceivably be developed. Although Alex had never wanted to be in the real estate business, his new wife understood that while owning the land that the resort used literally every day was not as sexy or marketable as a new lift, purchasing it simply had to be done in order to assure an orderly, predictable future for the company. Although Nancy and I disagreed about many things, her insistence on acquiring the land around O.V.I. was an essential and strategic business move.

The late '80s and early '90s was a period of great expansion at Squaw Valley as skier visits increased and the sophistication of the resort operation improved. We got serious about providing excellent customer service. Alex and Nancy hired a very energetic pair of "guest relations" trainers and required all the employees to go through their class, which the staff sardonically dubbed "Charm School." We installed Kleenex dispensers in every lift line and had comment cards that urged unhappy guests to "Tell Alex." Alex implemented a "No Waiting in Line or Your Money Back!" guarantee and produced television commercials in which he was the spokesman—he was surprisingly good as a TV pitchman. The most visible and widely ridiculed symbol of the "new Squaw Valley" was new uniform for the staff: black with a red diagonal stripe across the front, that said, "We Care." Anyone with a bit of sense would not have dressed people working outside in black—it is sunny nearly every day in the Sierra, and the employees were slowly roasting in their all-black outfits. Black is also extremely hard to keep looking clean, so the sweaty employees frequently looked a little bit dusty as well. Snowboarding was just starting to gain acceptance, and Squaw tested the waters by allowing snowboarding during the last month of the 1988 season and the last two months of 1989, because, as the Olympic Plaza food and beverage guru, Tom O'Neill, wryly put it, "Alex didn't think we had enough graffiti." The next year, we were all in for snowboarding as the sport really took off and attracted a new and dynamic group of guests to the mountain.

The construction of the Resort at Squaw Creek in the late 1980s was a giant step toward moving Squaw into the category of a destination resort. There had been lodging in the valley since the very beginning, but the number of rooms, variety of types of lodging, and overall quality had never approached what could be found at competing resorts. The Resort at Squaw Creek would offer over 400 rooms with accommodations ranging from hotel rooms to suites, restaurants offering everything from casual family-oriented options to haute cuisine fine dining. In addition, the property would offer state-of-the-art conference facilities, an 18-hole golf course, an ice skating rink and boutique shopping—all delivered with world-class service. It was quite a concept and the level of sophistication it would bring to Squaw Valley was truly a profound impact for the resort and the community. The concept was that the hotel would be a ski-in, ski-out property connected to the rest of the mountain with a chairlift right at the hotel's back door and a network of trails providing hotel guests

Alex used his annual season pass solicitations to engage and entertain his 'tribe'—a group of people that he referred to in the letters as the "Squaw Valley Faithful." Some of the vocabulary in his letters caused me— and I suspect that I am not alone—to reach for the dictionary.

A small sampling of Alex's special words and their definitions:

Largesse—generosity
Mundane—ordinary
Euphoria—intense happiness
Proclivity—inclination
Hubris—excessive pride
Lachrymosity—weeping
Misfeasance—transgression
Miserly—cheap, thrifty
Admonition—warning
Forebearance—restraint, tolerance
Aficionados—enthusiasts
Parsimonious—cheap, stingy
Curmudgeon—sourpuss
Cognoscenti—people 'in the know'
Vicissitudes—difficult turn of events
Unpretentious—humble, modest

Two large dozers working in tandem to build a wide trail toward Red Dog Face from the Squaw Creek and Red Dog lifts.

with access to and from the property—with skiing for all skill levels and reliable snow. Not much to ask. Of course, none of these facilities existed and the terrain was, at best, high intermediate to low expert. The ski resort agreed to a partnership with the hotel to build a new lift from the hotel to the top of the ridge, construct a new Red Dog lift with a top terminal adjacent to the new Squaw Creek lift, construct new beginner and intermediate trails, cut trees for expert trails on the north face, and install snow-making throughout, provided with water from large ponds and a pump station next to the golf course. The project amounted to building from scratch a ski area of about 400 acres with two moderately long fixed-grip triple chairlifts and full snowmaking on a steep, mostly tree-covered mountainside. I had a contract with Squaw Valley to move tens of thousands of cubic yards of dirt and rock to construct an area large enough for the top terminals and unloading areas of the two lifts and to build trails on both sides of the peak, leading to the hotel on the east side and the existing trails at Squaw Valley on the west. Given the nature of the terrain—virtually all of it steep and with several deep gullies—it was a major project. We used a D10—the largest bulldozer Caterpillar made at the time—and a Komatsu D455A, which was about twenty-five percent larger than the Cat machine: Two machines made for moving lots of rock and dirt, as well as a smaller D6 dozer for finish work. The grading went well, thanks to outstanding work by Bruce Colburn, John Moors, and Wilbur Meyer, who put in long days on the dozers and transformed the steep, rocky, uneven terrain into trails that could be skied with a minimal amount of snow. The lifts were installed and the air and water lines for the snowmaking system followed. Making snow on the trails connecting the hotel and the resort base area would be the first priority each year, so that Thanksgiving hotel guests could be guaranteed skiing. It is one of the few places on the mountain where so much grading has been required to develop skiable trails, and the results are well thought out, challenging, and fun to ski.

The partnership with the Resort at Squaw Creek was something of a mixed blessing. The hotel management had some unrealistic expectations about the quantity and quality of snow that a snowmaking system could produce with marginal temperatures early in the season. Squaw Valley locals had to a large degree been vocal in their opposition to the hotel—in particular, the golf course—and a lot of them regarded the black glass tower as an eyesore. The fact that the hotel provided a lot of jobs locally should have been a point in its

We did a lot of very large grading projects, including this one that dramatically widened and improved the groomability at the top of the Tower 20 Traverse and Burkhart's. The Siberia lower terminal is in the upper left of the photograph, Broken Arrow lift on the right. The crew is getting ready to do a large blast to the right of Cupcake Rock.

We also did a difficult and costly widening project on another important bottle neck on the mountain: the Bellevue run that sweeps around Mogul Hill toward the bottom of the KT-22 Saddle. The run had been little more than a Cat track and this project turned it into a wider and much safer skiing experience for intermediate skiers.

The new runs from the top of the Squaw Creek and Red Dog lifts to the hotel were a major project.

The shop in Verdi allowed us to store Squaw Valley's equipment and materials in a location with less snow—and more space—than was available in the Valley.

Alex was always adamant about moving any equipment that would not be needed during the winter out of potential parking spaces by the Lower Vehicle Shop at Red Dog. I would make a number of trips to Verdi with a low-boy to store it for the winter in my yard and then haul it back to the Valley in the spring. Nancy somehow interpreted this as providing me with a significant benefit.

The Verdi shop also provided workshop space—here Sepp Immos, one of the Garaventa crew that installed the tram in 1968, supervises a rebuild of the tram carriages.

favor, but it also had the effect of increasing pressure on an already stressed long-term rental market, further raising rents paid by employees who were making modest hourly wages. Before long, the hotel found it necessary to recruit many of its employees in Reno and operate a transportation system to bring them to work.

Rebuilding the Tram carriages was a major project—having a large indoor area to organize the components and keep everything spotlessly clean was essential.

Nancy and Alex were thrilled with the addition of the Resort at Squaw Creek to the lodging inventory in the valley and the prestige that such a property afforded the ski resort. Dealing with the hotel management was another story. Alex had never been a particularly cooperative "partner." He preferred to make decisions unencumbered by the operational needs and opinions of others—and the hotel's agenda rarely coincided with Alex's—so in short order his legal obligations to the hotel became problematic and frustrating. There were several agreements between the hotel and the Ski Corporation that became so contentious that they wound up in court. The hotel didn't quite grasp that if there was no snow anywhere other than on the run right out their back door, even their guests would be unhappy, but when they could see the golf course ponds draining at night and no snowmaking guns on "their" run in operation, they would call and complain, eventually bringing suit against the Ski Corporation. Operation of the Squaw Creek lift was another bone of contention. But the most ridiculous was the battle over the tennis courts at High Camp.

The High Camp tennis courts may have been Alex's least successful idea of all time.

High Camp complex during installation of the Sprung structure to cover the ice rink. Beach volleyball courts at the top of the picture, bungee tower, pool complex, ice skating rink and the straw-covered portion of the Bailey's Beach run at left is being covered with plastic matting on which Alex hoped to provide year-round skiing... The ill-fated tennis courts would be below this photograph and the soccer field to the left.

Alex had an irrational devotion to the High Camp complex, dubbing it "The Eighth Wonder of the World." Perhaps it was because at the top of the tram, there was room on which to construct facilities that would have displaced either parking or skiing at the bottom of the mountain, but High Camp received a disproportionate amount of attention and investment. At one time or another, High Camp boasted an Olympic-sized ice skating rink, a swimming pool and hot tub complex, a bungee-jumping tower, six regulation-sized beach-sand volleyball courts, a full-sized soccer field, and six championship tennis courts— Alex had proposed even more, but these were the facilities that we actually constructed.

The bungee-jumping tower was surprisingly popular. After it was constructed, the concessionaires who operated it offered me the opportunity to try it. I'm sure they thought there was no way I'd take them up on the offer, but I did, and it was a lot of fun. My daughter Mekala was at High Camp one day and presented herself at the bungee tower and told the attendant that she wanted to jump—she was about six. She told them she had my permission, but when they weighed her, she was too light for any of the bungee cords: The cord wouldn't stretch enough to give her a soft rebound. She went away very disappointed but reappeared a short time later and insisted that they weigh her again. This time—miraculously—she was just heavy enough. Suspicious, the bungee people looked in her little backpack and found that she had gone to the kitchen of the restaurant in High Camp and filled it up with potatoes.

Alex had a plan to offer skiing year-round on the Bailey's Beach lift, using chipped ice produced by the ice-making refrigeration system for the ice-rink, but—although we gave it a game try—the chipped ice production capacity of the plant was no match for the California summer sun, even at 8,200 feet. He also experimented with a golf driving range, where patrons would drive golf balls from the southeast corner of the High Camp building into the Tram Bowl. There was no plan to collect and reuse the golf balls, and, even today, you can probably find the odd golf ball in the bottom of the Tram Bowl from the few dozen balls hit into the canyon as an experiment. Eventually, someone found a source for golf balls made from fertilizer and seed, but by then interest in the driving range had cooled.

Mekala bungee jumping—legally—at age 7.

The tennis courts were a considerably more costly experiment. The year after the ice rink was completed, we built five or six tennis courts on the slope below the rink. Alex loved tennis—and admitted that he was a much better tennis player than skier—and had pitched the Resort at Squaw Creek with the idea of giving hotel guests access to the tennis courts at High Camp and of providing a tennis school at the High Camp location. I'm not sure who imagined that guests at the hotel would want to ride a shuttle bus from the hotel to the Tram Building, ride up the tram, and then take tennis lessons at 8,200 feet, but perhaps Alex's enthusiasm for the "Eighth Wonder of the World" was that infectious. The tennis courts didn't hold up well, however—the fences around the courts had to be taken down for the winter and then reinstalled for the summer season, and the playing surface didn't resist the conditions at the top of the mountain all that well. Although the tennis courts were virtually never used by their guests, the Resort at Squaw Creek sued the Ski Corporation over the condition of the courts; a monumental waste of time and money for both parties.

While the Cushings were generally extremely private, one element of Alex and Nancy's relationship was highly visible—for a while, she would take Alex jogging. Alex was closing in on 80, and while he gamely went out in the morning and gave it his best, the sight of this very tall, elderly man in a ball cap trying to keep up with his much younger wife as they jogged down Squaw Valley Road was rather pathetic. The staff was convinced that the jogging was Nancy's attempt to kill Alex, not keep him healthy.

Although Squaw Valley was economically successful in the early '90s, we faced a number of challenges that tarnished our image to a significant degree. There were several terrible snow years and a diesel fuel spill that polluted an area near the Red Dog lift and seeped into Squaw Creek. It was not handled well, and the regulatory agencies came down hard on the company, alleging that this episode was yet another egregious example of Squaw's cavalier attitude toward the environment, and imposing heavy fines and mandatory mitigation.

In an effort to turn the fine, which was imposed by the California Regional Water Quality Control Board (Lahontan Region), to more positive effect, we proposed using it to design and construct a stream restoration project in the stretch of Squaw Creek that the U.S. Army Corps of Engineers had "channelized" between the confluence of the north and south forks of the creek (adjacent to the Squaw Valley Hostel building) and the east end of the parking lots, where the creek returned to a more natural meander. The channelized portion of the creek was an eyesore, and we were only too happy to make the creek a more appealing and integrated feature of the west end of the valley.

Lahontan wanted to put an end to the snow removal regimen that we used, which resulted in a huge berm of compacted snow along the edge of the creek channel that would persist well into the summer. The solution was to keep moving the snow to the north, across Squaw Valley Road, and blow it up onto the hillside, so part of the project needed to be the construction of a couple of bridges that would allow us to push snow across to Squaw Valley Road where it would be stockpiled for the blowers.

You would think that a project mitigating an environmental deficiency that would also provide aesthetic, flood control, and recreational benefits would be an easy thing to permit, because all the agencies would be in favor of the work and would move it along, but this project was the single biggest waste of time and money of my entire career. In addition to consuming a tremendous amount of staff time at the resort and at the agencies, it was monumentally expensive: Lahontan had fined us $500,000, which they agreed to allow us to apply to the stream restoration project, but we blew through that in the first year in engineering and design costs. Despite all the work that we invested in it, we were basically no closer to a permit than we had been when we started, because the regulatory agencies had such differing agendas and requirements. The project had to be reviewed for potential environmental impacts and regulatory compliance by several dozen different agencies at the federal, state, and county levels and in many cases, a modification to the design of the project intended to satisfy a comment or requirement from one agency would trigger an adverse reaction from another.

The amount of paperwork was simply staggering. One example that seems representative is that during the design process, we were provided with a document from the U.S. Department of Transportation, Federal Highway Administration that had been prepared by the U.S. Department of Agriculture's Technology and Development Program (Report No. FHWA-FL-90-006): a detailed analysis titled "Fish Passage Through Culverts." It was a large and well-illustrated booklet, thirty-six pages in length. The conclusion? "Fish use culverts. The design and length of a culvert affects how readily fish pass through it." I'm paraphrasing, by the way—the authors never expressed their observation of fish behavior in such simple, direct terms.

When we built the aerial tram in 1968, there was a designated process for permitting the construction of "lifts, trams, rope tows, or like facilities" on the state-owned Squaw Valley State Recreation Area. It was a model of practicality:

> "(1) Company will notify the Park Supervisor of Squaw Valley State Recreation Area in writing of intention to construct a particular facility. The Park Supervisor will notify the United States Forest Service through its District Ranger and arrange for an on-the-ground inspection of the proposed site. If the site is found to be satisfactory, Company will be so notified in writing within 10 days of receipt of the letter of intent."

In contrast with this procedure, where the officials of the state and federal agencies who had regulatory authority for the project met with the Ski Corporation, evaluated the project together by looking at the conditions at the site, and then approved it within ten days of a letter requesting approval, the stream restoration project—even after years of effort, thousands of hours of staff time, and millions of dollars—was never permitted or constructed. Simply put, bureaucracy and the mind-boggling complexity of the permitting process killed what would have been a great project.

I logged countless hours dealing with Placer County and even when we scrupulously followed the rules in every aspect of the operation over which the County had oversight, there never seemed to be any recognition of our cooperation. Alex had disrespected the County so many times that there was a widespread conviction on the part of the County employees that even when we did everything they required, they felt that we were trying to get away with

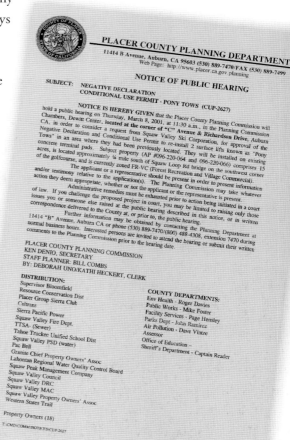

In 2001, we decided to reinstall a pair of small wire rope tows in a location where they had previously been used—not a teaspoon of dirt would be disturbed. The Placer County process solicited comments from 26 different agencies and 18 property owners before we could be allowed to reinstall the tows.

something. We were always driving to Auburn for yet another meeting. I think Alex kind of enjoyed the 'cat and mouse' aspect of the relationship with the County and I think he liked the time that we spent driving back and forth to meetings and the opportunity to spend some time chatting with me and, just maybe, having some time apart from Nancy. He loved McDonald's French fries, a treat that he must have been denied when they were together, so every time we turned off I-80 at the Bell Road exit to go to the County offices, he would say, "Don't forget to stop at McDonalds…."

Through the '90s, Nancy asserted an increasingly authoritative role in the management of the company, creating confusion and anxiety among the employees. As an employee myself, I understood the feeling, because it was difficult to know that you had job security at the company or that your contributions were appreciated or even understood by "Mom and Dad," as some members of the staff referred to the Cushings. The traditional model of ski resort employment was changing—we had gone from being a company primarily focused on winter operations to one that was offering products year-round as the lodging base within the valley expanded and, as a result, the proportion of our staff who were permanent, year-round employees had changed significantly. More and more of our staff were on salary, were married with families, and were putting down roots in the area for the long term. Although we paid competitive (but by no means generous) wages and offered health insurance, there were no provisions for retirement or even a 401K program. I asked Tony Reid, the corporation's chief financial officer, to investigate the costs of providing a 401K retirement plan with an employer match, and he reported back that the one time he had discussed such a program with Nancy, she had "bit off his head." Unfortunately, the employees making the most valuable and unique contributions to the company were made to feel disrespected and marginalized by the Cushings, who knew just enough about the jobs performed by those people to know how to make them feel inadequate and insecure. It was not an effective way to motivate people and run a successful business.

I did the best I could to keep the people in the areas of the operation reporting to me from being affected by this demoralizing approach to management. We had a fundamentally sound and solid operation and had come a long way in terms of customer service and guest satisfaction: This was reflected in the annual ratings issued by the national ski press. Snow Country magazine, which went into operation in 1988, did a particularly capable and fearless job of ranking ski resorts throughout North America, and we consistently scored well nationally and either first or second in the Far West region. My secret weapon during this period was Donna Brenner, who was a versatile and polished writer, a sympathetic but formidable gatekeeper, and relentlessly well-organized. My office was in the Far East building—once the Nevada Visitor Center for the Olympics—and it was no coincidence that it was about as far from the Tram Building and the Blue House as you could get and still be on Squaw Valley's "campus." Nancy had moved into my old office on the lower level of the Tram Building and Donna and I along with Hardy, Fred Schmidinger, and a couple of other key people, had moved into the Far East building with a beautiful view of Red Dog, KT-22, Olympic ski jump hill, and Lower Vehicle Shop. The level of tension in our offices was a great deal lower than across the parking lot, and the coffee was much better as well. In addition to her outstanding secretarial and writing skills, Donna had also mastered the process for hiring highly specialized technical workers from Europe and filling out the State Department documentation to keep their work visas valid. Donna's other superpower was that she could read Alex's handwriting, which became less legible as he aged. His annual season pass letters were all written longhand, and only Donna could decipher Alex's scrawl and turn it into the witty and occasionally revealing letters to "the faithful" that he so relished producing. Donna was a critical and very valuable member of the team.

In contrast to Donna's calm, steady nature, Alex was far more mercurial, and, as described by a newspaper reporter, "tetchy."[5] He was basically shy and uncomfortable around people he did not know, but he was very capable of rising above his reluctance to engage with people outside of his normal circle and being very charming and outgoing. He was confident in the things he knew, but sometimes thought he knew a lot more than he really did, and this could get him into trouble. His attention tended to move quickly from one thing to another, and once he was excited about something, he wanted to move it along right away. This was an ongoing problem when it came to dealing with the Placer County Planning and Building Departments, which moved at a more deliberate pace. As an attorney, it would be reasonable to expect that he would have been able to navigate regulations and standards, but he generated more business for other lawyers than anyone I know; it seemed like he was always suing someone or being sued, and the amount of wasted time and money resulting from these usually fruitless lawsuits was staggering to contemplate. In many situations, Alex used the calculation that it would be more efficient to do a project without permits than to delay the project by following the prescribed review process, and then to pay whatever fines were assessed (after fighting them in court, naturally…). People joked that we never got a building permit until we were ready for the roof to go on, and this was not far from the truth.

Early in his career, Alex had been the youngest lawyer to argue a case before the Supreme Court of the United States, so he should have been a master at giving depositions, but he was a nightmare client for the attorneys representing him, and an all-you-can-eat banquet of unexpected delights for the attorneys on the opposing side. A deposition is a fishing expedition for an attorney, and Alex would not only chase down the lure, he'd bite an un-baited hook, then virtually throw himself into the boat—he just could not stop himself from volunteering information the opposing attorneys should have had to pry out of him. His attorneys were eventually able to prevent him from being deposed by claiming that he was unable to hear the questions.

One of Alex's worst traits was that he had the idea that no deal was ever really done, even after all parties had signed the contract. It was as if he always felt that he should have gotten more and would try to alter the terms of the agreement to squeeze a little more out of the deal. This came back to bite him more than once, and kept Squaw from being as successful as it might otherwise have been. For example, plans were well along for a second summer music festival with Bill Graham Presents—even though Bill Graham had been killed only a few months after the first event—until Alex got into a frivolous but bitter argument with Bob Barsotti over participant camping. Just like that, the opportunity evaporated.

I do not mean to make it sound like I did not like Alex, or that working for him was not exciting or interesting. We had a lot of differences through the years, but our interests and skills complemented one another. He had a lot of interesting and sometimes crazy ideas, and I had the ability to tell him which ones could be implemented, and then make them happen. For someone like me, who loved wire rope and lifts, working for a man who loved nothing more than building bigger, better lifts, and lots of them, was a dream come true. During the times that Alex followed his own advice and allowed me to run his company based on my experience in the industry, according to my principles and standards, Squaw Valley was a successful and well-regarded resort; but Alex's tendency to micro-managing became more pronounced once Nancy entered the picture and started created her own niche within the company. She seemed to think that for her to be successful at creating a financially secure position with ownership equity in the company, she had to move me out, even though I had no interest in anything more than managing the operation, supervising the construction of new facilities, and receiving compensation for doing so. I had no interest in an ownership position—if I had wanted that, I could have started building one by asking for stock or options back in the '60s. I believed Alex when he said that it was his wish that Squaw Valley would continue to operate as an independent entity after his death, and that he had set up the corporate structure so that it "could never be sold." Maybe this was why Nancy felt that she had to find a way to get rid of me—because I was the only person still in the picture to whom he had expressed this wish. In any event, it was clear that Nancy and I were like oil and water, and that she was looking for ways to make me look bad and eventually become Alex's only link to the operation of the business.

Juniper Ridge

In the late '80s and early '90s, Alex and I had discussions about building a hotel on the mountain at Squaw Valley. My experiences at small, owner-operated hotels at ski resorts in Europe convinced me that there was a niche for such a lodging option at Squaw Valley—especially if it were located mid-mountain and served by the aerial tram or gondola. From time to time, Alex had said that he wanted to express his gratitude for my dedicated work at Squaw Valley by giving me the opportunity to create a portion of the operation that would be mine to own and operate. Alex had a particular attraction to setting Squaw Valley apart from other resorts by having things that no other North American resort offered. We both thought that a high-end, European-style lodging property with a small restaurant would be a unique and sophisticated addition to the resort, provide an appealing lodging alternative for our guests, and be an economic success in a relatively short period of time. I had worked out a business plan and was confident that I could get construction financing.

The site we discussed was between High Camp, at the top of the tram, and Gold Coast, the upper terminal of the gondola. There was a knoll that had a great southern exposure, could be graded to create a generous building site, and had excellent ski-in, ski-out access without impeding any of the existing ski traffic. It was high enough to have great views, but sheltered enough to be spared the worst of the wind on the upper mountain. The only way I was willing to make the necessary investment of time and capital was to own the land, and

229

Alex was willing to create a separate parcel and convey it to me with a deed. Alex liked to refer to the hotel as the "Schloss," which means castle in German: he called it the "Schloss Burkhart."

I had Carl Gustafson—a civil engineer who lived in Squaw Valley—survey the site and draw up a topographic map in anticipation of doing an architectural rendering and getting a building permit. I hired an architect in Austria to design the building and drilled a couple of water wells on the site—wells that Squaw Valley is still using! All this time, Alex was completely on-board with the concept. I would remind him from time to time that I needed a deed in order to be able to continue, and he was always totally agreeable and reassuring that he was supportive of the project and that the transfer of the land would be forthcoming. I was reluctant to make too big a deal of it, because that could have been interpreted as a lack of trust on my part, and during this period, our relationship was particularly good. I saw no reason to introduce anything contentious. We had discussed all the logistic issues of having a hotel at the mid-mountain site: guest access to the hotel outside of the operating hours of the ski resort, emergency access and procedures, food service and provisioning—we had even discussed hauling the trash and connecting the hotel to the sewer line. We had figured it all out.

Paul Minasian drew up an agreement for the transfer of the land and gave it to Alex, but it languished on his desk for a long time. When I asked him about it, he would say, "Oh, yeah—I think I've seen that…." But nothing ever happened. Finally, a long time later, I got a note from Nancy saying that in order to make the transfer of land, Alex would have to secure

View from the proposed site of the Schloss Burkhart toward Headwall.

The Schloss Burkhart was planned as a small, Bavarian-style boutique hotel on the mountain.

the approval of the board of directors. At that point, I knew that the project was doomed, because if Alex was going to do something, he just went ahead and did it, and if the board needed to approve it, he got the approval retroactively. Telling me that the board "needed to approve it" was a long-form way of saying that Nancy did not like the project and had talked Alex out of proceeding with it. It appeared to be going nowhere, which was too bad, because I had invested a lot of time and money in it and the "Schloss Burkhart" would have been a great addition to the mountain.

In the European tradition of small, family-operated lodging properties, I had my daughter Kathrin lined up to operate the Schloss - she would have done a great job!

Rock and Roll in Squaw Valley

In early 1991, we were approached by the legendary rock and roll impresario Bill Graham, who was working on a plan to produce outdoor music festivals at several ski areas that summer. Alex was onboard right away, recognizing that an alliance with Bill Graham would be a unique and powerful marketing opportunity, and when Alex was enthusiastic about something, it was likely to happen. Bill and several members of his staff met with us and explained the concept of two concerts that summer: one at Squaw; one at Telluride. Each festival was multi-day with different performers each day, so attendees would likely purchase a multi-day ticket and stay in nearby hotels or campgrounds. It sounded like quite a bonanza for the lodging industry. The Resort at Squaw Creek was brand new, and we thought they would be thrilled at the prospect of selling out a weekend in July.

The logistics seemed very manageable. We had a good location at Gold Coast and would grade out a level pad for the stage near the bottom of the Emigrant lift. Power for the stage lighting and sound system could be tapped from the lift. The concert ticket price would include transportation on the gondola or tram. Our food and beverage concessions could operate in the Gold Coast lodge, and Graham's organization would have food and beverage concessions set up outside. They would provide an emergency medical capability at the site, as well as fencing, staging, lights and sound, and a certain number of security people. It was interesting to see how the Graham organization approached the project: They were the most successful concert management organization in the world, and yet they had a very lean management structure, just a handful of people. They were very casual, and yet they clearly knew exactly what they were talking about—how to configure the site, manage the crowd, manage marketing and ticket sales—and they were very matter-of-fact and open about how they approached it. They wanted a happy audience and happy performers, and they knew just how to achieve that. Bill Graham had a reputation for being a tough negotiator and an abrasive person, but he was cordial and articulate about the details of putting on a show such as this—it was a master class in managing a large event and crowd psychology.

The dates for the festival were set for August 24 and 25, 1991. This gave us almost all summer to prepare for the festival, and it gave the Bill Graham Presents staff an opportunity to try the concept out at Telluride in July, more than a month prior to the Squaw Valley event. The revegetation crew seeded and set up an elaborate watering system on the "Concert Bowl" so that the audience would have comfortable grassy seating on the hill under the East Broadway lift. The area for the stage was graded and oriented so the audience would have sun overhead and the performers could be shaded and protected from the prevailing wind while playing. The weeks leading up to the festival were a flurry of activity on the mountain as the staging was hauled up

The "Gold Coast Concert Bowl" with North Bowl and the Palisades in the background.

and constructed along with lighting trusses and a large sound system. The show was quite a windfall for local businesses, with hundreds of portable toilets rented to augment the bathrooms in Gold Coast and thousands of pounds of ice purchased from Crystal Dairy—there was truck traffic up and down the summer road all day.

Our first inkling that the show might be more than we had anticipated was when people started showing up and camping in the resort parking lots a week ahead of time. All week more and more of them rolled in—it seemed like every Volkswagen camper van in North America had converged on the Squaw Valley parking lot. The atmosphere was very mellow and friendly, but it was getting increasingly difficult to get around. By Friday, the parking lots were filling and the U.S. Forest Service campgrounds along the Truckee River were overflowing with people, tents, trailers and a party atmosphere. We started getting phone calls from Squaw Valley residents about people camping in their yards, in the meadow, and in Shirley Canyon.

Saturday morning—the first day of concerts—was a beautiful summer day, and there was a large and enthusiastic crowd waiting for the gondola and tram to open and carry them up to the concert site. Despite the size of the crowd, everyone was very cooperative and friendly, and a lot of people opted to walk up the mountain. There were evidently people walking in from other directions—sans tickets—to attend as well. A line of hikers coming from Five Lakes traversed across Cornice II and Headwall and a large contingent swarmed out of Shirley Canyon. The Bill Graham Presents crew, ever the capitalists, sent a couple of staff members up to intercept the hikers and sell them tickets—they figured that word would get out that no one would be getting in without a ticket, and it might reduce the number of people trying to sneak in. Squaw Valley Mountain Manager Jimmy King drove to the top of the Siberia lift to intercept and sell tickets to a group that hiked over from Alpine Meadows.

The concert was a great success—a beautiful day, great music, and a happy audience. We had not anticipated the effect that Jerry Garcia's presence on the bill would have. A lot of the people at the show were Grateful Dead fans—"Deadheads"—who basically followed the band on a full-time basis, and although the other members of the Dead were not performing, having Jerry on the program was all it took to attract thousands and thousands of Deadheads. The Jerry Garcia Band performed late in the afternoon on Saturday. As is typical for summer afternoons in the mountains, the wind had picked up and the sunshade over the stage was flapping and there was some wind noise in the sound system, but he put on a great show after having arrived in Bill Graham's Bell Jet Ranger helicopter.

We were concerned with the logistical challenge of moving the whole crowd down the mountain at the conclusion of the show. While people arrived in the base area at different times during the morning—allowing a long period to move them up to the concert site—when the show was over it was over, and everyone would want to leave at once. We had rented dozens of self-contained lighting units—a generator and telescoping light tower on a trailer—that were positioned to illuminate the portions of the summer road not lit by the night-skiing lights so that people could walk down, but we thought more than half of the audience would opt to ride down on the gondola or tram. It turned out that a lot of people walked down, and that while there were thousands of people waiting to ride down on the gondola and tram, everyone was very calm and cooperative and simply waited their turn to load into the cabin and ride down. The Squaw Valley staff people working at the gondola and tram terminals commented that skiers were a lot more aggressive and impatient than the rock concert audience.

A huge and happy crowd enjoying the concert.

David Grisman and Jerry Garcia performing.

Because the crowd arrived at the bottom gradually, the exodus from the parking lot was less frantic than it might have been, but it still took a long time, and there were a lot of people who simply camped for the night, although they were not eager to get to sleep. We were in the middle of construction season and in one section of the parking lot, there were strings of steel pipe 300 feet long that had been welded together in anticipation of being dragged into position and buried to supply water and compressed air to the snowmaking system. The overnight campers found the steel pipes irresistibly melodic and late into the night there were people making music and drumming on the snowmaking pipes while clouds of pot smoke drifted into the night sky.

The appearance of tens of thousands of Deadheads and other young people was what the local sheriff's office consider a "target-rich environment" and they set up a local command post at the fire station. Deputies disguised as concertgoers circulated through the parking lot attempting to buy drugs from those gullible enough to sell to them. There were plenty of Deadheads who were either greedy or naïve enough to sell a beefy guy in a bad wig and a tie-dyed shirt a joint or a balloon full of nitrous oxide, and they found themselves being taken over to the fire station, booked, and hauled off to jail, sometimes having their camper van impounded as well. The "Rock Med" group at the concert site saw a steady stream of people made ill from dehydration, allergic reactions, and drug issues, but there were few true medical emergencies during the weekend.

Overall, we felt that the weekend had gone well. A lot of people had a fun and memorable time. The music had been great, and the logistic issues that we had worried about were generally offset by the mellow and cooperative nature of the audience. The festival had filled every hotel and restaurant for miles and miles in every direction, and no one had suffered much more than a sprained ankle. There were those in the community who did not agree, however. Based on the comments in the newspaper the following Thursday, Bill Graham and Alex Cushing had released such a torrent of pestilence that North Lake Tahoe might never be the same—Cushing took most of the blame, because he was local. There were a handful of truly angry people who had in some manner been inconvenienced or adversely affected by the people attending the festival, and there were a dozen stories—repeated over and over and probably grossly exaggerated to begin with—that detailed the slothful, disrespectful, and disgustingly youthful conduct of the Deadheads. This became a real issue when, as a result of a few concerned citizens, Placer County held public hearings to receive comment on our application for a second music festival the following summer.

Tragically, Bill Graham, his girlfriend, Melissa Gold, and pilot, Steve Kahn, were killed on October 25, 1991 in a helicopter crash in a bad weather after leaving a concert at the Concord Pavilion. The opportunity to work with someone who was such a legendary figure in the music business was a unique and exciting experience. Bill Graham Presents continued operation, and we were in negotiation with them to present a second music festival the following summer, but could not come to terms, despite spending considerable time and energy convincing Placer County and the concerned citizens of North Lake Tahoe that if we presented a program without Jerry Garcia on the bill, their concerns over youthful exuberance would be answered. It would have been interesting to see if that turned out to be true.

Single Dad

By the mid-'90s, the child custody issues with my former girlfriend, Arlene McDonald, had reached an impasse. Our two daughters, Anika and Mekala, had always preferred living with me rather than living with their mother, but Arlene had filed several times to have a court award custody of the girls to her. The first two cases had been tried in Bend, where we had been living, but in 1994 I was living in Squaw Valley, and Arlene filed a petition in Placer County to be awarded custody of the girls. Perhaps she thought she would fare better under California law than she had in Oregon, where she had twice been unsuccessful at convincing a judge of her parenting skills.

My attorney, Trilla Bahrke, and I attended a preliminary hearing at the Placer County Courthouse in Auburn, and the judge—who was waiting for the legal records from the

Anika

Mekala

Oregon custody cases to arrive—ordered both Arlene and myself to submit to a psychological evaluation. I didn't know what that involved, and as we were driving back to Tahoe, I asked Trilla what I would have to do.

"It's about a four-hour process," she said. "They interview you and have you take a couple of different kinds of tests. It allows the psychologist to develop a profile of your personality and your mental health. Parts of it are kind of interesting and fun, and other parts will probably be annoying and seem repetitive."

Within a couple of weeks, I went to Auburn and sat through the process, which was just as Trilla had described, only a lot more difficult than she'd made it sound. It was hard, but I did what I had to do, and when I was finished, I thought that Arlene was going to have a much tougher time with it than I had. I told Trilla I thought that there was no way that Arlene could pass the tests.

We went back to court a little over a month following the preliminary hearing. After some introductory comments, the judge said that he had received the court transcripts of the previous custody hearings in Oregon and had reviewed them. He asked the attorneys for the results of the psychological evaluations. Trilla gave him the results of my evaluation, but when he turned to Arlene's attorney for her report, her attorney said that she hadn't done the evaluation. The judge asked why they had not complied with the court's requirement, and they tried to make some excuses that the judge found to be completely unacceptable. He dismissed their petition for custody and advised them against filing future such petitions in Placer County, awarding me full custody of Anika and Mekala.

As the girls got older and were teenagers, I sometimes wondered how accurate the psychological evaluation could have been. The tests presumably showed that I was sane and reasonably well-adjusted but raising 8- and 12-year-old girls single-handedly was a tremendous challenge and adjustment in lifestyle for a man of 58 whose profession demanded total commitment. Thankfully, there were wonderful women like Donna Brenner and Deon O'Leary who were great role models for Anika and Mekala and helped them grow into responsible adulthood.

The '97 Flood

One of the most remarkable events during my years in Squaw Valley was the New Year's Flood of 1997 because it was such an amazing demonstration of the power of nature. Although the flooding took place starting on New Year's Day, 1997, the events that allowed the flood to pack such devastation started weeks before. We had a solid storm with significant snowfall that started on December 20 and delivered a good four or five feet of snow. Then there was a break of a few days, and another storm started just after Christmas, dropping several additional feet—the skiing for the Christmas holiday was excellent. Another storm was forecast and, unlike the others that had originated in the Gulf of Alaska, this one was the classic "Pineapple Express" storm track coming from the warmer regions of Hawaii. It started to rain on December 30, although the snow level was about 7,000 feet, so the upper mountain at Squaw Valley continued to accumulate snow. The rain at lower elevations continued the following day, New Year's Eve, although as the main body of the storm reached the Sierra, the snow level started to rise, saturating the snowpack on the upper mountain with rain. It rained hard overnight and continued to warm, so that in the morning of January 1, 1997, the snow level was about 10,000 feet.

The Truckee River rose for several days as the rain caused flows in tributaries to the river to increase dramatically. The dam at Tahoe City was releasing about 2,200 cubic feet per second, but downstream, the flow in the Truckee was several times that volume. The rising river had trapped a few residents in their homes and was threatening some of the bridges between Squaw Valley and Truckee. The Truckee River tributaries were starting to over-whelm the culverts that carried their flows under State Route 89—some of the streams, like Pole Creek and Brush Creek, were flowing across the highway rather than under it. Late in the afternoon, the saturated ground above Sandy Way in Squaw Valley started to erode and slump. It turned the small creek at the top of Wayne Road muddy, and created a larger flow of mud and debris that soon blocked the road to the depth of several feet. That flow oozed down the hill between homes on Lanny and continued downhill until it covered Squaw Valley Road with a layer of mud. Heavy rain continued into the evening, and the flow in

Squaw Creek flooding the first floor of Squaw Valley Lodge—it filled the hallway to the ceiling with rock and mud.

The Blue House with Squaw Creek running right through it.

Squaw Creek increased hourly as the warm rain melted the snowpack all the way to the top of the mountain. As the flow in Squaw Creek increased, the normal streambed—unable to contain the abnormally large quantity of water it was carrying—grew wider and the eroding banks contributed mud, rock, and debris to the flow coming down the mountain. The small bridge over the road to the Granite Chief subdivision became clogged with debris, causing the south fork of Squaw Creek to start backing up and looking for a new path. This was when the excitement really started.

Alex and Nancy were at home in the Blue House, listening to the rain and fretting about what effect it would have on the skiing and operation of the mountain. Sometime close to midnight, the clogged bridge a hundred yards downstream caused Squaw Creek to overwhelm its normal channel, and the Blue House began filling with water, slowly at first, but once the flow began, it was impossible to stop. In a panic, Nancy called me to come help get Alex out of the house and to a safe place. The front door—packed closed with mud—was out of the question. I was able to get in a side door and noted that Alex's piano was just about ready to float in the living room. Nancy and I managed to push and pull Alex through a side window and, wading through rushing water, make our way to the parking garage of the Squaw

Alex's beloved Steinway concert grand piano didn't float well and was seriously damaged by the flood.

Valley Lodge. The lowest level of the parking garage was below grade and it was already full of water, but they were able to get their car out of the middle level and down Squaw Peak Road, which was awash with most of the south fork of Squaw Creek—water about sixteen inches deep. I led them over to the Resort at Squaw Creek, which, miraculously, was able to give them a room where they could dry out and spend the night.

Because the south fork of Squaw Creek was basically dammed up at the Granite Chief bridge, the entire (and very substantial) flow was rolling down Squaw Peak Road, and the back doors into the lower level of the Tram Building were taking on a lot of water. I wondered about the motor room of the tram, which is more than a full story below the level of the road. Sure enough, the motor room was filling up with water and—although the electric motor that drives the system was a couple of feet off the floor—the motor and generator of the AC-DC converter are a lot closer to the floor and were in imminent risk of being submerged, which would be disastrous and would put them out of service until they could be dried out and rebuilt. I set about finding any pumps I could get my hands on to pump the water out of the motor room, which was not a simple task, since in the middle of a flood, the one thing everyone is looking for is a pump. I rounded up a couple of different small pumps and got them working to try to at least stabilize the water level in the motor room. Fortunately, what was making its way to the motor room was mostly water, not mud.

The night was far from over for me, because as I had left my house on Sandy Way, I had noticed water and mud flowing down Navajo Court that, it appeared, would soon be filling my garage. I managed to build a quick berm with a backhoe to prevent the garage from taking on too much water and to direct the flow into a gully between my house and the next home to the east. Meanwhile, the other end of Sandy Way was completely blocked with mud, and a minor river flowing across the road, so the residents in the middle were trapped.

A mudslide across from the entrance to the Valley had taken down a major power line, and once Squaw Creek was finished trashing the Blue House, it created a new pathway through the first floor of one of the Squaw Valley Lodge condominium buildings, eventually filling the hallway to within a few inches of the ceiling with rocks and mud, then filling the Lodge swimming pool with mud and debris. When January 2 dawned, the extent of the devastation in Squaw Valley was apparent: The Meadow was a huge, muddy lake, roads were blocked, trees and power lines were down.

The underground utilities that served the mountain and mountaintop facilities were in bad shape. The ditch with snowmaking air and water lines, high voltage electric, and the propane and sewer line for High Camp and Gold Coast had been washed out, and the utility lines exposed. Several towers on the Squaw One lift had been undermined and were leaning, held up by the haul rope. It was just unbelievable.

As bad as things were in Squaw, in other places they were even worse. The Shell station in Truckee was under water, as was much of downtown Reno. The Truckee River was several blocks wide through downtown Reno, and downtown casinos were flooded. In the industrial area of Sparks, businesses were under five or six feet of water, and the Helms quarry had filled with water that could never be pumped out—it became the Sparks Marina Lake. The Reno-Tahoe International Airport was flooded. Half of the bridges along the Truckee River between Squaw Valley and Truckee had been either washed away or severely damaged. A dozen or more large propane tanks had simply disappeared. Miraculously, no one was killed.

The Gold Coast snow study plot had received twenty-two inches of water in a matter of a few days—by far the largest amount of precipitation recorded for the storm at any of the locations at which rainfall data had been gathered. In addition, the snowpack had lost three inches of water content, so a staggering twenty-five inches of water was available for runoff in the Squaw Valley watershed. It looked like it had all come down the mountain—and probably right through Alex's living room.

Rotary recognition

Hans Burkhart, general manager of Squaw Valley Ski Corp., received the Rotary Club of Tahoe City's Man of the Year award. Presenting the award were, standing, from left to right: Joe Curletti, Tom Kelly, Don Robbins, Liz Dugan, Mekala Burkhart, Hans Burkhart, Donna Brenner, Joe Marilac. Kneeling is left, Curtis Crooks and Wes Schimmelpfennig.

Burkhart named Rotary's Man of the Year

Hans Burkhart, general manager of Squaw Valley Ski Corp., was recently named Rotary Club Man of the Year by the Rotary Club of Tahoe City.

Nominated by Nancy Wendt, President of Squaw Valley Ski Corp., Burkhart's efforts and leadership during the severe snow storm just after Christmas 1996 were cited as particulars for his nomination. Burkhart, with assistance of others, is credited with clearing a mudslide which isolated Squaw Valley and Alpine Meadows, keeping roads cleared while homes and businesses were threatened, providing sand bags to those in need and restoring auxiliary power to skiing facilities and thereby ensuring the jobs of 2,000 employees and skiing opportunities for many skiers.

The nomination included this quote from Burhkart during the time, "This mountain is about superior service. This holiday season we have families from all around the world here to experience the wonders of Squaw Valley, USA, and we have got to have our mountain open for them. Our neighbors also need help. This is going to be a very trying couple of weeks. Please stay out of my way."

The nominating statement concluded, "Since his arrival in 1961, Hans has continually been tested, not only by nature, but by his peers and he has never fallen short of exceeding the expectations set upon him." The award is an annual award made by the Rotary Club for "Service Above Self" given to the community. Wes Schimmelpfennig presented the award plaque on behalf of the Tahoe City Rotary Club.

I was very honored to receive the Tahoe City Rotary Club's "Man of the Year" award for our team's rapid and effective action following the New Year's flood event.

Squaw Creek created a trail of destruction on Tower 20 Traverse, destroying culverts, power and telephone conduits, night lighting, snowmaking pipelines—even the sewer line from the upper mountain to the bottom—a total disaster.

The Funitel

During the winter of 1995-96, the upper mountain at Squaw Valley was closed for forty-eight days due to high winds and our inability to operate the gondola. This was thirty percent of a season lasting an average of 160 days. This was dissatisfying to resort management and especially to our guests. Although the Poma six passenger gondola was only ten years old at this point, Alex and I both felt that we needed to do better, and we started looking at alternatives. One possibility was modifying the tram to make it more wind resistant. After the 1978 accident—and even more recently—we had received all kinds of proposals for improving the tram's ability to operate in high winds, including: increasing the gauge of the track ropes; installing hydraulically-damped "landing gear;" installing ballast systems; even putting in gyroscopic stabilization, which, the proponent pointed out, are used in ocean liners and space vehicles. The wildest was a proposal to install jets on the cabins to "counter-thrust the swinging moment created by cross winds."

Alex and I were not sure that installing jet engines on the tram cabins would provide our guests with a greater feeling of safety, so we took a trip to Europe to see what other transportation solutions might be available. Building a funicular seemed like a solid option. Such an inclined train operating on rails would be totally unaffected by wind, although because the installation would require tunneling in some areas, installation costs would be quite a bit higher than an aerial lift. Still, a funicular at Squaw would be unique in North America, and Alex still had a passion for owning the newest, biggest, most unusual lifts.

We were willing to consider nearly any option to provide more reliable operation in windy conditions—a monorail was given serious consideration.

243

We rode a lot of different funiculars on this tour: Zermatt and Saas-Fee in Switzerland and then a couple in Austria, including one in Pitztal that was completely inside the mountain. Once you went into the lower terminal and got in the cabin, you did not see daylight until you walked out of the upper terminal. The windows in the train were small because there was nothing to see. Alex hated it—I think the dark tunnel made him claustrophobic—and he was so uncomfortable that he asked if there was another way down. Other than that, Pitztal's ski resort was an excellent and very modern resort with attractive architecture and the latest lifts, but Alex said: "I'm not going to have my customers riding in a submarine!!" The funicular idea did not seem to be the answer, although the ability to have a curved line was quite attractive.

We met with Garaventa in Switzerland, and they suggested we look at a new concept that they had developed with cabins supported between parallel haul ropes, which gave them a lot of stability and resistance to swing, even in strong wind. (The "funitel" was a hybrid of "funicular" and "telepherique.") Garaventa had built two funitels, and they happened to be in Verbier and Crans-Montana—separate resorts on opposite sides of a large Swiss valley.

Although the uphill capacity was somewhat limited by the number of cabins the Swiss resort operators were running on the line, Garaventa assured us that we could increase the number of cabins and improve the uphill capacity of the 2,400 passenger-per-hour gondola by better than 50 percent while improving our ability to operate in the wind. After a good bit of discussion with Garaventa about cost, construction scheduling, and the cabin design, we signed a letter of intent to construct a funitel at Squaw Valley —the first in North America.

I had no idea then what a difficult project it would be; but I did know that we could not do it in one building season, so we would have to figure out a way to spread construction of the funitel over two seasons while continuing to operate the gondola. That seemed like an impossible idea at first: we wanted to use the same line, and the upper terminal location had to be at Gold Coast. The lower terminal, too, had been in the same place for thirty years, and the flow of skiers from the lodging properties and parking areas was well established. The terminal for the funitel would need to be somewhat larger than the gondola terminal, and I saw that the solution to increasing the size—without cutting into the available retail footage in the Olympic House and Plaza—was continuing right through the back of the existing gondola terminal and over the Plaza, and building the lower terminal behind the ticket booths. This location would provide the size needed and would also allow us to build the new lower terminal for the funitel without interrupting the operation of the gondola. We could build the lower terminal—start to finish—in the first year and do the rest in the second building season. It would be ambitious, because in the second building season we would need to remove the existing Poma gondola, fabricate and install all the towers, and build the upper terminal. It could be done—weather permitting—but it was a tremendous amount of work, and there were tasks that could not be performed out of sequence to accommodate weather or a delay in the delivery of parts.

Garaventa provided specifications for the outlines of the loading area, the control room, and the motor room as well as for a basic building design, which Squaw Valley's draftsman, Fred Schmidinger, and I immediately started to redesign. The building looked like a shoe-box, and Freddie and I both knew that it would not work with the existing architecture in the base area, so we incorporated more windows, wide eaves, native stone facing on the walls, reflective glass, and a natural wood soffit around the eave to make it better match the surrounding structures and please the eye. Freddie went through any number of revisions and new drawings to get the building to look the way we wanted it to look—we worked on it for a couple of months. In the end, it turned out to be an aesthetically pleasing and func-tional building. I knew that if I showed it to Alex and said, "What do you think of it?" he would have to change something, so when I showed him the renderings, I said, "Here's the lower terminal," and he liked it! Not bad work for a couple of amateurs.

For the upper terminal, I asked Garaventa for something that did not look like a shoe box, and they referred me to a Swiss architect out in the country near Zermatt, who had done some work for them that they thought was outstanding. He came over to look at the existing Gold Coast lodge building. He analyzed how the funitel terminal would have to

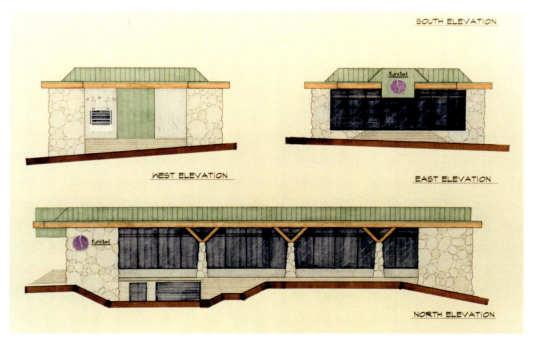

Fred Schmidinger's rendering of the lower terminal design that he and I developed—really an excellent job for a couple of amateurs!

attach to it and examined the flow of passengers into and through the existing gondola unloading area. He shipped us some renderings that I liked very much—a contrast to the very angular, industrial look of the main building. I thought that the offbeat, modernistic shape would appeal to Alex as well—it was a unique look—and I was right. He liked it and we had a deal.

From the time we got a permit and started construction of the lower terminal for the funitel in August 1997, I worked on it for seventeen months straight: I took two days off during that time. There was a tremendous amount of concrete work which we did in-house— literally 4,200 cubic yards of concrete. Fortunately, I found a labor force that was up to the challenge. They spoke Spanish, which was a new experience for me, but they were excellent workers, and there was no complaining about working too many hours or working seven days a week. I paid them well and I worked with them every day. We built all the forms and set and tied all the rebar.

One day in September, we were making really good progress on the forms and had scheduled a lot of concrete for the next day.

Tom Kelly, Squaw Valley's director of operations, showed up at the job site and said, "Hey, Hans—Vice-President Gore is going to ride up the tram and would like it if you would ride up with him!"

The vice-president was in Lake Tahoe for the first "Lake Tahoe Summit," and he and his wife were going to ride up the tram and hike over to The Cedars, near Serene Lakes.

Building the lower terminal in the first building season was the only way to complete such a large project on time.

I passed up a Tram ride with the Vice-President of the United States to work on the foundation for the lower terminal—it was a huge job.

There was no way I could leave the job for an hour or so, and I think maybe I was a little stressed trying to get the forms ready for the pour the following day, because my reply to Tom was, "You'll just have to tell the vice-president I can't leave now—I have work to do!"

We had a roof on the lower terminal before it snowed, which was a good thing because it snowed a lot in the winter of 1997-1998. We were constantly fighting the snow, digging things out which would get reburied right away. We installed all the drive equipment during the winter. There were I-beams in the ceiling of the motor room with electric hoists on rolling carriages that allowed us to lift a piece of machinery off the bed of a truck backed into the doorway, then move it across the room, and lower it into place. The catch was that everything had to be assembled in sequence from the floor to the ceiling, and if you forgot something, it was going to be difficult to move it or lift it vertically with other machinery already in place above it. In this respect, the project was much more difficult than either the Squaw Valley or Snowbird trams because the motor room in the funitel had a lot more equipment packed into a smaller, more densely configured space with a relatively low ceiling.

Moving large pieces—like this bullwheel—into the motor room required planning and lots of rigging.

I had some excellent help building the motor room—David Mercer worked on the project as a break from flying helicopters, Scott "Big Daddy" Miller always had a positive attitude and, of course, Hardy, who, at age sixty-something was commuting to school in Sacramento to get his doctorate in divinity. Garaventa sent a crew of technicians from Switzerland to install the lower terminal drive equipment—they did a superb job of installing the equipment and fine-tuning the alignment of the enormous yet intricately arranged components in the motor room.

Celebrating Jonny Moseley's Olympic gold medal with the lower terminal of the Funitel in the background.

NEAR-DEATH EXPERIENCE #10
VERDI CULVERT

In 1972, I bought a four-acre parcel of industrial land in Verdi, Nevada. I had some equipment that I had acquired for the tram project in Snowbird, and I was anticipating further contracting jobs in the lift industry, and I needed a place to store equipment that would be out of the snow in Lake Tahoe. Verdi was the first town in Nevada when you traveled east on I-80 from the Tahoe area, and it was convenient and had a good climate. North of my yard in Verdi was a small hydroelectric generating plant that diverted water from the Truckee River through a flume, ran it through the hydroelectric plant, and then returned it to the river. On the south edge of my property was a small creek bed that carried bypass flows from the flume when the river was running especially high or to which the flow in the flume could be diverted to allow the plant to shut down for repair or maintenance. When I first bought the property, I had installed several lengths of eight-foot diameter culvert in the creek bed so the driveway to the yard would remain accessible even when there was water in the creek. The culvert could almost always carry all the flow that was diverted to the creek without allowing the driveway to flood.

As I worked on other projects and expanded from lift construction into other kinds of contracting and trucking, the Verdi yard took on a larger role, and I built several buildings and acquired more equipment and inventory. The yard became an ideal location for the fabrication of lift towers and terminal structures and for a variety of other functions—it was even a winter home for my daughters' horses for a few years.

One evening in February 1998, I pulled into the yard in the Kenworth, and when I got out to unlock the gate, I could tell from the sound that the creek was really running. It had been storming, and as I had followed the Truckee River down from Squaw Valley, I had noticed from the highway that the river was running high and fast. High flows in the river resulted in excess flows in the flume, and I wanted to get a look at how full the culvert was so that I would have an idea of whether the driveway was likely to flood. If it looked bad, I did not want to strand the Kenworth tractor on the other side and risk not being able to get it out of the yard until the water level subsided. I pulled the truck forward and left it idling on the driveway while I walked upstream of the culvert a little to look at the water level. The bushes all along the creek were frozen and covered with ice from being splashed by the creek, and I made my way to the edge of the creek to look downstream. There was a large flat rock at the edge of the creek, and I stepped on it so I could lean out over the creek and get a look at the water level in the culvert. As I put weight on the rock, it dropped a couple of inches—nothing had been holding it in place but pressure from the flowing water—and I lost my balance. I went into the fast moving, freezing water and was swept downstream by the current. I was dressed in winter work clothes with boots, and all that extra bulk kept me from being chilled right away, but because of it, I was not able to come to the surface and get a breath until I was inside the pitch-black culvert. That was just as well, because the water was moving fast, and if I had popped my head out quickly, the sharp edge of the upstream end of the culvert would have taken it off.

I came out on the other end of the culvert—water now having soaked through my clothes, so I could tell just how cold the water was—and started trying to get out of the water. I grabbed at the branches of the willows and bushes along the edge of the creek, but they were of little help, being all coated with ice. I finally managed to get out of the water and staggered toward the shop where I could warm up, trying to get the keys out of my soaking wet pocket with frozen fingers. I managed to extract the keys, open the shop, get inside and out of my wet clothes and into some insulated coveralls that were hanging there. When I looked at the water level in the culvert in the daylight a day or two later, there was only about six inches of difference between the surface of the water and the top of the culvert, reinforcing how lucky I had been to keep my head after getting swept through the culvert in the dark.

John Rollo drilling holes for blasting the counterweight pit out of solid rock.

It was the winter of the Nagano Olympics, and Squaw Valley athlete Jonny Moseley won the gold medal in freestyle skiing. We built a stage right outside the funitel building and held a "welcome home" celebration for Jonny. It was a welcome break from the work inside the lower terminal.

After a long winter with a lot of snow, I was anxious to start work on the upper terminal, but Placer County wanted us to wait until May 1 to start excavation work. I wrote a letter appealing this date, explaining that if we had to wait that long, I would not be able to get the project done on time for winter. They relented and allowed us to start on April 15. Scott Miller, John Rollo, and I hauled a track-mounted pneumatic rock drill ("air track") and a compressor to the site and started clearing off the snow and dirt on April 15. We started drilling and blasting not long after that. The biggest concern was the shaft for the counterweight. The lift would have an overall length of about 9000 feet and a profile varying from moderately steep to quite flat, so the design required a lot of counterweight travel. We would have to go down about seventy feet from the surface to be able to build a shaft deep enough to meet the specifications. Since there were rock outcroppings dotting the landscape in every direction from the site, it was a certainty that the shaft would be excavated out of solid rock.

The rock was a formidable enough obstacle, but what made the work tough was the weather. The site was generally located on a side hill, and there was a tremendous amount of snow above it still, to say nothing of the rain and snow that continued to fall from the sky as we worked. This translated into a very, very muddy worksite. Normally when excavating a shaft like this, you drill into the rock the depth of the "deck" or level that you will be blasting and removing. In a multi-deck project, it does not pay to drill too deeply all at once, because the rock will fragment poorly and be more difficult to remove, so you drill in eight-, ten- or twelve-foot increments, using a pattern that will provide the outline of the shaft that you need to make. You normally drill the holes and plug them with cones of rolled-up asphalt felt tarpaper or ordinary traffic cones to keep debris from falling into them. When you have drilled the full pattern, you go hole to hole, removing the cone, lowering explosive charges into the holes using the wires from the blasting cap or the explosive primer cord that will fire that hole, then filling the hole with explosives and fine dirt "stemming" to confine the explosion, which will provide the fracturing effect in the rock.

That is how you proceed normally, but there was nothing normal about this project. As soon as we finished drilling a hole, we would load it with explosives and tie the wires from the blasting cap to a rope trunkline on the surface, because if we had left the hole, it would have filled with mud or been impossible to find or, most likely, both. With ropes running across the work area that had wires tied to them every few feet, you had to be incredibly careful where you stepped. Scott and Rollo did a great job with the drilling: it was hard, noisy, repetitive work, but they never complained. To remove the fractured rock from the shaft, we opened a kind of canal on one end, so that the spoils could just be pushed out by a dozer, rather than scooped out, bucket by bucket, by an excavator—it was a large shaft, and this was a far more efficient way to remove the material.

We used a tremendous quantity of dynamite in the excavation for the funitel. When we did a large blast, we would occasionally use all the explosives we had in stock in the various magazines around the mountain. At one point, we completely ran out and I called the vendor in Reno to order more. They were expecting a shipment the following day, and I arranged to drive down and pick up a load at their terminal. I drove to Reno and, sure enough, the vendor had a ton of dynamite for me—forty cases each weighing fifty pounds neatly stacked on a pallet and shrink-wrapped in plastic. I had one of their guys set the pallet in the bed of my pickup with the forklift, then push it forward so all the weight

Steve Lamb preparing a blast in the counterweight pit with the primer cord for each drilled hole tied to a rope so that we could keep them from disappearing into the mud.

Siller Brothers Sikorsky S-64 "Skycrane" preparing to remove one of the old gondola towers with the Squaw Valley Meadow and Resort at Squaw Creek in the distance.

Welder Danny Sprague getting into his work—literally inside one of large tower bases.

was not on the rear axle. I shut the tailgate and headed for home. I had to stop for the traffic light at Glendale Avenue and Rock Boulevard in Reno—a large intersection with Baldini's casino on the southwest corner. When the light changed, I started into the intersection and heard a loud "thud." The pallet of dynamite had slid back, knocked the tailgate open, and fallen onto the street. I stopped quickly and assessed the situation. A few of the cases of explosives were still on the pallet, but the rest were all over the intersection, and the traffic was just driving around them. I backed up a little, got out, and started loading the boxes back into the truck as quickly as I could. A factor in my favor was that the cardboard boxes were very sturdy, and none had popped open and spilled sticks of dynamite all over the street, because then someone would surely have figured out what it was. The other positive was that none of the cars behind me had run into or run over any of the boxes. I kept waiting for a police car to show up—I figured they would get a look at the boxes with "DANGER—HIGH EXPLOSIVES" printed all over them, go crazy and call the bomb squad—but none ever came. The light changed and the Rock Boulevard traffic drove carefully around the boxes as I continued to load them back into the pickup. Finally, I got everything reloaded, put the pallet on top and drove away. No muss, no fuss, no bomb squad and no help from anyone in getting it all reloaded!

The weather continued to be a challenge as we removed the old gondola, which we had sold to Lake Louise, Alberta, but the drive was dismantled and moved out of the upper terminal, and the lower terminal structure was dismantled to make way for the funitel line, which made the job of disassembling the conveyor and carriage much easier.

Rather than shipping a lot of large pieces over from Switzerland, we manufactured the large structural pieces for the funitel at my yard in Verdi. Unlike the lattice towers on the funitels in Crans-Montana and Verbier, we planned to use tubular towers, which would require a smaller footprint on the ground and would be constructed in sections that would bolt together on site. Garaventa supplied the blueprints, and Danny Sprague, two other welders, and another man cutting and fitting steel worked for months doing the fabrication.

When the pieces were finished, they were trucked to a company in Woodland, California to be galvanized. There was a limit on their capacity, however, and some of the

Massive Tower 3 nearly complete and ready for the tower head and line machinery.

largest pieces were sandblasted and painted in Verdi, then trucked to Squaw Valley for installation. We went through a lot of steel—it seemed like the truck from PDM Steel was in Verdi every other day. The charge to Garaventa for the parts that we manufactured (on a "time and materials" billing) and the surveying that I did was $875,000. Some of the materials they had specified were nearly impossible to find. The external struts on towers 3 and 5, for example, called for 8-inch diameter pipe with ¾-inch wall thickness. When I asked for this at PDM they laughed—they said there was no such thing. I was able to find a mill in Texas that made the pipe to the specification for me.

Once the counterweight pit was excavated, the "Mexican army" took over, forming the counterweight and the enclosure for the counterweight shaft. Reinforcing steel—known universally in the construction industry as "rebar"—is manufactured in varying diameters and the thickness of a given type of rebar is expressed in eights of an inch—so ½" rebar is called #4, one inch is #8, etc. The specifications for the Funitel counterweight pit enclosure called for #12 rebar—the largest made at 1½" in diameter. Each twenty-foot long piece of the #12 rebar weighed 306 pounds and in many parts of the enclosure it was

Looking down the line. The old gondola terminal is still standing; Funitel terminal has the green roof.

placed on 7" centers. The crew came up with a procedure for placing and tying this mammoth and extraordinarily heavy rod in place—six of them would lift the bar and hold it, while six others standing between the lifting team would rapidly tie it in place with tie wire. It was an efficient, if labor-intensive method, but they worked quickly and cheerfully and the rebar 'cage' was erected and then the forms that would create the smooth concrete walls were put in place and braced. The forms were sixteen feet tall, so we did five lifts—pouring the forms full, allowing the concrete to cure for a week, then stripping the lower forms, placing and tying rebar on the next section up, moving the forms up, pouring that section, etc., etc. It was a tremendous amount of labor, but no complaints from the men, who were happy to have as much work as we could throw at them.

Once the counterweight shaft was done, we poured foundations for the upper terminal so that the subcontractor building the structure of the upper terminal could get started with their work. Once there was a structure, we would go back in and set machinery, but the focus shifted to tower footings so that the work on the line could stay on schedule. Compared to most lift towers, the footings for the funitel towers were massive and contained an enormous amount of rebar.

Even the tower footings had extensive and complex rebar layouts.

Fabricating towers at the Verdi yard gave us a head start on the weather and more room to work.

The upper terminal for the Funitel nearing completion . It nearly doubled the size of the Gold Coast complex.

Unloading the spools of haul rope was a maximum lift even with two large cranes.

Cheerful, efficient and ready to work—there was no challenge too difficult for these guys. The 'Mexican Army' did a phenomenal job.

The Garaventa crew was right at home at great height assembling the towers.

Splicing the Funitel haul rope in the lower terminal.

Digging down seventy five feet at Squaw Valley without hitting solid granite is virtually impossible, so after removing the minimal amount of soil on the surface, the rest of the depth of the counterweight pit was gained by drilling and blasting the rock. The excavation was large enough to allow two track-mounted drills to work at the same time.

Unstable rock had to be removed from the walls of the pit so that the workers could safely form and pour the floor and walls of the counterweight enclosure. The only way to do this was by rappelling down the walls and prying potential hazard rocks loose.

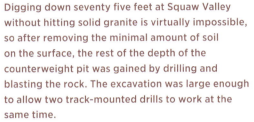

Once excavated to full depth, we drained the bottom of the pit as much as possible before pouring a concrete pad on which to form the floor.

Pouring the floor of the counterweight enclosure.

Forms for the outside of the first lift have been installed.

Rebar, inner and outer forms have been constructed along with a catwalk to allow the crew to pour the first 'lift' of the counterweight enclosure.

Pouring the first sixteen foot section of the enclosure.

The forms have been stripped off the lowest section and moved up for the next lift.

The forms have been moved up again to pour another lift.

Forms in position to pour the top section of the enclosure. Out of the ground and dry!

Counterweight Pit Collapse

The installation of the funitel at Squaw Valley was an extremely difficult, complicated job in many ways, none more than the construction of the counterweight at the top terminal. From the surface of the ground below the site of the top terminal, we had to go down about eighty feet—eight stories—to have an adequate amount of travel for the counterweight, because the haul cable is one gigantic loop of wire rope that is about 36,000 feet—almost seven miles—long. Once we removed a couple of feet of dirt, we hit solid rock. Totally solid rock, and that is what we had to work with for the reminder of the excavation. It was drill and blast, drill and blast, down and down. The weather was consistently terrible—snow and rain and mud. As soon as we finished drilling a hole, we had to load it with explosives right away or the hole would fill with water and mud. It was the most challenging and frustrating blasting work I have ever experienced, but the crew—Scott "Daddy-O" Miller and John Rollo—kept at it, day after day, week after week.

The most efficient way to remove the broken rock from the excavation was to push it out with a dozer, so we built an opening in the east end of the shaft where the dozer could just push the broken rock out after every blast until we were back down to solid rock again and the blasters could bring in the air track and drill down another ten or twelve feet. We were deep—probably fifty feet—when one of the blasts created a little undercut on the south side of the shaft—it was not much, just a small niche in the rock wall on that side about four feet deeper into the vertical rock than the wall above it. We kept working and were well below that overhang—almost to the full depth of the shaft—after several subsequent blasts.

I had a brief conversation with Ron Mancino, who was operating the dozer, and I stepped under the little overhang to get out of the rain while Ron made passes pushing material out through the opening in the east end of the shaft. One of the guys at the top of the excavation yelled something down to me and I could not hear what he said, so I walked out to see what he needed. The dozer backed into the excavation past me to make another pass and as he did, the entire wall above the overhang collapsed into the pit, crushing the front of the cab, the engine cover and the blade. It made a tremendous noise and as the dust cleared, we were relieved to see Ron climb out through one of the windows on the back of the cab, unhurt. The collapse consisted of gigantic blocks of rock, several of them (which

The counterweight pit with the crushed D8. There are some pieces of plastic conduit on the left that are where I had been standing just before the wall collapsed.

The Caterpillar D8 dozer was destroyed—we were very relieved to see Ron Mancino crawl out the window as the dust cleared.

fortunately missed the machine) larger than the D8. The Cat was far enough away from the wall to have been hit with what was only a glancing blow by (relatively) smaller pieces at the front edge of the collapse, but it was enough to crush the D8 beyond repair. The amount of rock that had collapsed right onto the area where I had been standing only a few seconds before was mind-boggling—close to a half-million pounds of granite.

After our experience on the counterweight and counterweight shaft, forming and pouring the tower footings seemed simple and fast, especially because we were able to drive to all the tower locations, so we could use a crane to install pre-tied rebar mats, and could either "tailgate" the concrete directly into the forms from the truck or use a small pump to place it.

Building the towers, too, went quickly and smoothly. We had staged tower sections in the parking lot at Squaw Valley, and from there it was a matter of hauling them to the tower sites and building the towers, section by section, then installing the crossarm, lifting frame and line machinery. The large sizes of the tower sections—although heavy—made the assembly process relatively quick, but the crossarms and sheave trains were awkward as well as heavy and were in some cases right at the limit of the crane's reach or capacity. We could manage all but one of the towers with my crane, but I had to hire a larger truck crane from Carson City to set the line machinery on Tower 3—it was just too heavy for me to set with the extension on the crane. The Swiss guys from Garaventa had some interesting ideas about doing the line work, though. One day we were working on a very tall, exposed tower and the weather started to look threatening with lightning in the area. I was in the crane and I called them on the radio and told them they had to get off the tower—there was lightning.

"No, we're not coming down," they said. "If we come down, we'll just have to climb up again."

"I think you better come down," I said.

"No; we'll be okay," was their reply.

The haul rope—two inches in diameter—came in two pieces that were each over 18,000 feet long. The spools were so heavy we had to use a crane on each side to lift them clear of the lowboy trailer, which then drove out from under the spool. We staged the spools between the funitel building and the locker room so we could pull the rope through the funitel terminal and onto the line, around the top tensioning assembly, and back down. We then made the first of two splices—we were able to do the splice in the terminal—and pulled the other section of rope around, then made another splice to complete the huge loop of haul rope.

With the terminals completed, the towers and line machinery installed, and the rope spliced and tensioned, it would seem like we had a working lift. If that had only been the case. We had discovered that Garaventa had made an error in calculating the height for Tower 4—it was four or five meters too low. Although under normal conditions, cabins would clear the ground, the distance from the bottom of a loaded cabin to the ground allowed for no accumulation of snow, which was unrealistic: in any normal winter, snow would accumulate in that part of the line and we could not work around the issue by plowing the snow out of the way before operating the lift. Making Tower 4 taller seemed like a possibility, but any modification to Tower 4 would change the loading on both towers 3

The Funitel was an immediate hit with Squaw Valley skiers and the lower terminal that Fred and I designed is an attractive addition to the base area.

and 5. We needed to remove about ten feet of rock under the line below Tower 4—there was simply no way around it. After years of testy relations between Alex and the Placer County Planning Department, there was no way that the county planning department would do anything to expedite a permit for this work, and they would have been on shaky ground legally to issue a permit without some level of environmental review. The Squaw Valley opponents in the community would have taken them to task for it and the county would have been forced to defend itself for essentially doing Alex a favor. That was not going to happen. I went to Alex and explained that Garaventa had admitted that they had made an error and we needed to correct it so that the lift would be ready to run on time.

He told me to do it. "I'll take care of it," he said.

I did not waste a lot of time thinking about how he could "take care of it"—and in the end, it was Tom Anderson and myself who took the heat at the public meetings—but we drilled and shot the rock shelf below the line and pushed the material out of the way. The removal of about ten thousand cubic yards of granite created a controversy that followed us for several years.

The other unexpected complications had to do with the United States codes regulating lift design, installation, and operation—the American National Standards Institute (usually referred to as "ANSI") B77 Code. Since the Squaw Valley Funitel was the first of its kind in the United States, it might have been anticipated that it might conflict with the B77 Code in some manner, since the code adapts to technology, but rarely anticipates technological

Somehow, the height of the rock between Towers 3 and 4 had been overlooked when calculating the line height. Removing the rock would become a major—and controversial—additional project.

It takes a lot of drilling and blasting to move 10,000 cubic yards of solid rock, but it had to be done.

Drilling and blasting fractured the rock, then the excavators came in and moved it out of the cut.

After weeks of work, there was barely enough clearance for summer operation with a loaded cabin. There was no way it would be adequate in the winter....

Celebrating the opening of the Funitel with two Squaw Valley legends—Tom O'Neill and Alex Cushing.

changes. In the case of the Squaw Valley Funitel, Garaventa had specified a fifty millimeter (two-inch) haul rope, which provided a breaking strength safety factor of 4.8:1—the rope was 4.8 times as strong as the maximum tension that might be exerted on it. That was fine, except the B77 Code called for a five-to-one safety factor. We went through a series of hearings with the State of California Occupational Health and Safety Board to get approval of the four-point-eight-to-one safety factor, and eventually secured it.

Similarly, the B77 Code called for a conductor to be provided for each cabin on a lift that accommodated seven or more persons. This seems laughable today, but in 1998, the only lift cabins carrying more than six passengers were on aerial tramways, so the code required a conductor. Since the funitel cabins could each carry twenty-eight people and we had forty-six cabins, providing a conductor in each cabin would be quite an expense. We sought a variance to the requirement, and received one after the requisite number of hearings and many letters back and forth between the ski resort and the State of California. It is never easy to be the first.

The funitel project was tremendously challenging. Other than rebuilding the Squaw Valley Tram following the 1978 accident in five months, it was certainly the most difficult of my career. It was satisfying to complete the difficult installation on time, even though the legal challenges due to the Tower 4 grading, the safety factor of the haul rope, and the conductor issue lingered long after the lift was open. And skiers loved the new lift.

One particularly meaningful outcome of the funitel project for me was being invited to present a paper on the lift and the details of the installation at the 8th OITAF Congress in San Francisco. OITAF stands for "Organizzazione Internationale Trasporti A Fune" (International Organization for Transport by Rope) and it holds an international congress every six years. The congress was held at the San Francisco Marriott in May 1999. My paper described the characteristics of the ski resort, the kinds of weather and wind we encountered, how those factors informed the selection process for the new lift, and why we concluded that a funitel was the best choice. Then I described how the project schedule led me to conclude that by building the lower terminal while the old gondola was still operating, it would be possible to provide uninterrupted service while constructing the upper terminal and installing line equipment in a single construction season. The paper and presentation were well received, and it was very gratifying to be recognized by an international group of my peers—people who could really appreciate the complexity of the project and the challenges that were overcome to complete it.

35

Ski Patrol Unionization

I n 2001, there was a surge of interest in unionization for ski area employees. Whether the idea had originated with the unions or with the employees was uncertain. Labor unions had certainly lost ground from their peak period of influence when the United States was a highly industrial country. To a large extent, the gradual shift to an economy based more on service industries and technology had left the union movement behind, and it had been less than successful at convincing employees in those industries of the value of union membership. It was more difficult and time-consuming to organize employees in smaller companies with relatively few people in each job description for collective bargaining than in large corporations with hundreds or thousands of people performing similar tasks.

In the ski industry, the idea to join a labor union began with year-round skilled employees like mechanics and electricians, some of whom may have worked in union shops before being employed by a ski area. Seasonal workers were generally disinterested in union membership, because within a few months they would be moving on to new jobs at new employers, and they had little interest in reducing their already meager take-home pay with union dues.

At Squaw Valley, the one department in which the idea of unionization gained traction was the ski patrol—the one largely seasonal department with employees who returned year after year. Because Squaw Valley is a Class A avalanche resort, a big part of the job of the ski patrol is avalanche control. It is a job that takes years to learn because patrollers perform avalanche control all over the mountain under dramatically varying conditions before they develop the skills to correctly assess and effectively mitigate avalanche risk. Of course, it is a dangerous job, as well.

The Squaw Valley Ski Patrol had been in contact with the patrol at Heavenly Valley, which was considering, along with a bunch of the Heavenly mechanics and electricians, joining the Teamsters Union. The ski patrol director and assistant director came to me and told me that the patrollers were serious about joining the union as a means of improving their wages, benefits, and working conditions. My belief was that adding a third party to negotiate on behalf of the employees would add a lot of unneeded complexity to the situation, and that the employees—while paying union dues every month—would be no better off financially than they were now. I told them that I thought someone from the company should have the opportunity to meet with the ski patrol members before they voted, and hear what they had to say, give them management's position on the matter, and make sure that a true majority of the group was in favor of it, and that no one was being coerced. The patrol director agreed.

I called Alex and told him about the situation.

"Oh, no—we don't want that," he said. "You have to talk them out of it."

"Me?" I said. "Why don't you send Nancy; she's the lawyer."

"Oh no," he said. "That would be a disaster. You talk to them."

I arranged to meet the patrollers in Bar 6 that afternoon. They were all there, along with the mountain manager, Jimmy King. I talked to them for two hours—no one else said anything. I do not think I had ever talked for two hours before in my life. I told them how important we believed their work was and how much everyone who worked at Squaw depended on them and respected them. I told them that—when it came to seasonal employees—they were already at the top of the salary scale and because of that, even if they entered into a collective bargaining agreement with the union negotiating on their behalf, it was unlikely that wages would increase enough to offset the dues that they would have to pay to the union. I reminded them that during storm periods, they received a significant amount of overtime pay, and that because union dues are typically a fixed amount per member per month, the union's agenda would be to hire more people, which would dilute the earnings of existing employees, rather than increasing them.

When I was done, they said that they were going to discuss the idea further and would get back to me with their decision. I really did not know if I had made much of an impression or not—it was a difficult group to read. The ski patrollers went to the Cantina to continue the discussion, because it provided the opportunity to meet in somewhat more private surroundings. I got a call from the ski patrol director later that night to tell me that the patrollers had voted against the idea of joining the union, so I guess what I said made sense to them and they believed that I had their best interests at heart, which is what I believed, too.

36

Janek Kunczynski, Part 2

My relationship with Jan Kunczynski, if not warm, was at least one of mutual respect. After the Squaw Valley Tram accident, Jan was one of the only people who would help us get the lift operating again—he was instrumental in achieving that goal and I appreciated it. I could not really blame Jan in 1983 when he successfully pitched Alex to build a prototype gondola at Squaw Valley: My attempts to persuade Alex to buy a proven product from Doppelmayr fell on deaf ears—Jan was married to Alex's daughter, Lily, and more than that, he was a great salesman.

When the "Yandola" turned out to be unreliable and a complete customer service disaster in its first year and Alex called me in a panic in the summer of 1984 telling me that he wanted to take the gondola out and replace it, I talked him off the ledge, assuring him that Jan would correct the deficiencies that had so plagued his centerpiece lift. I never said "I told you so," even though I had told him, in so many words, that the first year of operation of the prototype lift would be unreliable and a customer service disaster. Janek, however, never lifted a finger to fix the problems, ruining his relationship with one of his best customers. Jan was too busy building fifteen lifts around the country and installing another gondola— the only other one he would ever build—at Keystone, Colorado.

Jan was on to bigger and better things, and the Yandola had been only the beginning of his ambitions—but it was indicative of things to come at Lift Engineering. In hindsight, Jan's company and his personal reputation had reached their zenith in 1983. Things would be all downhill from there.

By the 1980s, Jan and Lift Engineering had developed a reputation for building a very solid, reliable fixed-grip chairlift that was sturdy, inexpensive, efficient to install, and straightforward to operate and maintain—and in high demand around the country. The electrical systems were sophisticated and innovative, and Jan found ways to improve the lift each year, both mechanically and aesthetically, which gave him a distinct advantage with resort owners. In the early '80s, the Yan lift was the best-selling chairlift in the U.S. Through the years, about 200 Yan fixed-grip chairlifts were constructed. At Squaw Valley, we had Yan lifts that have been installed three times in different locations and are still in service. Jan was not satisfied to keep building the same product, however, and started looking for ways to equal the cutting-edge lifts coming over from Europe. The detachable Doppelmayr triple we built at Mt. Bachelor put that resort on the map and showed resort owners what a detachable lift had to offer their guests.

Jan came up with a detachable chairlift design, using a grip sourced from another company, and did his first installation in 1985. Unfortunately, the excitement and acclaim that might have accompanied Jan's the first detachable lift from Lift Engineering was over-shadowed by an accident that winter at Keystone, Colorado when the bullwheel on the year-old Teller lift (a fixed-grip Yan triple chairlift) separated from the driveshaft at the top terminal and fell to the ground, killing two people and injuring forty-seven. Faulty welds on the bullwheel were blamed, and after Jan rebuilt the chair lift for nothing, Keystone renamed it. In a move that may or may not have been related, after a single year of operation, the resort dismantled the River Run gondola and replaced it with a gondola from Von Roll. Elsewhere, Yan detachables earned a poor reputation with ski resort operators for a variety of deficiencies; even so, Lift Engineering sold thirty-one of them between 1987 and 1995. Jan blamed bad maintenance for the problems.

In 1993, a fatal accident involving a Yan detachable chairlift at Sierra Ski Ranch near South Lake Tahoe, California took the life of a nine-year-old boy, and a 1995 accident on the Quicksilver lift at Whistler, British Columbia killed two people and injured eight others when chair slippage caused four chairs to fall from the haul rope. These accidents effectively put Lift Engineering out of business as lawsuits from the accidents forced the company into Chapter 11 bankruptcy.

Janek forged ahead. He had been working on a design for a "people mover" which would expand potential markets significantly beyond the ski industry, and had formed a new company called Yantrak to market, manufacture, and install the systems. In 1997, he got a contract from Las Vegas mogul Steve Wynn to build one of the elevated trains between the Bellagio, Mirage, and Monte Carlo hotel-casinos on the Las Vegas strip. While testing the system at his Carson City factory in February 1997, one of the units malfunctioned, kill-ing a Yantrak employee and injuring two others.

The final blow was a fatal accident at the Angel's Flight funicular in Los Angeles. In 1995, Yantrak had been hired by a company that had contracted to overhaul the almost century-old system (it first opened for business in 1901). While replacing the old equipment, Yantrak had requested variances from the approved design for the rebuild and lobbied hard to omit a track brake, claiming that, "This track brake is frequently eliminated on modern high-speed (more than ten meters per second) tramways." Parsons Brinckerhoff, which had designed the drive system, argued that some sort of emergency braking system or backup cable had to be provided in the event of a failure of the haul rope. In the end, the company hired to manage the project accepted the Yantrak installation even though no redundant safety systems were provided. Parsons washed their hands of the matter, stating:

> *"The submitted documents [see below] show evidence that the proposed design is not in compliance with the required scope of work as related to the safety of the system. As written, they pass on to the Owner, or his representative, the responsibilities/liabilities of a non-compliant and non-failsafe design."*[6]

The funicular reopened for passenger traffic in the winter of 1996. On February 1, 2001, an uncontrolled descent of the upper car resulted in the death of one passenger and injuries to 20 others. The National Transportation Safety Board found several factors that contributed to the accident—many related to the construction of the system by Yantrak, but several that could have been related to improper maintenance or operation by the operators. The accident was the last straw for Yantrak. Janek closed the company and moved to Mexico. It was an awkward and embarrassing final chapter for an engineer and a company that had started from scratch and achieved real success, contributing so much to the advancement of American ski resorts and the lift industry. It was a case of simple overreach; allowing ambition and financial consideration to overrule the duty of care and vigilance in engineering and quality control in manufacturing. That it had cost people their lives was tragic and horrible.

Squaw Valley, the End

In 2002, Squaw Valley appeared to be reaching its full potential. The Village at Squaw Valley—after years of wrangling and reluctance on the part of the community—had finally broken ground. The developer—Intrawest—had a track record of successful development in other resort communities and their staff had done a credible job of addressing the concerns of the Squaw Valley community and Placer County, which was no small achievement. The village was to be constructed in four phases, and Alex and Nancy had sold Intrawest the land for Phases I and II, which signaled that while Alex had always talked a good game about Squaw becoming a "destination" resort, for the first time there was reason to believe that it might happen. A company with significant holdings in other resort communities and the financial horsepower to purchase the land was a good bit more credible than the "joint venture" with Mainline almost thirty years previous. Alex enthusiastically promoted the new village in his season pass letter in May, promising that it would be "better than Whistler" and that, unlike Vail and Beaver Creek, there would be no "rumbling of interstate trucks here."

Of course, Alex could never allow someone else's project to overshadow his own, so he dangled the prospects of a 100-room hotel at High Camp, the forty-room "Schloss Burkhart," and a funicular linking Gold

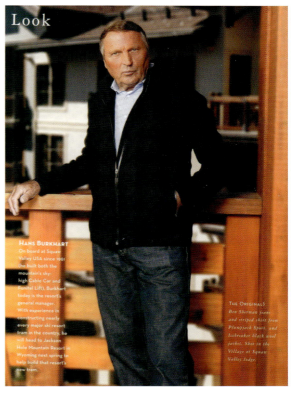

I was photographed for a fashion feature in Reno Magazine—the beginning and end of my modeling career!

Coast, High Camp, and the two upper-mountain lodging properties, as well as a detachable six-passenger chairlift on Shirley Lake, a detachable quad on Links, and other projects. He announced a reorganization of the management of the company to achieve these projects—Ernst Hager would take over as general manager and I would oversee the construction of the new amenities. Alex used typically effusive language in making this announcement, calling me his "friend of over forty years" and "a great mountain man, who has been principally responsible for all we have built in Squaw Valley over the last forty years."

Although Alex characterized the reorganization as a means of facilitating the construction of several complex projects, that was a small part of the overall picture. In truth, at almost ninety years of age, Alex's physical and mental abilities were declining, and Nancy was running the show. I had made it clear that I worked for Alex, not Nancy, and the atmosphere between Nancy and me was increasingly poisonous as I watched her manipulate Alex to achieve her agenda. Even though Nancy had been in the picture for fifteen years at this point, her credibility with the employees was still poor—they saw right through her, and the transition from my management to Ernst's brought their opinion of her to a new level of cynicism. The transition was widely regarded as another step toward Nancy taking full control of the company—it was obvious that the idea of reorganization had originated with Nancy, not Alex. While Alex may have been sold the idea that it would expedite completion of the projects that were so important to him—and while I went along with it on that basis—it was widely understood that Ernst would be forced to accept that he worked for Nancy, not Alex, and that was the real motivation for the change. Ernst was between a rock and a hard place if he wanted to be general manager. Nancy was always "on-message" and her relentless efforts to undermine my authority in the company and my credibility with Alex were a distraction from the work I needed to be doing. I hoped that the transition would take the heat off me by putting the general manager under her direction and would allow me to perform the work that interested me most with a minimum of drama or interference, which had been considerable.

Squaw Valley Ski Corporation's business operations were always short of space. At the west end of Olympic Valley, there was no place to build new buildings without displacing either skiing or parking. The shortage of space was so profound that when Tony Reid was CFO of the company, his office was literally in a stairwell in the Cable Car building, and there were offices, employee locker rooms, and other functions shoehorned into virtually every nook and cranny throughout the company. At a particular premium was workshop space—the vehicle and lift mechanics worked in extremely crowded conditions at both the top of the mountain and the base area. As a result, when there was a special project, it was not unusual to use my yard and shop space in Verdi to rebuild things like the carriages for the tram, fabricate towers as we had for the Funitel, and warehouse lift components that had been taken out of service—or to store heavy equipment and vehicles for the winter. The Verdi yard is only about thirty-five miles from Squaw Valley, and receives a fraction of the snowfall that the ski resort typically sees, so it was a practical solution to Squaw's chronic overcrowding for maintenance and storage functions.

Nancy's lack of understanding of the "nuts and bolts" functions of the business led her to think that the use of the Verdi yard—and the Squaw Valley employees who occasionally drove there to work on Squaw Valley's equipment—personally benefitted me. She went so far as to order an accounting department manager to spy on me and report to her anytime a Squaw Valley employee or vehicle went to Verdi. Neither Alex nor Nancy had ever been to Verdi and did not understand that it was, for all intents, an extension of the company's facilities. They made it sound as if work performed there was in some way inappropriate. This was a sneaky way to undermine my relationship with Alex and to insult and discourage me. The spy from the accounting department apologized to me for his role in it: "I was only doing what she told me", he said.

Consequently, when Alex called me in August of 2002 and asked me to come to his house in Newport, Rhode Island so we could formalize our plans for the transition and agreement for future work, I got on a plane. We had a good meeting and positive discussions about the various projects—the "Schloss" seemed to have new life and the funicular connecting Gold Coast and High Camp would be another first at a North American ski resort. Alex's old friend, architect Henrik Bull, had drawn up a rendering of an elegant hotel

One of Henrik Bull's concept drawings for a hotel at High Camp.

to be constructed north of the High Camp complex along the Tram Bowl with stunning views of Lake Tahoe and Shirley Canyon. The large, mainstream hotel operated by Hyatt or Marriott would complement the Schloss and give prospective upper-mountain guests more variety in lodging and dining, and the funicular and funitel would provide weather-resistant, twenty-four-hour access.

The Newport house was right on the water, and Alex would swim in the ocean every day. He invited me to go for a swim one day, and even though the ocean there is very cold, I agreed. It turned out to be less of a "swim" and more a "dash into the water, get wet, and dash back out." The result of the meeting was a seven-point agreement covering the projects, my compensation, the transition to Ernst as general manager, office space, a vehicle, and an assurance that I would be on-call for major maintenance and repairs for the funitel and tram. The agreement did not appear on paper until early November, and neither of us ever signed it, but it was an agreeable framework for my continued employment with the company, and I continued to do my job even though the agreement was unsigned.

November 23, 2002—a Saturday evening—I went over to the Blue House to meet with Alex about a few items. Ernst was easing into the general manager role, and he was well regarded by the employees, understood the operation well, and would be thoughtful and deliberate about making changes. Nancy answered the door and as I walked in, I mentioned that I had not been paid on Friday, thinking that there was a glitch in the payroll because of the transition. "That's because you didn't do anything," she said. I was temporarily speechless, because no one had ever said anything like that to me in my life. I had always worked hard, given excellent value for what I was paid, and prided myself on over-delivering, if anything. I chalked it up to Nancy's snarky personality.

I went into the living room, where Alex was waiting. For a few years, the understanding had been that to get Alex at his sharpest, you had to see him in the morning, because he tired during the day and would be less "with it" in the afternoon. This was probably not a good time to talk to him, but I had no choice. Nancy's remark really offended me, and while Alex knew very well that we did not get along, he and I had an agreement and I expected him to honor it.

"Alex," I said, "I went along with this reorganization because it's what you wanted and so that I had the time and flexibility to manage the projects. I have always delivered for you no matter what it demanded of me personally, but I do expect to be paid."

"You didn't do anything—that's why you didn't get paid," came Nancy's voice from the other room.

"That's right," Alex parroted: "You didn't do anything."

"Alex," I said, "I'm done. That's bullshit and you know it. Nancy has wanted to get rid of me for years, but I always thought you trusted me and could see through her lies. If you can no longer do that, I can't work for you. After almost forty years, you should know better. I don't want your money and I'm not interested in doing any more projects for you, so don't call me."

I left and never spoke to or saw Alex again. I couldn't really be mad with him because he had become so susceptible to Nancy's influence in his final years. He had been lucky rather than clever

Alex died of pneumonia in August 2006 while in Newport. He was ninety-three. There was a funeral for him there and I called Nancy and said that I would like to attend, but she told me I would not be welcome. Squaw Valley held a large, outdoor memorial service for him several months later which was attended by several hundred people: current and former employees, long-time Squaw Valley skiers, and members of the community with whom Alex had quarreled for decades. It was a diverse crowd, and it was appropriate that it would be composed of some who saw Alex as a hero, some for whom he was a villain, and many who had seen him in each role at different times.

The memorial was held on a sundeck on the site of the lower terminal of the three Squaw Valley gondolas: the original 1963 PHB installation that had brought me to the valley and given me my first job for Squaw Valley Ski Corporation, the "Yandola" that had prompted my departure in 1983, and the Poma gondola that brought me back in 1985. It was fitting, too, that the Funitel went right above the audience for Alex's memorial. My last major project for him, and one of my most challenging, had once again put Alex and Squaw Valley at the very forefront of the ski industry.

Alex's death brought into sharp focus the uneasy relationship between Nancy and Alex's three daughters from his first marriage. Ownership of the land and improvements that comprised Squaw Valley USA was divided among several corporations, including Squaw Valley Development Company and Squaw Valley Preserve. Alex had raised capital to start building the ski resort in the 1940s by selling shares of stock, and had created trusts for his first wife, Justine, their daughters and, later, his grandchildren. The trusts, combined with his own stock holdings (also held in a trust), represented a voting majority of the shares of stock. Alex had frequently bragged in his season pass letters that he had reinvested every dime of profit and that his shareholders had never been paid a dividend, which was true. Thanks to this, the total value of Squaw Valley's stock had gone from less than a half million dollars in 1949 to upwards of a hundred million dollars in the 2000s. Now that Alex was gone, his heirs and other investors were wondering when they would start to see some return on their inheritances or their investments. Alex had frequently told me that he had set up the trusts so that "Squaw Valley can never be sold." As ski areas across the country were being acquired by a small handful of large corporations, it was his hope that Squaw Valley could continue to be a family operation. Nancy seems to have been committed to this as well, because as the beneficiaries of the family trusts—Alex's children and grandchildren—sought to secure some financial benefit of their grandfather's vision and hard work, she appears to have fought them tooth and nail.

A problem was that the family trusts had been run in a somewhat sloppy manner through the years. When Alex had set up his own trust and one for Justine in 1973, the documents establishing the trusts had specified that a trustee could serve only until the age of seventy, at which time they would—together with the other trustees—select a successor. Although all three of the original trustees—Alex and the other trustees—his friends Hazard Gillespie and Fran Breen—had reached the age of 70 in 1983, 1982, and 1986 respectively, no successors had ever been named. In 2007, Nancy and Reno attorney G. David Robertson—the trustees for the nine other trusts Alex had created (one for each daughter and grandchild)—had petitioned the court to be designated trustees of all eleven family trusts, but Alex's daughters and grandchildren—the "beneficiaries"—had filed a formal objection with the court. Since the majority of Squaw Valley stock was held by the family, it amounted to a major shareholder revolt. The fact of the revolt and the details have been cloaked in secrecy.

According to court documents, Alex's daughters had on many occasions asked Alex—and later the trustees—for financial help and had been turned down. While they were all millionaires on paper, the manner in which the corporation was operated didn't afford the beneficiaries of the trusts with dividends or other ongoing financial benefit from their inheritance. As he had since the founding of the company, Alex—and later his board of directors—had reinvested every dime of profit. The Squaw Valley accounting department paid Alex's bills, but his daughters, as they started families, bought homes and incurred private school and college tuition costs and the other costs of ordinary life, had financial needs that would have been much more readily managed had they received some financial benefit from the company that would eventually become their inheritance.

In 1998, with Lift Engineering on the ropes as a result of the fatal accidents on several detachable chairlifts and the Yantrak people-mover system, Jan and Lily Kunczynski tried to sell their Squaw Valley stock to raise capital with which to keep the company solvent. They first offered to sell the stock back to Squaw Valley, but the offer was rejected. Vail Associates was willing to buy some of the stock and to provide a loan against other shares encumbered in a voting trust, but Nancy and Alex filed suit to prevent the sale, claiming that the Kunczynskis had agreed to be part of a voting trust and, while that agreement would expire within months, the Kunczynskis had a duty to renew it. The Cushings further asked the court to require the Kunczynskis to forfeit their stock holdings back to Alex's ownership. While the court eventually ruled in favor of the Kunczynskis, the delay and complexity created by the lawsuit effectively killed the deal with Vail Associates and contributed to the collapse of Lift Engineering.

The crux of the objection by the beneficiaries in the 2007 case was that as trustees, Nancy, Robertson, and Lee DiPietro (the third trustee and the husband of a Cushing cousin) had not adequately represented the interests of the beneficiaries, and had failed to exercise the fiduciary duty required of them. The beneficiaries alleged that the trustees had, on several occasions, acted in a deceptive or adversarial manner to the detriment of the beneficiaries. The family had requested representation on the Squaw Valley Board of Directors: they believed that since they were the largest bloc of shareholders, they deserved a voice in determining the future of the company. The trustees countered with an offer to give the family a seat on the board provided family members agreed to take no legal action against the board of directors or trustees for five years.

A reverse stock split gave the Board of Directors the opportunity to rid itself of a few dozen small shareholders and potentially provide enough of a financial benefit to family members to shut them up for a while. The outstanding shares were split 400-to-one—the pre-split share value of $35 had been determined by an "extensive appraisal"[7] which suggested a range in value of $32.69 to $35.51 per pre-split share. Shareholders with more than 400 shares of stock were to be given one "post-split" share—valued at $14,000—for every 400 shares owned, and were paid cash for the balance of their position, while shareholders owning fewer than 400 shares were paid off at $35 per share for their holding. After almost sixty years, some shareholders finally saw a return on their investment!

The valuation was not universally hailed as generous. It was based on an overall estimate of $88 million for Squaw Valley, while the actual value was believed by many to be a good bit higher. While the expenditure of up to $7 million to buy back shares from as many shareholders as could be accommodated by that budget doubtless tidied up the bookkeeping for the company, it also increased the percentage of shares under the direction of trustees of the various trusts from 49 percent to 53 percent, a consideration that had to have been significant in the decision to make the offer.

The reverse split and tender offer did little to diminish the concerns of Alex's daughters, although they probably received a little cash as a result of the "rounding" to blocks of 400 shares. They had little to show for the tremendous success of the family business, and their requests to the trusts for financial assistance in the form of a dividend had consistently been rejected, even though the trusts had been established to pay "for the education, comfort, support, or maintenance[8]" of beneficiaries of the trusts. Members of the family trusts were by no means the only shareholders who were disenchanted with the machinations of the Board. Clinton Frye, Jr., executor of the Laurance Rockefeller Estate (Rockefeller had been one of the very first investors in Squaw Valley), was very frank in his comments on the management of the corporation. In a letter to G. David Robertson, Frye wrote:

"You imply that Laurance Rockefeller should have been pleased with his investment. I can tell you that he was not. Investments in new ventures carry high risks, and are justified only by much higher returns than are expected by established companies on the stock market, and that is what he expected. Mr. Rockefeller's investment was instrumental in attracting other investors, in giving Alex Cushing credibility in making his Olympic bid, and, at various times, in bailing out Cushing from various liquidity crises. What Mr. Rockefeller received, despite periodic urging, was basically nothing—an interest in an illiquid property run as a monument to Alex Cushing, or perhaps, to benefit insiders, but certainly not to benefit the shareholders."

Frye concluded his letter:

"Your enthusiasm for Squaw Valley jumps off the page, as if it were self-evident that every shareholder should be grateful for the stewardship of this Board. No shareholder I know agrees with this."

Despite a lengthy discussion in the court filings of the trustees' failures to execute their fiduciary duty to Alex's children and grandchildren, and detailed rebuttals on the part of Nancy and Robertson, I never found out how the case resolved. I heard that it was going to go to trial in Minden, Nevada. (Although several of the trusts had been set up in New York, the trustees had moved the "situs" or legal jurisdiction for the trusts, to Douglas County, Nevada—rather inconvenient for the beneficiaries residing in New York). I drove over to Minden and had a short but pleasant visit with Alex's daughters Justine, Lily, and Alexandra in the hallway of the courthouse, but then Dave Robertson came up and told me I wouldn't be allowed in the courtroom and that there would be no trial, because they had "settled."

Nancy continued her role as president of the company for a couple of years and then brought in Andy Wirth from Steamboat Springs in July of 2010—a move publicly billed as her "retirement." Wirth had come up through the ranks at Steamboat and had worked there for twenty years when Steamboat was acquired by Intrawest in 2006.

For several decades, a large black on chrome rendering of the Time Magazine cover of Alex Cushing had hung in the lobby of the Tram Building. It was a fitting location for such a tribute, because the Tram was such an icon: It had been a symbol of distinction and success for Cushing and the company and had also been the site of tragedy and humiliation. Cushing's portrait, high on the wall in the Tram lobby was the first thing you saw as you came up the stairs and stepped into the three-story tall space and it was an imposing sight— the Founder as a young man looking down in approval on his creation. After Andy Wirth took over as President of the company, the plaque suddenly disappeared. Nancy simply had to have been consulted about the removal of the tribute to Alex, and to the Squaw Valley faithful, it was shocking and revealing that the Founder could be tossed aside so casually.

Clearly, big changes were in the wind in the valley, although it was a shock when it was announced in November that KSL Capital Partners was the new owner of Squaw Valley. What had tipped the balance and led to such a dramatic move on the part of the Squaw Valley Board of Directors, all of whom understood and presumably agreed with Alex's conviction—which he had expressed so many times and with such passion to me—that Squaw Valley would never be sold? Did the shareholder revolt move the board in that direction? Did pressure from the family provide Nancy the cover she needed to make the sale? There are people who know, and someday the whole story will be revealed.

As he had in Steamboat Springs, Andy Wirth went to work for the new owners without missing a beat. One day shortly after he had taken over the presidency of the company, I stopped by Andy's office to say hello and offer my assistance any time it was needed. I knew that Nancy had been able to provide a limited amount of information, since she had been in the picture only since the '80s, and I could provide more background on the operations of the resort, which had never been her strength.

Andy was cordial in meeting me—he clearly had read up on the history of the company and understood my role in bringing Alex's ideas to fruition and in the daily operation of the resort year-round for decades. We talked about the company, the great employees who, in some cases, had devoted decades of their lives to making Squaw Valley a success, and the devotion of Squaw's skiers to the mountain and the unique experience it offered. I told Andy to feel free to give me a call if I could ever provide any advice or assistance. He replied, "I've got this under control. Piece of cake."

I was shocked. It had been fifty years since I had first set foot in Squaw Valley at the 1960 Olympics, and any time I thought I had seen everything the mountain could dish out, a new and humbling surprise would come along to set me straight. That someone in the CEO role at a mountain that was totally new to them would be so casually dismissive of an open offer of assistance meant that they were either a genius or hopelessly stupid.

...I found myself acutely aware of the dangers of overcrowding at Squaw. Nothing we could ever build in the future could equal what we already have... Our Valley is certainly one of the most beautiful places in the world. Bumper to bumper traffic all day long is not in our future. Because we control over 4,000 acres, we can keep it that way, and we intend to do so. No further development for an indefinite period, except for environmental projects... Our emphasis will be in beautifying what we have. The Village is the right size and will remain as it is for the foreseeable future.

Alex Cushing, from a Squaw Valley newsletter

Golden Sage

The story of Golden Sage is complicated, confusing and packed with frustrating, factual experience. I include it in the hope that my children, grandchildren and other readers can learn from my discouraging and costly experience and not have to go through something similar. If you ever need to hire an attorney, be very careful about choosing the right one. If a friend or relative offers their services, don't hire that person. Nine times out of ten that does not work and could turn into an absolute nightmare—no different than doing other business with family or close friends—it's simply a bad idea.

I have been involved in both situations and regret the experience to the point that I feel responsible to warn my children and grandchildren about the unpleasant facts of life. Should you need an attorney (a 'third party' only!), research their background and reputation and their experience relevant to your case. Too many attorneys think they know everything and that's where the problem starts. The attorney I hired and paid very well called me "my friend" and then forgot the most basic responsibility of an attorney: if you accept a client's case and their trust, work for them to the best of your ability, representing their interests to the exclusion of all others and telling them the truth. I have worked with many attorneys who have common sense, ethics and a moral compass and they have done good work for me, but, as this story illustrates, they are not all equally ethical or capable.

The attorney I hired to represent me in the Golden Sage transaction, despite decades of experience and that fact that we had a relationship of trust long before this story starts, failed miserably to exercise even the most basic duties to protect my interests. I cannot explain this breach of ethical and professional responsibility, I only hope you can learn from it at less expense than I did.

By the early 1990's, I had closed the trailer manufacturing business in Bend and found a tenant for the shop property when I went back to work for Alex at Squaw Valley. As the decade ended, I was busy at Squaw Valley with no time to devote to a piece of real estate 400 miles away. Bend had undergone tremendous growth and was now a large and remarkably successful town: it had come a long way since the early 80's when the lumber mill that was the primary economic engine in town had closed. Fortunately, people like Bill Healy had the vision to see the potential of a new economy based on tourism and technology and a revitalized Bend became one of the most desirable places to live in the Pacific Northwest and was a consistent "Top 10" choice in magazines rating the "Best Places to Live in America" and "America's Best Resort Communities." My shop property had appreciated quite a bit in value, and I sold it in April 1998. I started looking for land in which to reinvest the proceeds of the sale. The I.R.S. allows an exchange of business property without incurring capital gains tax provided the new property is acquired within only a few months, so the clock was ticking.

I looked at a few pieces of property in the area surrounding Reno before settling on a one square mile section of land south of Mt. Rose Highway in South Reno. The 640-acre parcel had the potential to be developed into high-end home sites with excellent views of Mount Rose, Washoe Lake and the city of Reno. There was a water tank on the parcel that could supply water to the lots and the rest of the utilities ran to the western edge of the parcel. I closed on the land in June, well within the I.R.S. 1031 tax exchange requirement. I felt that I had made a good investment, even if I did nothing with it right away.

After leaving Squaw Valley in November of 2002, I had the opportunity to start planning the development. I hired a Reno engineering company to survey and map the parcel, designed a street network and bought water rights for the lots. There would be 37 generously sized lots for custom homes, all with excellent and unique views. There was shopping nearby, an excellent golf course at Montreux and the state was planning to extend Highway 395 beyond Mt. Rose Highway, so there would be limited-access freeway all the way from Reno to Carson City. Things were falling into place that would make this little subdivision a very desirable location: you could be at the Reno Airport or in the parking lot of the Mt. Rose ski area in about 15 minutes, in downtown Reno or Carson City in about 20 minutes, at Lake Tahoe in about 25 minutes.

Although the planning and permitting process was lengthy—I even had to get aviation rights, because the departure pattern from Reno-Tahoe Airport goes right over the property—I was enjoying the challenge

The view from the Golden Sage site looking south toward Washoe Lake and Carson City.

of the project. By the time the planning and permitting were just about complete in 2004, I had invested about $2.4 million. I was so engrossed with the project by this point that when I got an offer for $6 million for the property with the engineering and permitting work we had done so far, I turned them down—I wanted to keep going and complete the work. At this point I was ready to start constructing infrastructure so I could sell lots. My engineering company, Stantec, had estimated $2.5 million with a 20% contingency to construct the improvements needed for 37 lots.

The next offer—for $9.6 million—stopped me in my tracks. The buyers were a pair of former executives who had done very well working in fields unrelated to real estate development and were looking for an investment—I'll call them "the Developer." I did not know that much about the intricacies of structuring a purchase and sales agreement and a promissory note for a deal this large, so in April 2005, I hired a lawyer, whom I'll refer to as "the Attorney", to write the sales and loan documents. The purchase agreement was signed on January 31, 2006, and the promissory note on February 27, 2006.

Later in 2006, the Developer contacted me and said that they were planning to decrease the lot size and increase the total number to over 300. They would need to provide a second means of ingress and egress, because while the homeowners along Fawn Lane had no issue with the minimally increased traffic impact the 37-lot subdivision I had proposed would have created, a subdivision of more than 300 new homes was a whole different matter. Homeowners along Fawn Lane had made quite a fuss at the County meeting to consider the project. The Developer believed they could provide a second means of access by purchasing a piece of undeveloped property on the Mt. Rose Highway that was owned by a church and then building a mile of road through National Forest land before reaching the subdivision, but they also needed new engineering, and would need to buy additional water rights before they could propose a new tentative map. The bottom line was that they needed to borrow $3.7 million for the new work. They had a lender who would loan the money, but the lender wanted the promissory note that the buyers had issued to me to be 'subordinate' to the new loan. I did not understand the implications of this proposal, so I turned to my attorney, who pointed out that increasing the number of lots would significantly increase the value of the project, but that this was only possible if the Developer could fund the water rights and engineering work that would allow the project to be permitted by Washoe County. Once the permitting was approved, the Developer could start selling lots, generate cash flow and continue making payments to me.

The Attorney was very clear that allowing the subordination was necessary to keep the modified project moving ahead, which is how it would allow the Developer to sell lots and make payments to me. He admitted that there was an element of risk, but risk is present in every aspect of life—calculating the degree of risk for one option against the risk of another option is why we hire experts to assist us in business transactions. A reasonable person does research to assess the risk, however, and I later discovered that the Attorney had done nothing to assess the risk that the subordination agreement presented, had done no research on the Developer's financial situation or their ability to meet the increased financial obligations created by the new loan or how the Developer had determined that $3.75 million was an adequate amount to get the project to the point where it would be able to generate revenue or how the loan proceeds would be utilized—nothing. The Attorney did not advise me to hire someone to research or investigate those or any other questions.

Another unpleasant surprise that would be revealed later was that the Developer did not have an attorney—it appears that the Attorney was representing us both, because invoices sent to me for legal work associated with the project had been paid by someone other than me—tens of thousands of dollars in fees. On October 26, 2006, the Attorney stated in an evening email to the Developer, "I have worked extensively with Hans on the refi issue…." The Developer replies a few minutes later saying, "…you must realize I am in the unfortunate position where I must make this deal with Hans" and "…any help you could provide to get Hans back to the table… would be most welcome." The following day, the Attorney e-mailed, "Hans is trying to work with you as best is possible, however understandably is concerned about subordinated debt being placed on the property." The Developer responds, "Thanks for taking the time with Hans to put this together." I had to wonder whose interests the Attorney was representing—mine or those of the Developer—there seemed to be a conflict of interest. In addition, it appeared that the Attorney was involved in negotiating the purchase of water rights for the project—I know this because I was mistakenly sent the invoice for the Attorney's work in negotiating water rights on behalf of the Developer. It appeared that the Attorney was working for multiple parties involved in the transaction—a very profitable arrangement for him.

I signed the subordination agreement on November 21, 2006—the same day that the Developer signed a promissory note and received the $3.75 million in funding from their lender—the "Third Party", providing the Developer the funding they needed to get the project rolling… or so I thought.

Looking north at the Golden Sage site.

This money could have been impounded or placed in an escrow account, then distributed only for specific, project-related purposes to provide security despite the subordination, but the Attorney never suggested such a measure, which would have provided me a measure of protection.

Things proceeded normally for 18 months. Payments from the Developer arrived on time, and it seemed as if the drama was behind us. In February of 2008, I had a call from the Third Party, who asked about the church property at Thomas Creek Road and Mt. Rose Highway. During the conversation, the Third Party asked who was doing my legal work. "The Attorney," I replied. There was an uncomfortable pause and then the Third Party said, "Oh. He's my lawyer, too."

The check for the April 2008 payment from the Developer was returned by the bank because of insufficient funds, so I called the Developer to ask what was happening. The Developer sent another check for April which deposited with no problem, but in May— while I was in Jackson Hole—no payment arrived. I called the Developer and he said, "I'm out of money, but I'm going to recapitalize, so it should be no problem if you just give me some more time." I called the Attorney, told him what was happening and asked what I should do. The Attorney said that it was too complicated to discuss on the phone, but that he would send me a letter explaining my options.

At the end of May, I received a memorandum written by a different attorney at the Attorney's firm who, to the best of my knowledge had no previous involvement with the project. The memorandum provided a detailed explanation of the different situations that might follow. The oddity of this memo was that it required that the writer to have "examined" and "reviewed" the documents governing the transactions—documents that had been written by the Attorney, whom I had paid to write them. It was as if the law firm was seeing them for the first time and was trying to figure out the financial and legal implications that the documents created for me. It seemed like they should have understood this.

While the Attorney had stated that there was 'some risk' in agreeing to the subordination agreement, what he had not bothered to explain was that if the Developer defaulted on his $3.75 million loan from the Third Party, the lender would get title to the land, and I would have to pay any monies the Developer owed to the Third Party to get the deed to the property back. The Attorney finally got around to telling me this—through his colleague— two years later when the deal had imploded. All of the signs pointed to a major conflict of interest, because the Attorney and his firm appeared to have been representing several parties in the transaction. Since I had hired them, I had the apparently quaint notion that I was entitled to their exclusive representation of my interests. When I brought this to their attention, a flurry of denial and backtracking ensued. They quickly sent me a letter hotly denying any conflict and claiming that they had, indeed, warned me of the risks of agreeing to the subordination agreement. The interesting thing is that in this letter there is no reference to documentation that would substantiate their claim that they had expressed serious reservations about the wisdom of allowing the subordination, a claim that *was* made in a subsequent letter from the firm, stating that a memorandum had been provided to me in "October 2006." I have never had an attorney refer to the date of a document in such vague terms—they always refer to a document by the *exact date* on which it was prepared, especially when many documents are being sent within a short period of time. I was immediately skeptical of this statement because it had never been mentioned previously and I had never seen such a memorandum. I asked for a copy of it. When I had not received anything several weeks later, I called and again requested a copy of the memo, which I finally received seven months after I initially confronted the Attorney about his failure to adequately represent my interests in the subordination. It seemed very suspicious that it took until January 19, 2010 to find a copy of a memorandum that had supposed been written on October 18, 2006.

The other thing that convinced me that the memorandum was back-dated was the fact that I had been billed $1,386.50 in May of 2008 to "review the file" and "consider strategy and prepare memo" concerning issues that had supposedly been explicitly addressed in the October 18, 2006 memorandum written by the same attorney.

I am convinced that the fact that their first letter made no mention of any such memorandum, the second letter claimed that one had been provided to me but didn't specify a particular date and the lengthy delay in finally producing the document indicates to me that the memorandum was created more than two years after they claim it was written and was backdated to cover their tracks.

When confronted about the Third Party's statement that the Attorney "…is my lawyer, too", I received two separate letters denying any conflict of interest in that relationship, because the Attorney claimed that the Third Party's company had not been a client of his law firm at the time, but the law firm seems to have trouble keeping a story straight because each letter claimed a different starting date for their representation of the Third Party's company: one was August 31, 2007 and the other claimed that the Third Party or his company were not their clients until "the fall of 2009"—a pretty wide range of dates. The denials of responsibility in these letters are remarkable reading, if only for the creativity with which they attempt to absolve the firm of any responsibility. In one letter the Attorney claims to never have given "business" advice, but this contradicts their statements about the subordination agreement permitting development and lot sales to proceed, providing the developers with the ability to resume making payments to me. In addition, one of the letters suggests that had they advised against subordination, I probably would have acted contrary to their advice—the Attorney wrote, "Even if I had strongly counseled you not to agree to subordination, would you have accepted my advice or be in a better position today? I don't think so." "Even if I had" sounds very much like "…although I did not" to me. The unfortunate fact is that I always followed their advice, which turned out to be a disaster. They spent a lot of time and ink blaming the entire situation on the 2008 downturn in the real estate market, which had little bearing on my situation. The bottom line was, if I had not followed their advice, I would have retained the land and the money invested in my ability to develop it.

The Developer subsequently declared bankruptcy. In order to have any hope of preserving my standing as a creditor, I needed to hire a bankruptcy attorney. Despite's the Developer's repeated pleas to give him more time to attempt to "recapitalize", the lender had foreclosed and taken title to the land. The only way I could get it back would be if I paid the balance of the Developer's loan to the Third Party, as well as the past-due interest and property taxes on the land—several hundred thousand dollars owed to Washoe County—which the Developer had never paid, and which could have been reserved out of the loan proceeds from the Third Party as a condition of the subordination. The total would have been about $4 million to get back the land that rightly belonged to me. I investigated getting a short-term 'bridge loan', but it was 2008 and the financial markets were quickly headed for an epic meltdown as a result of incautious real-estate lending—the worst possible time to look for somewhat unconventional financing.

To make the situation even more complex, the lender's title company eventually held an auction to dispose of the property. My understanding is that the Third Party was the successful bidder at the auction, which seems strange until you consider that the property would be reassessed by the County to the auction sale price—$600,000—and the property taxes would be reduced by a significant margin.

To this day, although a new parcel map was issued, dividing the property into five parcels—the largest of which is still owned by the Third Party—the property has not been developed to this day.

The bottom line in this sad story is if I hire an attorney and pay them a lot of money—literally tens of thousands of dollars in this case—I have every right to expect that they will represent me exclusively and to the very best of their knowledge and ability. It would have been a simple matter to research the Developer's financial situation and let me know that it was precarious and that they had little or no reserve with which to make payments on the additional financing on which they depended and if they defaulted, how that would affect title to land that I owned. The attorney in this case had my trust, was given full authority to act on my behalf and— despite decades of experience—failed miserably.

Home Building

Verdi

It's in my nature to always want to have a project—something to be working on and thinking about—and most of the time there is more than one. I had purchased some land in Verdi—a building lot in an upscale gated community and property on the hillside behind it—and I came up with the idea of building a log home. A log home would be very different from the other homes in the neighborhood, but I thought it would be a really good fit in the setting where the foothills of the eastern Sierra Nevada give way to the desert, and it would be historically accurate as well. By this time in 2003, there were a lot of companies marketing log homes, and there was a lot of information about the types of logs to use, different fitting methods, how to assemble the structure once it was delivered to the site—it was an interesting and absorbing process with a lot of options. I looked at a lot of floorplans and pictures, but I couldn't find anything that exactly matched my vision for the home that the building site needed, so I started working with an architect in Boise who had designed a lot of log homes, and we developed a plan that would be perfect for the location. It would take advantage of the dramatic views of Verdi Peak and the Truckee River Canyon to the south and nestle against the foothills of Peavine Peak, which sloped down to the back of the site.

There were a lot of log home vendors who would build a home according to the drawings. They'd fit and stack all of the logs, then disassemble the structure and truck it to the building site to be assembled and finished. The company that most appealed to me was located in British Columbia. It was a Canadian First Nation tribe that built log homes as one of their tribal businesses. I flew up to Kelowna, B.C. and drove out to their plant to watch the process and talk about my project with them. The key to building a quality log home is the care and skill with which the log for a particular location is selected and fitted. It takes a long time to be able to look at a stack of logs and select the correct one, and then place it, scribe it, and fit it to the log below. The Canadians were very patient in the fitting process; stacking and removing each log, trimming a little here and there, then restacking

The construction of the Verdi house started with footings formed on the site, stacking the pre-cut logs and finally the logs stacked and ready for rafter framing.

and checking the fit until it was correct. I was impressed with the quality of the logs they were using—it was all dry "standing dead" timber that had been part of a large area of beetle kill—and the craftsmanship that the finished product displayed was exactly what I was after. I gave them the plans and placed an order that would take months of painstaking work on their part to fill.

Although the logs were delivered—seven truckloads of them—for the following building season, we stacked them in the Verdi yard for a year so that they could dry to the local climate and stabilize before stacking them. This is a crucial step that is often omitted when building a log home, and I was determined to be patient and respect the materials to get the best possible outcome. Log homes that have survived for hundreds of years were not built using chain saws, mechanized skidders, and cranes, and the slow, methodical manner in which their builders were forced to build them contributed to the craftsmanship and durability of the finished structure. We didn't need to be in a hurry—there was plenty of work to be finished on the site while the logs dried from the moist climate of British Columbia to the extremely arid surroundings of western Nevada.

We levelled the building site, installed utilities, and dug footings for the house, then poured a slab gridded with hydronic heat tubing and all of the utilities for the house stubbed out where they would be extended up into the walls. Electricians hate wiring log houses,

The Verdi house with the upper of two ponds on the south side. To the left is an outdoor dining room.

The north side of the Verdi house has a large salt-water pool, hot tub and waterfall.

because the process is so much slower than pulling wire through exposed stud bays in frame homes. Each log has to be drilled and a pull string fished through, and there is a lot of standing around waiting for the next log to be placed. I was lucky enough to find a German electrician in Verdi who was willing to learn how to do it, and Hardy was the mastermind for the hydronic and boiler system that would heat the house.

One man came down from British Columbia to help us assemble the house and—while you might think he would come with a truckload of specialized tools—he arrived on a plane with only a suitcase and a loop of chainsaw chain. He told us what kind of chainsaw he needed (Stihl 066) and what length bar it should have, however. He was a tremendous help in deciphering the marking system, which was critical to bringing the logs to the site in the sequence needed, to say nothing of stacking them correctly. Each log was then drilled and pinned to the logs below it with long steel pins. The chinking—filling the spaces between the logs with a flexible material that allowed some movement while weatherproofing the wall—took four months. Anika helped with it, and got to be very skilled!

It was quite a project and the house turned out to be magnificent, highly functional, and extremely comfortable. Allowing the logs to dry and stabilize for a year was an excellent decision. Between the patient approach to the execution of the project and the use of a unique mortised window mount, there was never a problem with the home settling—the windows and doors have always worked perfectly, which is a rarity in log homes.

We built two ponds in the front yard and a waterfall and swimming pool in the back, which my grandchildren enjoy very much. The deer and other wildlife that inhabit the hillside behind the house pay little attention to any of us.

Oberammergau

In the mid- 2000s, my daughter Kathrin expressed interest in spending time in Europe each summer while her three children were on vacation from school. They could get to know their cousins in Oberammergau, learn German, and develop direct knowledge and connection with the culture and family that been such a great influence in my childhood. Naturally, I thought this was a wonderful idea—my brothers and sisters still lived in the area and their grandkids and mine were similar ages. Oberammergau was still a pretty small town and it would be a nurturing and safe environment for the kids to explore and enjoy. I didn't want Kathrin and her family to have to stay with family members, though, so we cooked up the idea of building a house there that everyone could use when they were in Europe—it could be our vacation house and home base for travel elsewhere.

Kathrin pointed out that her cousins in Oberammergau spent a big chunk of their incomes renting apartments in town, and suggested that we add a couple of apartments to the house so that they had a comfortable place to live and weren't at the mercy of a landlord. It would provide income for the house, too, that could be used to pay a mortgage or recover the construction costs. It all made sense to me.

Kathrin, Anika and I took a trip to look at potential building sites and when we found one that was adjacent to an agricultural area that would never be developed and had a view of the mountain and the church in town, we knew it was the right one. A friend had

The Oberammergau house, seen from the street.

recommended an architect and I met with him and his wife, who was his working partner as well. She was about twenty years younger than he was and it didn't take me long to figure out that she was also the better architect. The first sets of sketched floorplans they gave me, though, reflected a very traditional, compartmented design—a kitchen, dining area and living room all in separate rooms off a hallway. I told them that I wanted it all open—no walls, no doors! They were taken aback at first—it was a real departure from the homes that they normally designed—but I had a lot of fun exchanging ideas with them. They were very detail-oriented and well organized and made efficient use of my time when I had flown all the way from San Francisco to meet with them. I planned to be the general contractor on the project and the architects were a good resource when it came to selecting subcontractors. The first contractor would do the excavation and concrete work for the basement and it was critical that they do an extremely careful job of waterproofing because of the groundwater level in the area. It was also a complex part of the job because there was a hot tub, sauna and wine cellar with a vaulted ceiling in the basement. The architects recommended a couple of companies and I met with the contractors and picked the one that seemed the best—really crossing my fingers and making the decision based on a brief conversation and my gut feeling. It turned out to be a great decision: they did an excellent job and used a process I have never seen in home construction when they brought in portable silos for the bulk materials and mixed the concrete right on the site. The basement and several feet above grade on

Vaulted wine cellar in the Oberammergau house.

A few more views of the house in Oberammergau.

the first floor is formed, mono-poured concrete, the remaining portion of the first story exterior walls are concrete block and the second floor is timber-framed or "post and beam" wood with well-insulated engineered panels between the uprights. It is completely unlike most single-family home construction in the United States and is both attractive and energy efficient. I found a small lumber operation in a little country town that used a computer-aided process to mill and cut all the lumber, including the complex angles in the framing. Everything was pre-cut, so the carpentry work on-site was assembling the pieces—they built the entire roof in a single day. It was a remarkable process to watch.

I made a lot of trips between California and Germany in 2005—8 or 9 over the course of a year. I would drive from Tahoe to San Francisco and leave my car in the long-term parking lot near the San Francisco airport while I was in Europe and I bought a car in Germany and stored it with a company near the Munich airport that would bring it to the airport when I arrived and would put it back in storage when I left. I spent a tremendous amount of time selecting the components for the house—windows, doors, tile, electrical fixtures

One valuable byproduct of building the Oberammergau house was the opportunity to spend time in the mountains with family, like this outing with my sister Herta, my aunt Anny and daughters Kathrin and Anika—at 4,000 meters in the Alps.

and appliances. I went to Austria and picked out the models and finishes of light fixtures that I wanted in the showroom at the plant where they are manufactured—very different than buying 'Made in China' lighting fixtures at a Home Depot in the United States. The company that did the landscaping built a pond in the back yard with aquatic plants growing in it—the pond doubles as a swimming pool.

Although it was a complex and costly project, the quality of the subcontractors in Germany and the European focus on energy efficiency made it a very satisfying project. The windows on the cold side of the house are triple pane and the hydronic heat and domestic hot water are powered by a recycled wood pellet-fired boiler. There is a pellet room—a room-sized indoor hopper in the basement that automatically feeds the boiler with an automatic auger. The pellets are replenished each year by a truck that comes and fills the storage room. It turned out to be a very beautiful and comfortable home—the traditional exterior is in marked contrast to the modern, open interior design and amenities.

Once finished, the cousins moved into the apartments and were very happy with the size and the quality with which they had been designed and built, although they complained about the cost of utilities, so I absorbed some of the costs. Kathrin and her family went to Europe and spent a few days in the house that first summer on their way to Italy. I spent some time there as well, in between commitments in the U.S., but the house was not getting the amount of use that we had anticipated. My nephew Toni offered to manage it as a short-term rental—AirBnB or Vacation Rental by Owner—and we started advertising it on that basis, figuring that it would be one of the best properties in Oberammergau and that it would command a good rental rate. It was rented some of the time and got great reviews, but when Toni gave me a summary of the income versus the expense after the first few years of operation, I was shocked to find that I had netted a total of five Euros for five years of operation—we had a profit of exactly one Euro a year!

Meanwhile, Kathrin's kids were getting older and had busy schedules with commitments during their school vacations that didn't allow them to spend the summer in Europe, so I made the difficult decision to sell the house, it had been an interesting and absorbing project.

Jackson Hole Tram

Construction on the original Jackson Hole Tram started in 1964, and the lift opened in 1966, a year after the opening of the resort. The access to the terrain provided by the tram unlocked the potential of the resort. The original tram—like the 1964 aerial tramway at Grouse Mountain—was manufactured by a company called Voest. It had a capacity of fifty-three passengers and rose over 4,000 vertical feet in less than eleven minutes. To say that Jackson Hole skiers loved the tram would be an understatement—they were crazy about it—and the amount and quality of ski terrain it served was unsurpassed, even though the uphill capacity was *very* limited, about 260 passengers per hour. The tram was the only way to get to the top of the mountain and the lines for it could be very long, even though the original cabins had been replaced with sixty-two-passenger cabins in 1989. In 2005—after forty years of service—inspection of the track ropes determined that it was time for them to be replaced. As the resort considered the cost of replacement of the track ropes and the limited capacity of the lift, they concluded that a better alternative would be to replace the entire system with a tram with greater uphill capacity—larger cabins and higher speed. Garaventa was selected as the vendor for the new equipment.

I had known the original developers of Jackson Hole—Paul McCollister and Alex Morley—for some years. McCollister had done very well in the San Francisco Bay Area and had "retired" to Wyoming because he was in love with skiing and the Grand Tetons. McCollister had first been to the area on an elk hunting trip in 1942 and bought some land there ten years later. He started skiing in the Sierra in 1952 and, after attending the 1956 Olympics in Cortina, Italy, decided to sell his home in California, retire from his radio advertising sales job, and move to Wyoming to develop a ski resort. He became president of the Jackson Hole Ski Club, then formed a corporation to investigate the development of a ski resort. McCollister acquired land at the base of the mountain in the late 1950s and early '60s and, with investments from Alex Morley, a contractor from Cheyenne, Wyoming, and Gordon Graham, a business associate from California, formed the Jackson Hole Ski Corporation in 1963. They started construction in the spring of 1964 and opened for

The Jackson Hole area has a uniquely western heritage, echoed by this wonderful old barn with the magnificent Tetons in the background.

business in 1965. The original aerial tramway opened the following summer.

McCollister frequently came to Squaw Valley to ski in the spring and would stop at my office and chat. We would compare notes on the snow that winter and the kind of season that we had had, and his comments about Jackson Hole were always the same: "Too steep, too remote, and too cold!" Compared to Squaw Valley, he had a point.

After almost 30 years of "retirement" as a ski area operator in 1992, McCollister sold Jackson Hole resort to a family with huge coal-mining interests in southern Wyoming, the Kemmerers, who invested substantially in upgrades to the lift network and base area facilities. Like McCollister and Morley, they were actively involved in planning and operating the resort. Reducing the long lines for the tram and upgrading the lower terminal were priorities, so a larger, faster aerial tram following the same line was a logical evolution that would be easy for the U.S. Forest Service to approve. A documentary filmmaker—Peter Pilafian, who lived in nearby Wilson, Wyoming—believed that the tram was such a local icon that he followed the project from the last run of the old tramway to the first run of the new system and produced a film called "Cable to the Sky" that aired on the National Geographic network. It turned out to be a very interesting and detailed record of the project although at times a bit dramatic.

Construction on the new tram started as soon as the ski season ended in 2007. The top terminal was accessed by a long, very steep road, and it would have been virtually impossible to drive concrete trucks to the site, so Jackson Hole's concrete subcontractor and the resort came up with an ingenious system for transporting concrete for the new top terminal—use the old tram. They cut holes in the floors of the cabins, attached a hoist to the ceiling and, after an initial attempt at hauling buckets of concrete from the bottom to the top, settled on transporting huge bags of dry cement and aggregate mix to the site using the tram. The dry mix could then be stockpiled at the top and mixed as needed by emptying the bags into an all-wheel-drive concrete truck they had driven and towed to the site. The truck mixed the dry concrete and water just as it would normally be mixed at a batch plant, then poured the concrete into forms or a pump for placement. It was a creative and efficient way to provide a large quantity of concrete on-demand at a remote location without having to haul it in buckets with a helicopter. Although the Las Vegas-based concrete subcontractor had not yet finished the concrete work for the upper terminal by the end of the 2007 building season, the Garaventa crew took down the track ropes, spooled up the haul rope for later use, and dismantled the drive equipment at the base before returning to Switzerland for the winter.

I was contacted by Garaventa because they needed a crane operator for the project, and they were having some issues with the crew. I asked enough questions to figure out how large a crane we would need, and the answer was the largest rough-terrain crane available. Some of the towers were nearly 200 feet tall and others were not as tall, but the access was difficult and it would be impossible to position the crane optimally, so we would need more crane than would ordinarily be required. In addition, the road was terrible and had sharp turns and steep corners that would require an all-wheel-drive rough-terrain crane with four-wheel steering to get where it needed to go. I found a Link-Belt 8090 that met the requirements and that I could rent on a monthly basis, so I went to Texas to be trained to use it over the course of a few days. It was a very sophisticated crane—the features and electronics were far more complicated and comprehensive than any crane I had operated before. It was a good thing I had the opportunity to learn how to use it, because the standard method—where a truck driver unloads the crane in the parking lot and tosses you the keys—would never have worked. I arranged to have the crane delivered to Jackson Hole, excited at the prospect of having such a great tool with which to build the tramway. Even though I had been operating cranes for forty years, I had never had any formal training and had not been certified as an operator. Certification to operate a crane had become an OSHA requirement and a big deal in California, so I went to a class in Sacramento for five days to learn all the things I needed

to become certified and take the test. At age seventy-two I was more than twice the age of most of the people in the class, and three times the age of several of them. The class was a good review and the certification exam was a breeze, even on an unfamiliar

The old cabins at Jackson Hole may have been serviceable and quaint, but the new cabins look fantastic and accommodate more than double the number of passengers.

After a long spell of miserable weather, sunny skies allowed for rapid progress on the towers.

piece of equipment. I received my diploma: Graduation day attire was hardhats and jeans instead of caps and gowns.

It had been a long winter in Jackson Hole and the weather gave no sign of relenting; the arrival of the Garaventa crew from Switzerland seemed to be the bait for a new round of cold and snow. As we started work on Tower 1 in the first week of April, a cold storm moved in with snow and high winds, not a recipe for safety or efficiency in building a tower nearly 200 feet tall. The Swiss guys responded with characteristic determination and toughness and, working long hours, got the tower done, prompting an improvement in the weather. Next, we had to get the crane to Tower 3 and the roads on the mountain were buried in eight to twenty feet of compacted snow. The Jackson Hole crew plowed with snowcats, dozers, and excavators to get the road open, which then became muddy and slimy from the runoff of the melting snow. Adding crushed rock as a surface helped the crane get traction, and we were able to drive the crane up the road and into position to erect Tower 3. The road up the mountain was extremely rough and it was a long drive to some of the tower sites—several miles. I had been driving a one-ton pickup truck up the hill every day, but the road was beating it to death. I bought a Honda ATV and started riding that up to the tower sites, which was faster, more fun and a lot less wear and tear on both the truck and on me. By mid-June, the snow and cold moved on and we had perfect weather until mid-September. I impressed on the young crew from Garaventa that we were in Jackson Hole to work, not party and they responded with enthusiasm and dedication. Getting the crew in line was perhaps the most easily solved problem, because we discovered that some of the most critical portions of the work that had been done by the concrete contractor from Las Vegas the year before were deficient and would have to be removed and redone. Only once that was achieved and the new concrete cured for 28 days would we be able to pull the track ropes.

Jackson Hole is located, to a great extent, on National Forest land and the construction process on the mountain was the subject of constant scrutiny of the local Forest Service representatives, who were adamant in their objection to the construction of a single foot of road more than necessary. What this meant was that rather than allowing us to build a road another fifty feet toward the base of the tower, they would say, "No, that's close enough—you'll just have to work from there." Easy for them to say, because they were not sitting in the crane, which was totally maxed out and teetering on the brink of tipping over and falling down the side of the mountain. I had quite a few anxious moments very cautiously lifting heavy components into place, trying to bring them in smoothly and safely for the Garaventa guys perched on the tower while the alarm buzzers and chimes were going off in the crane letting me know that I was at, or slightly past its capacity in that configuration. I got very adept at cancelling the alarm and overriding the warning devices so I could concentrate on positioning the load.

The Garaventa crew assembled Tower 2—which was in a totally inaccessible location—using the traditional "needle and winch" method of construction. They flew the tower components in using a small Kaman "K-Max" twin-rotor helicopter, which flew the structure of the old tower out as a backhaul. They flew in the winches and needle parts and spent a couple of days building the needle and rigging it to trees and stakes, then got busy building Tower 2, which went surprisingly quickly. The needle was then dismantled.

When I got ready to move the crane up the road to Tower 4, we found that the four-wheel drive was not working. There was power to the front wheels, but not to the rear. One of the Jackson Hole Mountain Resort mechanics came up to the site and discov-

The view from the top terminal is magnificent.

ered that we had broken a universal joint in the rear driveline. He did not have the U-joint, and the rear axle would have to be substantially disassembled to install the new one, which was not an option in any case: I needed to get the crane to the Tower 4 site with four-wheel drive or without it. We towed the crane with a Caterpillar D8 much of the way and drove it through the sections it could manage without the rear wheels driving. Once at the tower site, it did not matter whether the drivetrain worked correctly or not—when the crane was set up in position to assemble the tower, it did not need to move. Tower 5 was a good bit riskier than Tower 4—the ground where the crane needed to sit sloped strongly toward the tower and I had to build pillars of rocks and cribbing—stacks of heavy timbers—under the downhill stabilizers to level the crane. It was so precipitous that I borrowed Jackson Hole's dozer and parked it behind the crane, stuck the blade into the ground and tied

We had to strip down the saddles in order to (barely) have enough crane capacity to set them.

The Garaventa crew building a tower the old-fashioned way, with a 'needle'.

The three large winches—tied off to rocks, stakes and trees—provide the crew with the ability to position and lift loads into position with the needle.

the crane to the dozer with cable. If the crane fell off the cribbing, at least it would not slide downhill and fall over the cliff. The up-side of this was that the mechanic could come and replace the universal joint while the crane was jacked completely off the ground—he had plenty of headroom in which to work.

Once the towers were completed, we moved to the upper terminal and assembled it, which was easy compared to the towers. Once the upper terminal was ready, we could pull the track ropes. The track ropes had been shipped from Switzerland to Texas, then trucked on special heavy-haul low-boy trailers to Wyoming. Each spool came on a separate truck because each spool of cable was monumentally heavy—ninety metric tons or 198,000 pounds (the normal maximum weight for a tractor-trailer combination is 80,000 pounds).

This only looks precarious because it is, although tying the crane to the large dozer on the uphill side provided a measure of protection in case something went wrong.

A very unusual design for a tramway tower with a narrow midline base and struts to one side—but it works!

We unloaded them with my ninety-ton crane on one side and a 110-ton truck crane on the other side—we lifted them clear of the truck and had the truck drive out from under the spool. Even positioned optimally for the lift, the ninety-ton crane was working hard to lift its side, while the 110-ton crane handled the load well. The spools were placed behind the lower terminal and were aligned with where the rope would be going when we pulled it—we did not want to have to move them again. The Garaventa crew was very efficient at pulling the ropes and had shipped over excellent equipment with which to perform the job. Once the track ropes were in place, the haul rope was pulled in, and a "splicing bridge" would be hung from the track ropes so that the haul rope could be spliced. The only problem was that it was late enough in the project that I had sent the large Link Belt crane back to Texas and we had nothing with which to hang the splicing bridge. I looked all over for a large boom truck but could not find anything closer than Salt Lake City, so I flew down to Salt Lake, picked up the rented boom truck, and drove it back to Jackson Hole—anything to finish the job!

The use of a continuous loop of haul rope allows the ski area operator to park both cabins in the lower terminal when bad weather is anticipated: valuable for an installation like Jackson Hole where the upper terminal is a simple open platform without shelter for the docked cabin. In this system, the carriage supporting each cabin is attached to the haul rope with a sophisticated clamp that can be released to allow the haul rope to move freely through, so the resort can dock a cabin at the bottom, release the clamp on the docked cabin, then move the other cabin to the bottom of the line as well. One safety system that this arrangement does not support is the use of a track rope brake, which is mounted on the carriage and automatically clamps on to the track ropes if slack is detected in the haul rope, which prevents the cabin from rolling out of control down the track ropes in the unlikely event that the haul rope breaks. I suppose Garaventa believes that the likelihood of a haul rope breaking is so remote as to render the track rope brake obsolete, or that the utility of being able to store both cabins at one terminal is a reasonable compromise.

The splice bridge was nicknamed the "Stairway to Heaven" by the Jackson Hole crew who assisted Norm Duke in making the splice. The pieces were lifted into position with the boom truck, hung from the track ropes, then pulled uphill toward the first tower—a lengthy and repetitive process—and then were tied off to buildings on each side of the line to minimize the swaying of the bridge as the crew worked. It took a good bit longer to put up and take down the splice bridge than it did to perform the splicing operation. Compared to a traditional aerial tramway system with upper and lower haul ropes attached to the cabins with sockets, the continuous haul rope system has operational advantages, but shortening the rope takes considerably longer than pulling tension and pouring new sockets, which can be accomplished overnight by a capable crew. The installation of the splicing bridge, pulling

The splicing bridge assembled just uphill of the lower terminal—the crew dubbed it "The Stairway to Heaven."

tension and splicing the rope will take the better part of five days—an amount of downtime which won't be acceptable to many installations that don't benefit from the ability to bring both cabins to the bottom terminal. It's an interesting technology but my suspicion is that it will probably only find modest acceptance.

With the cables now in place, the cabins could be placed on the line and the systems tested. The cabins—built in Switzerland by CWA—were kept draped to conceal their appearance until the new design would be revealed at the grand opening. Jackson Hole did an excellent job of building suspense and excitement among the locals for the grand opening, and it was a great success with dramatic lighting, fireworks, and Santa rappelling out of the cabin to the cheers of a crowd of several thousand rabid Jackson Hole skiers.

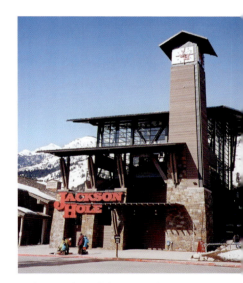

Jackson Hole aerial tramway lower terminal.

Operationally, the new tram did not disappoint. Operating at a speed of ten meters per second, it reduced the travel time to the top of the mountain to about nine minutes, which allowed local skiers to score more tram rides in a day, the local measure of success for a successful day of skiing. Although it was a tough project—after perfect weather through the summer, the temperatures plunged to as low as -30 in October and November- it was satisfying to replace a historic and well-loved tram with a modern version that enhanced the operation of the resort and thrilled its guests. It was satisfying, too, to be tested against a tough mountain under demanding conditions, and to prevail once again.

Troy Caldwell and White Wolf

On July 1, 1862, President Abraham Lincoln signed into law the "Pacific Railroad Acts of 1862," which provided financing and granted land for the construction of a transcontinental railroad from Council Bluffs, Iowa to Sacramento. The railroads were granted a right of way for 100 feet on each side of the track, as well as five sections of land (each one mile square) on each side of the track within ten miles of the railroad right of way for each mile of track constructed. What this meant was that for the length of the new, transcontinental railroad, the railroads were given half the land within ten miles on each side of the track—6,400 acres per mile of track, 175 million acres of land in total; an area larger than the state of Texas. The railroads made quite a bit of money through the years selling this land off—it was made much more valuable by the fact that the railroad was within ten miles.

Fully 125 years later, the railroad still owned some of the land that it had been granted in 1862. Squaw Valley had been renting from Southern Pacific Railroad since 1958, when the last 700 linear feet and the top terminal of the KT-22 lift had been built on land owned by the railroad. A few years later, almost 1,000 linear feet and the top terminal of the Olympic Lady lift was constructed on the parcel. In all, about seventy-five acres of railroad land were within the boundaries of the ski resort. When the railroad's real estate operation decided to liquidate the parcel in 1987, it called and offered Squaw Valley Ski Corporation the entire 460-acre parcel, but somehow the opportunity was fumbled, and a young contractor from Alpine Meadows, Troy Caldwell, was able to acquire the property.

That Alex was peeved at somehow having missed the opportunity to acquire land that he had to pay rent on would be an understatement. It's been suggested that someone else at the company made the decision—but it seems extremely unlikely to me that anyone but Alex would have decided not to make a deal with Southern Pacific—and totally in character for Alex to have done so. Squaw Valley's missed opportunity opened the door for Caldwell and his wife, Susie, a chance at their dream of building a family-operated lodge and boutique resort that could conceivably provide access to both Squaw Valley and Alpine Meadows.

When I met Troy Caldwell, I was immediately impressed with his forthright personality and work ethic. He gave the impression of a guy who knew how to work and enjoyed a challenge. He drove an old Toyota pickup truck that probably had 150,000 miles on the clock. He was wearing sun-bleached Carhartt work pants and a somewhat threadbare fleece jacket—nothing fancy. We talked about lifts—he was trying to work out a deal in which he would issue a credit for the lease of the seventy-five acres of land within the ski area boundary for the old KT-22 double chairlift. Troy had what he felt was a good alignment for the lift that would make good use of the parcel. What he had not counted on was the challenge of working with Alex or—even worse—with Placer County.

In 1996, a new method of determining the value of the land lease—based on the linear feet of lifts installed on Caldwell's land and the operational status of those lifts—led to a dispute over the amount of rent that Caldwell was due. Based on the operation of the lifts over the previous five years, Alex determined that he had drastically overpaid, and that Troy owed him $26,449, which he was willing to apply to future rent or purchase of the land. Predictably, Troy called foul, and even more predictably, Alex filed suit against him for breach of contract. While that lawsuit was still in the works, they decided to exchange the land for the much newer Headwall triple chairlift, which had been removed to make way for a detachable, but after agreeing to the trade, Alex thought better of the deal and substituted the elderly Cornice II double chair, which prompted Troy to sue Alex for breach of contract. They eventually settled on trading for the Headwall chairlift, but when the Placer County Planning Department got wind of the plan, they instructed Caldwell in no uncertain terms that he could not even store the components for the lift on his property without a having a minimum five-million-dollar liability insurance policy in place, so the Headwall lift, when it was taken down, was stored in Verdi.

The County placed such extraordinarily restrictive conditions on Troy's proposed family-operated inn and resort that it seems unlikely that it will ever succeed. (For example, that only twenty-five people can ski there at any given time. If this same condition were imposed on Squaw Valley, only 217 people would be allowed on the mountain each day.) But I wish Troy and his wife, Susie, well. If anyone can make it work, they can.

United States Citizenship

In the mid-2000s, I traveled frequently between the U.S. and Europe. I had purchased the piece of property in Oberammergau in 2006 and was building the house that my kids and I could use when we went to there to ski, hike, and spend time with family, so I was making frequent trips to manage that project. After being away most of my life, it was a good time to reconnect with my roots in Bavaria and spend more time in Europe than I had been able to spare in the past. But after the 9/11 attacks in 2001, international travel became a lot more challenging. Every trip went less than smoothly because I would buy an airline ticket with my credit card, so the ticket said, "Hans Burkhart," but when I presented my German passport, it said, "Johan Burkhart," and the Immigration and Customs Enforcement people would want to have a conversation about the discrepancy. Although it would eventually be resolved, this slowed the travel process and was tense, time-consuming, and unnecessary. In 2012, I decided to apply to become a "naturalized" U.S. citizen, which would allow me to get a U.S. passport that would match my credit card and airline ticket, making for more efficient, less dramatic international travel.

When I told Hardy that I had applied for citizenship, he was concerned:

"You have to take a class," he said.

"What? Why do I need to take a class?" I asked.

"There's a test—they ask you questions about American history, the U.S. Constitution, the Bill of Rights, the presidents—things like that. You must pass to become a citizen, Hans. Everyone has to do it."

I wrote this off as typically Swiss over-analysis of the situation, and got an appointment at the federal building in Reno, figuring that after being in the U.S. for over fifty years, I could probably pass the test.

The interviewer from the Citizenship and Immigration Service was a nice older lady. She asked for my green card, driver's license, and passport.

"Wow," she said. "You've been here for a long time. I have to ask you some questions, but since you've been here since 1960, you shouldn't have any trouble with them."

She asked me who the first president of the United States was.

"Washington or Lincoln," I replied. "I think it was Washington."

"That's right," she said. "Okay, when is Independence Day celebrated?"

"The Fourth of July," I replied.

"Right," she said.

She asked me who the president was.

"That's Mr. Obama," I replied.

"Okay," she said. "You obviously speak and understand English very well; can you read and write in English?"

I explained that I had been general manager and president of Squaw Valley Ski Corporation for many years, and that I not only could read and write in English, I could read and understand legal documents and contracts in English, but these days I tried to avoid that whenever possible. She laughed.

"Okay, Mr. Burkhart. That's all I have for you. You will be getting a letter advising whether your application for naturalization is accepted or rejected within a month. Thank you for coming in—it was nice to meet you."

Within a few weeks, I got a letter stating that my application for naturalized citizenship had been accepted and that I should come to the Reno federal building to be sworn in as a United States citizen on September 10, 2012 at 11 a.m.

I spent that morning working at the yard in Verdi and drove over to the federal building on Keystone Avenue in Reno. I got there about fifteen minutes early, parked, and went into the lobby. There is a security checkpoint and the guard asked what business brought me to the building that day. "I'm coming to be sworn in as a citizen," I replied and showed her my letter.

"What?" she said, "You can't be sworn in like that!"

I was wearing work clothes—jeans and sneakers. The swearing-in had never occurred to me to be a big deal. Apparently, it was. "Okay, look," she said. "There's another swearing-in ceremony at 1 p.m. Go home and change and come back in time for that."

Even with two hours to work with, driving back to Squaw Valley, changing clothes and then driving back to Reno would be cutting it close, so I came up with another plan: I drove over to Wal-Mart, bought a dress shirt, a tie, a dark suit and shoes, had some lunch, took the tags off the clothes, changed into them and drove back to the federal building.

When I went to the security checkpoint looking like the world's oldest Mormon missionary, the guard cast an approving eye over my new outfit, said, "Now, that's more like it!" and sent me up to a courtroom for the swearing-in ceremony.

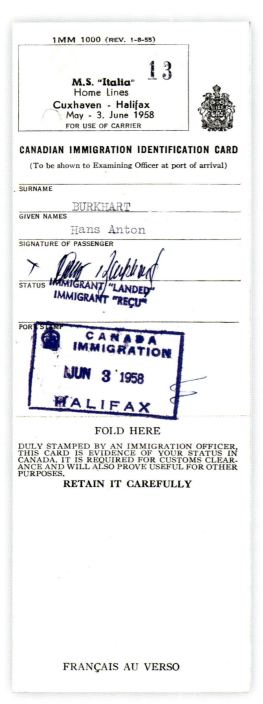

If you ask someone when their ancestor came to the United States or Canada, you usually get an uncertain answer. In my case, I know that I landed in Canada (Halifax, Nova Scotia, to be exact) on June 3, 1958!

The room was full of people at least as dressed up as I was—and their families. There were people from Vietnam, India, China, Thailand, and many from Mexico and Central America. I seemed to be the only one without a group of beaming family members taking pictures with their phones, and I was the only European. There was a short but well-produced video of President Obama talking about the responsibilities of citizenship and welcoming us as U.S. citizens, and then a federal judge administered the oath of allegiance to the United States and we were given our certificates of naturalization. Most stayed to take pictures with their certificate and the judge—it was clearly an incredibly special day for them and probably the fulfillment of a lifelong dream for many.

Although we arrived at the courtroom that day with different nationalities, experiences, and expectations, there was a characteristic common to all of us. Wherever we were from, however we had gotten to the United States, and however long we had been here, we had all been willing to work incredibly hard to make this day possible. It might have been working in a restaurant, a hotel, or on a farm, or roofing houses, pouring concrete, or building lifts, but that was the thread common to all of us, and the realization that all that hard work had paid off was a big deal indeed; something to be proud of and certainly worth a new suit from Wal-Mart.

Las Vegas Zip line

Certainly, my most unique and weird project was the construction of the second phase of a zip line on Fremont Street in Las Vegas. "The Fremont Street Experience" is an 'old Las Vegas' effort to compete with the mega-casinos on the Strip—the old, downtown clubs from the late 1940s and 1950s were in an area a few blocks long well north of the Strip. When these clubs were in their heyday, the Strip was largely populated with coyotes and rattlesnakes. The Fremont Street experience is an outdoor pedestrian mall that stretches for five blocks and has an arched roof that is also (according to the hype) the world's largest video screen. As hard as this is to visualize, the reality is even worse—kind of like being trapped in a video game or a slot machine. Someone had the bright idea to install a zip line starting at the east end of the mall and running for several blocks, and it was an immediate smash hit with the tourists who come to the mall. Although there is gaming in the clubs, the focus of the operation seems to be more oriented to entertainment than gaming, and since the unwritten law of Las Vegas is "bigger, brighter, louder, more" when your zip line is a virtual printing press for money, the only answer is to build a bigger, longer, higher, faster one.

The zip line operation is housed in a building designed to look like a giant slot machine, because the zip line is named the "Slotzilla." The original zip line is advertised as being "seven stories high" and it's about fifty feet above the ground. The new "Zoomline" was to add another thirty-five or forty feet in height, so it would start at an elevation just below that of the canopy. In fact, I had to point out that if someone raised their head (the riders are lying prone in a harness, so they fly like Superman), they could hit it on

Looking into the Fremont Street Experience canopy, this is above the launching pad for the zipline.

TREE TRIMMING

I have a house in Squaw Valley on Sandy Way—the top street on the north side of Olympic Valley. From the big windows in the house, there is a great view of the Resort at Squaw Creek, Red Dog, Exhibition, and KT-22, but a large fir tree behind the house blocked some of view. I decided if I limbed the tree a little bit more, it would open the view quite a bit. It is a beautiful, large tree and I did not want to cut it down, but removing some of the limbs would make a big improvement.

There were no limbs for the first fifteen feet at the bottom, so I needed to use a ladder to get up to where I could climb the rest of the way. When you limb, it is best to start at the top and cut your way down, so there is something to stand on while you're working. I was concerned that the falling limbs would knock the ladder over, leaving me no way to get down out of the tree when I was done, so I called my daughter Anika. She was coming over to Squaw Valley anyway, so I told her to come up to the house while I did the project. If the ladder got knocked over, she could put it back up when I was ready to come down. I put on a safety harness so that I could tie off to the tree and use both hands to run the chainsaw. I got an electric chainsaw and extension cord, and climbed the ladder into the tree, then up the branches until I got to the top of the area that I wanted to start limbing. At this point, my head was about sixty-five feet above the ground. I stepped onto a large branch on the right so I could clip the lanyard from the harness around a branch above me before I started cutting. Even though it was a large branch, and I was close to the trunk, the branch broke off and I fell. I bounced off branches on the way down, lying sort of flat as I kind of rolled through the branches—which I think slowed my fall a little—until I landed on the ground on the dirt and rocks. Anika watched the whole thing, and I think she was dialing 911 before I even hit the ground. I tried to get up and go up to the house, but Anika would not let me—she kept telling me not to move while she talked to the 911 dispatcher. In a few minutes, Squaw Valley Fire Department arrived along with an ambulance from North Tahoe. I was surrounded by firefighter-paramedics with scissors, all eager to cut off the harness and all my clothes. I recognized Captain Sal Monforte and asked him to keep the guys with the scissors from cutting the harness, but the warning came just a second too late. The firefighter-paramedics checked me over and decided that I would probably live long enough to get to the hospital, so they put me on a back board and carried me to the ambulance, then we drove down to the ski area parking lot, where the Care Flight helicopter was

Inside the canopy looking back toward the launching pad.

waiting. The flight to Renown Medical Center in Reno seemed a lot shorter than it really was, although it would have been more enjoyable had I not been lying on the rigid back board.

After being assessed, questioned, x-rayed and tested by the emergency department staff at Renown, they informed me that I had broken my back badly along with my pelvis and a bunch of ribs—just about everything. More than once, a nurse or doctor would look at the notes on my chart from the previous doctor or nurse, sort of scratch their head and ask, "How old are you, Mr. Burkhart?"

"Eighty," I would tell them.

"And what were you doing when this happened...?"

I would tell them the story, but for some reason I do not think they ever believed that I had been climbing a tree.

the canopy. We lowered the height of the cables somewhat to eliminate that risk. It was really a simple wire rope installation and tensioning project. Once installed, the four ropes would not move and would never wear out. The only tricky part was that we were doing the work above the lower zip line that was in daily operation and above the pedestrian mall at street level. It was important to not drop anything.

I made eight trips to Las Vegas, even though the project could have been done more rapidly if we had received parts shipments on a consistent basis. We would work until we ran out of parts and then stop until parts arrived—there was nothing else that could be done. The lower zip line was open from noon to midnight, so we worked from midnight to noon. There was a stage with live music right in the middle of the mall, so we never lacked for a soundtrack for our work. At times, it would have been handy to have hearing protection—as much for the quality of the entertainment as for the volume.

By far the weirdest aspect of the Fremont Street Experience was a restaurant right at the base of the starting tower for the zip and zoom lines called the "Heart Attack Grill." The Heart Attack Grill carved out its culinary niche by serving the unhealthiest meals it could concoct. It had hamburgers ranging from the "Single Bypass Burger" (with a half-pound burger patty) to the "Octuple Bypass Burger" (eight half-pound patties, 9,983 calories) as well as "Flatliner Fries" cooked in lard and full sugar Coca-Cola. Patrons put on hospital gowns as they entered, and the waitresses were dressed as nurses. Payment was cash only and the restaurant insisted that diners pay in advance because, "You may not live through the meal." Diners who were unable to finish their meals were subject to being spanked by the nurse/waitresses.

Our first passenger!

Pretty weird; but the weirdest and most disturbing aspect of the restaurant was that they offered diners weighing more than 350 pounds unlimited free food and would weigh them to make sure they met the minimum weight standard on a scale with a large, red digital readout, which the other diners in the restaurant cheered.

The number of people weighing more than 350 pounds in Las Vegas was truly astonishing. From our vantage point on top of the launching tower, we could see how many were going to the Heart Attack Grill, and it was both bizarre and sad. Fortunately, the customers coming to use the zip and zoom lines tended to be at the more athletic end of the spectrum.

The Heart Attack Grill—truly an "Only in America" phenomenon.

Aftermath

My fall from the tree left me—for the first time in my life—with serious injuries. The firefighters who responded to the scene and saw what had happened were convinced that it would have killed most people, regardless of their age. That I had survived it at eighty was almost miraculous. This was small consolation as I endured a month at Renown in terrific pain. At the end of the month, the doctors there told me that they knew what needed to be done to repair my ruined spine, but they did not have the confidence or experience to perform the surgery in Reno. They flew me to San Francisco, flat on my back in a fixed-wing air ambulance, which was a converted private jet. Kathrin came with me, and it was an amazingly smooth and reasonably comfortable flight—I could not even tell that we had landed. I was taken by ambulance to the University of San Francisco Hospital. An orthopedic spine surgeon—Dr. Ames—met with us and said that he wanted to operate as soon as possible. He did the surgery two days later, placing three long titanium rods along my spinal column from just above the small of my back to the middle of my neck. The rods would keep my vertebrae aligned and protect the spinal cord, but they eliminated much of the range of motion in my neck and head, so that I could turn my head only a few degrees to each side and only slightly up and down. The pain following the operation was severe—I couldn't sleep, and the nurses were the least sympathetic and caring of all of the healthcare professionals I encountered in many months of treatment and recovery. I would tell them that I was having a lot of pain and ask for a pain pill, and they would say, "Oh, no—we can't give you any before the time scheduled for the next dose—protocol!" As if that were some magical and irrefutable explanation. My daughters were fantastic: One of them was with me all the time I was in the hospital in Reno and in San Francisco. Kathrin could speak the arcane language of the doctors and nurses and go to bat for me, which made a huge difference. Anika brought her almost-year-old daughter with her and—despite the objections of the nurses—baby Elliana slept on a bunch of pillows in the corner of the room. Mekala also put her life on hold and came to San Francisco to look after and keep me entertained and in good spirits.

A few weeks after the surgery, the doctors wanted to do an MRI to assess the position of the rods and see how my spinal column was healing. I had lost about forty pounds—my weight was down from a fit 215 pounds to a gaunt 175—there was no cushion for my skeleton anymore. They transferred me from a gurney onto the platform that would gradually transport me into the tunnel of the MRI machine, and it was nothing more than a flat plywood or plastic shelf—no padding whatsoever. I asked the technician for some pillows—anything to provide some "give" under my back, but none was forthcoming. It was a thoroughly miserable forty-five minutes of unrelenting pain as the machine scanned my back.

After a few weeks in San Francisco, it was decided that I should be transferred back to Reno to go into a rehabilitation hospital. This time, it was not an air ambulance—I would be driven back to Reno in a ground ambulance. There were three young guys assigned to the ambulance—two rode up front and one in the back with me. It was January and raining in the city, which meant that it was probably snowing on Donner Summit—hardly the best time to make the trip, especially flat on your back on a gurney. The ambulance guys were not exactly engaging or helpful—they had no pain medication for me, even though the trip was lengthy, and they stopped several times so they could get coffee or go to the bathroom. I had nothing to eat or drink during the five-hour trip—it was another miserable experience.

By the time I got to Northern Nevada Medical Center in Sparks, I had become quite a connoisseur of hospitals and medical staff, and my first impression at Northern Nevada was not favorable. Shortly after arriving there, I was worn out and hurting from the ambulance ride from San Francisco. An occupational therapist came to my room and informed me that he was there to teach me to put my socks on. I thought I had heard him wrong.

"You're here to do what?" I asked.

He repeated that he was going to teach me how to put on my socks.

I was in no mood to deal with that, at least not right then: "Get out of my room!" I said.

We got to know each other later, when I was in less pain and a better mood, although I am not sure he ever showed me how to put on my socks. Overall, I eventually learned that the nurses and healthcare professionals at Northern

One day while I was a physical therapy, my friend Pete Bansen snuck this flock of flamingos on to the hillside outside my hospital room to give me something to look at.

Nevada were among the most caring, professional, and helpful of the dozens of people I encountered following the accident.

Although the doctors in Reno had told me that Dr. Ames in San Francisco was the best spine surgeon in the region, after the surgery in San Francisco, I found that my right hand was virtually useless. I could not write with it or grasp anything effectively. I am right-handed and my dominant hand just did not work. That had not been the case prior to the surgery at USF—it had been fine until the surgery. I asked the surgeon, Dr. Ames, about it and he said that the nerve had probably been pinched or damaged somehow when he installed the rods to stabilize my spine—he said that it would heal with time and that within a year or two I would be able to do anything I had done before. A year later, there had been little improvement and when I brought that to Dr. Ames' attention, he replied that it might take ten years to resolve.

"Ten years?!" I said. "I'll be lucky to still be alive in ten years."

He was unmoved and did not seem at all willing to discuss it further or even provide further follow up. "You don't have to come back," were his parting words. His arrogance in refusing to address the loss of function occasioned by the surgery destroyed my confidence in doctors. He was certainly not the best spine surgeon as evidenced by my results.

Now What?

After a lifetime of arduous and frequently dangerous work and a dozen or so incidents that could have easily killed me, the fall from the tree was by far the most serious and debilitating. It left me truly disabled in several ways—injuries from the accident have severely and permanently limited the range of motion in my head and neck. My right hand and fingers continue to be greatly impaired, and I doubt that I will ever regain adequate function in them. Nevertheless, I can still do almost everything, even if I have to change my technique a little. I was very lucky not to have been killed or paralyzed as a result of the fall and I'm grateful for that. I work every day—retirement is the leading cause of death—on a variety of projects in Squaw Valley and Verdi. I'm involved with agencies that provide water services in two different communities and I am actively involved in their operation as well as in formulating policy.

Looking back at my life and career, I feel extremely lucky to have discovered what kind of work was most interesting and rewarding to me as a young man. Many people go through life without ever doing work that they find meaningful or fulfilling; they just go through the motions to collect a paycheck. I *believe* in work—work is so much the core of my character and happiness that it would not be inaccurate to say that it's my religion—but I think as a society we need to develop a different perspective about work than what is currently accepted.

I have five grandsons, who are all bright, capable young men, all but one in their late teens and twenties. Their interests seem to be limited to computers and sports, however—none of them has ever asked me to show them how to drive a forklift, a bulldozer or a backhoe. They are simply not interested in building things or the tools and machinery with which it is done, and they don't seem to believe that making something has the potential to be fulfilling for themselves or seen as admirable by others. Sports and competition are great, but realistically, very, very few people can have a career as a professional athlete and those who have success as athletes find other work to support or entertain themselves once their career in sport comes to an end. It concerns me that none of my grandsons seem to have inherited the fascination with making things and that as a society, we seem to have lost respect for people who work with their hands. We would not be able to survive without them.

My grandsons are by no means unique. As a society, we are captivated by high-tech entrepreneurs, athletes and entertainers. We assign prestige to academic achievement—every parent hopes that their child will go to college—but we tend to look down on kids who pursue vocational or technical training, even though their earnings for the first decade or longer will likely exceed those who graduate from a college or university with a Bachelor or Master's degree.

Americans seem to be abandoning work as tradesmen, jobs which are eagerly filled by immigrants. The path I followed as an immigrant with limited language skills is now taken by immigrants from Mexico and Central America. When I first landed in Toronto, I met some guys who spoke my language that tipped me off to work as a farmworker and landscaper, an identical scenario for someone arriving today from Mexico or Guatemala, over sixty years later. As an immigrant's language skills improve, they're capable of finding work in more complex jobs—roofing, drywall or concrete work, for example—and as skills and savings allow, they may start their own company or move to trades that require a larger investment in tools or training or require more nuanced language skills.

My experience has shown that immigrants from Mexico and Central America are excellent workers who are eager for work, resourceful and willing to learn new skills. Their motivation and drive to succeed far exceeds that of the average American worker. Many, if not most of the building trades in this country are already performed by immigrants or the children of immigrants. This is a trend that I expect to become even more pronounced going forward.

Americans have greater respect and admiration for someone with education than they do for someone with training to perform a skill or analyze and solve a physical problem—college professor is considered a higher status role than electrician or machinist. Many more Americans hope to see their child become a physician than a diesel mechanic, yet the mechanic may have significantly greater job satisfaction, enjoy a more balanced and fulfilling personal life and may have a considerably higher income than a doctor. In every respect other than status, the mechanic may have a much happier and harmonious life than the physician. In an extreme example, teachers, who have such huge responsibility in the education and development of our children—the future of the nation—are afforded lower status and economic reward than even modestly successful business executives, not to mention entertainers or athletes.

Between disinterest on the part of American youth for doing anything that involves manual labor or working with one's hands, the drive for economic success in the immigrant community and the disorientation in how society assigns status to different jobs, we seem to be heading for a time of confusion and reckoning.

American society has always shown appreciation for artistry and craftsmanship in fine art woodworking, glass blowing and other pursuits that are closer to craft than industry, but the appreciation of excellence in something considered a trade occupation has been limited to people within those trades—a welder admiring a difficult and intricate weld, for example. A handful of scholarly books (although most have been written by craftsmen, not scholars…) have explored the satisfaction of working with your hands and the inherent value of making things, but more widespread appreciation of the benefits of the work of everyday tradesmen—both personal and societal—has yet to gain traction.

Building things and solving complex logistic problems—particularly those thought impossible to conquer by others—has been a lifelong fascination and something I found to be extremely rewarding. In my opinion, it would be beneficial if our young people had the opportunity to perceive a technical career as being as potentially prestigious and respected as that of a university-educated professional. In many European countries there are well-established and successful systems for vocational education and there's no reason why education in technical disciplines could not be equally successful in the U.S., but young people going into a technical field have to feel that their capabilities are valued and respected on a par with their academically-trained peers. Shouldn't we have the same regard for a plumber who does energy-efficient, technically flawless work that will last a lifetime as we have for a barista with a Master's in music education? Granted, the plumber makes a lot more money but shouldn't we see either path as equally desirable and prestigious for one of our kids?

The projects that I've done through my career have been the source of great satisfaction, both for me and for my clients. I developed a reputation as someone who could take on the most challenging projects—including several jobs that other contractors had deemed impossible—and bring them to completion on time and on budget. I'm very proud of that. I am really proud of the fact that in over fifty years as a contractor and project manager doing work that has at times been tremendously difficult and dangerous and under greatly challenging weather conditions, not a single employee has ever had more than a minor injury on any of my jobs.

I'm proud of the fact that throughout my life, I have never taken a dime of government assistance—no unemployment, worker's compensation or business subsidy of any kind. I'm proud of my children, who have grown up to be not only respected, successful members of their community, but responsible parents as well. I have wonderful grandkids—talented in so many different ways and with challenging lives ahead of them. I hope that my grandchildren are able to find the kind of satisfaction and success in their careers that my work has given me and I'm glad to get these stories down in writing so that they can enjoy them and pass them along to their children.

Appendix

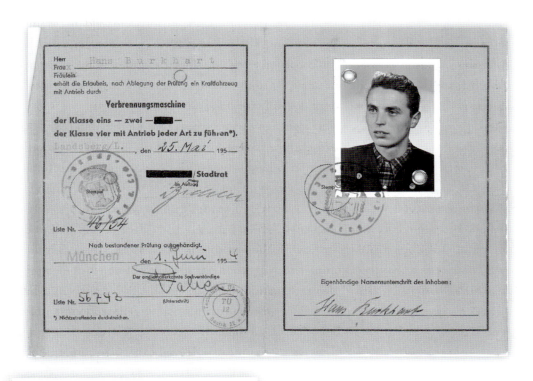

My German driver's license, issued in 1954, is still valid!
I spoke with Stein Eriksen on the phone, inquiring about a job teaching skiing for him at Aspen Highlands. In response, he sent me this letter inviting me to come to Aspen for a tryout in December, 1959.

STEIN ERIKSEN
Aspen Highlands
ASPEN, COLORADO

30/8.59.

Dear Hans.

The only way I can give you a job as an instructor, is to talk to you personally and to see you ski. I can not arrange for a visa for a guy I do not know personally. If you want to take the chance that you qualify as an instructor for me, you must have to be in Aspen before the 10th of December 1959. On the 10th, I start a pre season training course for my instructors, which lasts for 8 days. Write me and tell me what you think. I am interested in you, but want to meet you personally before I hire you.

Truly Yours
Stein Eriksen

Squaw Valley Work Halted

OLYMPIC VALLEY — Construction of a multi-million dollar tramway was likely to stop this week if a dispute between Iron Workers Union Local 118 and Squaw Valley isn't settled.

Work was halted today in the snowstorm.

Pickets appeared at the Squaw Valley entrance Friday to halt two truckloads of steel and a giant crane. Union officials said Squaw Valley Lodge employes instead of union members were being used to unload supplies.

John Buchman, a lodge official, said he believed a meeting between management and the union was scheduled for Tuesday.

The 120-passenger tramway was scheduled to open in December.

5-15-68

The picketing took place two days before the Garaventa crew arrived to begin work, but it didn't impede progress in any way.

Squaw Peak Ski Construction Set

TAHOE, March 5.—Long before the snow melts from the slopes of 8,900-foot Squaw Peak, work will be started there by the new Squaw Valley Development Company, it was disclosed yesterday by Wayne Poulsen, president of the organization whose plans call for the erection of one of the largest and most beautiful skiing resorts in the nation.

Alexander Cushing of New York is secretary-treasurer, and Cortlandt T. Hill, president of the Far West Ski Association, is chairman of the board of directors. The company is capitalized at $300,000, and many of the stockholders are easterners. They include Lawrence Rockefeller of New York, Dr. Frank Howard, of San Rafael, well known photographer who will make movies of the Squaw Valley project; Capt. Jack Hamilton and Capt. Bob Howard of Pan American Airways, and Jack Starratt of Tahoe City.

The road to Squaw Valley was built last fall and all but two and one-half miles have been graveled. Two concrete bridges were erected across Squaw Creek, which, like the road, winds through the picturesque valley. The road to the resort site branches off Highway 89 midway between Truckee and Tahoe.

Andre Roche of Switzerland accompanied Poulson to Squaw Valley via weasel last week to look over the site of the resort and giant ski lift. Roche is the Swiss government's technical expert on snow research and avalanches who was brought to America recently by the National Ski Patrol. He has just returned from an inspection tour of Mineral King, near Sequoia National Park.

Roche was well pleased with the Squaw Valley setup. He advised that the double chair lift the company planned to install on Squaw Peak at an estimated cost of $150,000 be run clear to the top of the peak instead of to the 7,500 foot level as originally planned.

This lift, when completed, will be the longest capacity ski lift in the United States. It will accommodate 600 skiers an hour and will have two intermediate "on and off" stations.

The lower section of the mountain is especially suited to intermediate skiers, while the upper slopes, from which you can view Lake Tahoe in the distance, will provide a long, fast run for the experts.

Another fast run for the experienced skier will start at the top of Deer Park.

The main resort building, which will nestle near the foot of the mountains, will be constructed in modern Swiss design with 3,500 square feet of space on the lower floor. In this will be included a large warming lounge with circular center room fireplace, a bar, restaurant, ski shop and locker and rest rooms.

The March, 1949 announcement of the development of Squaw Valley ski resort.

CAMPBELL CONSTRUCTION CO.

OF SACRAMENTO — ESTABLISHED 1906

TELEPHONE (916) 452-5371
2120 - 20TH STREET • P. O. BOX 390
SACRAMENTO, CALIFORNIA 95802

July 3, 1968

Squaw Valley Development Corporation
P.O. Box 2007
Olympic Valley, California 95730

Invoice #4175
Page 1 of 1

Attention: Mr. Jim Woods

Progress Payment Request No. 2
Tramway Terminal Building, Job #6805

Item No.	Description	Rev. Estimate Inc. C.O. #1	% Complete	Amount Due
1.	Preliminary & Temporary	$ 78,070.00	65	$ 50,745.50
2.	Excavation	5,250.00	85	4,462.50
3.	Concrete Work	377,278.31	35	132,047.41
4.	Rough Carpentry	6,211.00		
5.	Miscellaneous Items	10,311.00		
6.	Structural Steel & Misc. Iron	65,330.00	5	3,266.50
7.	Quarry Tile	11,130.00		
8.	Electrical	98,000.00	20	19,600.00
9.	Elevators	62,800.00		
10.	Composition Floors	6,000.00		
11.	Finish Hardware	3,500.00		
12.	Hollow Metal Door & Frame	5,000.00		
13.	Glass, Glazing & Aluminum Work	45,000.00		
14.	Masonry	11,414.00		
15.	Millwork	5,500.00		
16.	Finish Carpentry	3,850.00		
17.	Plumbing, Heating & Ventilating	56,840.00	20	11,368.00
18.	Painting	9,000.00		
19.	Roofing & Damproofing	13,000.00		
20.	Reinforcing	79,100.00	43	34,013.00
21.	Pre Stress Materials	15,275.00	25	3,818.75
22.	Install Garauentas Materials	1,500.00		
23.	Skylight-Sheetmetal	9,075.00		
24.	Toilet Room Partitions	1,156.00		
25.	Steel Rolling Door	2,510.00		
26.	Sitework & Seeding	1,500.00		
27.	Window Wall	60,700.00		
28.	Fixed Fee	45,000.00	24	10,800.00
	Sub-Totals	$1,089,300.31		$270,121.66
	Change Order #2	3,218.69	100	3,218.69
	Change Order #3	3,120.00		
	Totals	$1,095,639.00	24.9	$273,340.35
	Less 10% Retention			27,334.04
	Less Amount Previously Requested			164,201.12
	Amount Due			$ 81,805.19

The cost for the lower terminal of the Squaw Valley Tram—at just under $1.1 million—was more than the tram equipment and installation.

Safety on The Lifts At Squaw

From Page 53

erators and employes as a whole is a major contributor to the safety problem."

And from Mrs. Helen Fritz of Mountain View: "To many accidents are occurring at Squaw Valley ... Doesn't Alec Cushing have a moral obligation to protect his customers as much as possible?"

Cushing, who built Squaw Valley from nothing into a complex of 18 chairlifts and two tramways, agrees wholeheartedly thathe does have such an

"We feel so strongly about maintaining our lifts in a completely safe condition," he said yesterday, "that we continually make our own inspections and set much stiffer standards for ourselves than those established by the Division of Industrial Safety.

"Our maintenance program continues year round. In the summer, we have eight men who do nothing but work on the lifts.

"This year, I feel we've suffered from extremely bad luck. In 20 previous seasons, there were only two power-failures that affected the lifts at Squaw Valley. This winter alone, there were seven, and power-company negligence was responsible for much of the trouble.

"But you can't convince skiers who are stranded on a lift for a couple of hours that it's somebody else's fault."

According to Cushing, the Division of Industrial Safety's recommendation concerning the brakes on his Headwall lift last April 16 did not constitute a "warning."

"If they felt it was so important, they should have required us to redesign the

Squaw Valley

Differing Views On Ski-Lift Safety

4-3-70

By Bob Lochner

Are ski-lifts at High Sierra resorts, notably Squaw Valley, safe?

This was the question asked two days ago at the start of a brief series of articles stemming from the accident on Headwall chairlift March 7.

The answer, in two words, is "Yes, but . . ."

The "but" means they could be a lot safer.

Everyone, it seems, has his own particular horror stry about Squaw Valley's lifts. Most of them have basis in fact.

A Tahoe City "wife and mother" reported yesterday that she had "three children, all excellent skiers, and each child had one and more experiences of being on lifts when the chairs slid backwards at Squaw. Each and every one of these could have been disastrous, but thank God, was not."

John McCullough of Santa Rosa commented,, "The lifts are so unsafe that although I am an avid skier, I have foregone the pleasures of attitude of the op-

See Page 54, Col. 6

enclosure of all driveshafts that have previously been exposed to the weather, and thechange-over of many lifts so they can be operated at only one-half or one-third speed.

"Most of our lifts were designed for full speed only,' ' Burkhart said, "which means they would have to be shut down in high winds. With new drive

maintenance is still the key to safety.

"In the final analysis," said Davis, "inspections are worthless unless a ski-lift has been installed properly and a good operational-maintenance program is pursued."

About three-quarters of the lifts in California are on forest-service land, and

This 1970 article from the San Francisco Chronicle brought the lift safety issues at Squaw Valley into sharp focus.

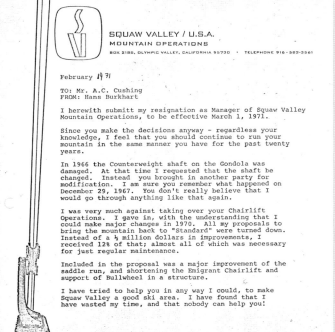

```
Snowbird, Ltd.
Hans Burkhart
9- 14- 70


Snowbird Tramway 1970- 71

Budget

100    Garaventa Contract (F.O.B. Nordseaport)      $  950,000.00
125    Dieselgeneratorset (incl. all necessary items)   19,000.00
150    Extra on 2 Tramway Cabins
        ( Special finish, sound proofing, padding,
         seats for summer operation, safety glass,
         water tank, electric hoist, etc. )           21,000.00
175    Additional extra items (reserve)               10,000.00

200    Duty, freight, insurance, inland freight, etc.
        ( approx. 20% of item 100- 175 ).            200,000.00  ←

300    Utah State Sales Tax
        ( 4.5 % of item 100- 175)                     45,000.00

400    Foundations of Tower 1,2,3,4,                  75,000.00
425    Foundations of Top Terminal                    30,000.00
450    Rock Anchors, drilling, grouting, stressing    15,000.00

500    Erection of Tramway equipment in 1971
        ( 900 tons of equipment, Lower Terminal,
         upper Terminal, Tower 1,2,3,4,
         Transportation to site, haul rope counterweight,
         Wages- erection crew, equipment and rigging tools,
         grouting, electrical installation, cable pulling,
         testing, final line up, commercial operation, misc.)
                                                      185,000.00
                                     ==================
                          Total   $  1,550,000.00
```

My cost estimate for the Snowbird tram project. This did not include the cost for the lower terminal building, which was the responsibility of the resort, nor did it include the costs for equipment and installation for the three Doppelmayr chairlifts we built at the same time.

SQUAW VALLEY / U.S.A.
MOUNTAIN OPERATIONS

BOX 2188, OLYMPIC VALLEY, CALIFORNIA 95730 · TELEPHONE 916·583·3561

February 19 71

TO: Mr. A.C. Cushing
FROM: Hans Burkhart

I herewith submitt my resignation as Manager of Squaw Valley Mountain Operations, to be effective March 1, 1971.

Since you make the decisions anyway - regardless your knowledge, I feel that you should continue to run your mountain in the same manner you have for the past twenty years.

In 1966 the Counterweight shaft on the Gondola was damaged. At that time I requested that the shaft be changed. Instead you brought in another party for modification. I am sure you remember what happened on December 29, 1967. You don't really believe that I would go through anything like that again.

I was very much against taking over your Chairlift Operations. I gave in, with the understanding that I could make major changes in 1970. All my proposals to bring the mountain back to "Standard" were turned down. Instead of a ½ million dollars in improvements, I received 12% of that; almost all of which was necessary for just regular maintenance.

Included in the proposal was a major improvement of the saddle run, and shortening the Emigrant Chairlift and support of Bullwheel in a structure.

I have tried to help you in any way I could, to make Squaw Valley a good ski area. I have found that I have wasted my time, and that nobody can help you!

My first letter of resignation from Squaw Valley. This followed a derailment on the Emigrant lift that Alex had repaired in an unsafe manner and several other unacceptable actions that I felt compromised the safety of our employees and guests.

I was fed up. It would not be the last time.

SQUAW VALLEY SKI CORPORATION

POST OFFICE BOX 2007, OLYMPIC VALLEY, CALIFORNIA 95730
TELEPHONE (916) 583-6985

Alexander C Cushing
Box 270
Old Tappan Road
Glen Cove, NY 11542

Re: Employment Contract

We have talked for several years now about an employment contract. My proposal is that if you want to be guaranteed that there are no disruptions, I will agree to be employed for a period of 5 years. The 5 year contract will be extended each year by one year, so long as I am able to work with you, and will run from May 1 to April 30. At any time that the corporation gives me written notice that it wishes to end the Agreement, the five years on the contract will start to run to the end.

During the 5 years, I will agree to provide the same level of effort and duties that I am presently providing. The employmnet contract includes that my wages will be increased each year in accordance with general standards in the principal areas such as Aspen, Vail and other areas and that my compensation during that five years will be at the level of those areas general managers and corporation presidents. If the corporation wishes to terminate the contract in shorter than five years, they will be required to pay to me a termination payment of three years of payments, payable at the same level as I would have received as salary.

The corporation recognizes that I am giving up otheropportunities in the construction and manufacturing businesses by retaining this employment for the term of five years and that I would not agree to stay now without this promise.

Dated: 5/12/82

Hans Burkhart

Squaw Valley Ski Corp.

_____

Squaw Valley Development Co.

_____

 VIII OLYMPIC WINTER GAMES

A 1980 proposal for an employment contract that Alex never signed.

FUTURE WORKING UNDERSTANDING

HANS BURKHART
at
SQUAW VALLEY SKI CORPORATION

May 3, 2001

The following is a candid recap of our discussions on April 30, 2001. I hope that we are in complete agreement on our combined goals. I am proposing a five-year agreement, incorporating several primary goals, which include reducing the debt liability from $20 million to zero, building the Scenic Shuttle from Gold Coast to High Camp, replacing the Shirley Lake lift with a detachable 6-pack, and moving the present Shirley Lake lift to Links.

My understanding is that you want me to run the entire operation. In order to accomplish the above-mentioned goals and to ensure that ongoing projects proceed efficiently, I must have total responsibility for running Squaw Valley Ski Corporation.

Legal matters and Intrawest's activities are in Nancy Wendt's capable hands. All other activities that make this mountain function (summer and winter) must be left to me without the nefarious and insulting meddling that has been going on.

I must emphasize that I am working *directly for you*, and no one else. You and I have had a long and good understanding and working relationship. You know that I can get the job done for you, but not if I am undermined or otherwise hindered. I must be able to run this entity as if it was my own business. I don't have anything to prove here; I have shown my ability for 40 years; but, I have to work on my own terms.

If we have an understanding, and if you want me to operate this organization, we must update the Organizational Chart. Personnel changes are needed if Ski Corp is to function in a healthy, productive, and positive manner. This will entail some layoffs and some recruiting of new hires. The people who report to me must be knowledgeable and professional. The best working alliances are built on mutual respect and support, and we need to revise our labor force to achieve a workable balance.

Please let me know if I am "on track" with your wishes. I would like to finalize this understanding as soon as possible. Please add any concerns you may have, and we will move forward with renewed enthusiasm.

Agreed: _____   _____
            Alexander C. Cushing   Hans A. Burkhart

A 2001 proposal for an employment contract that Alex asked for, but never signed.

HAB CONSTRUCTION, INC.

Post Office Box 801
Verdi, Nevada 89439

Phone (916) 583-9013

August 19, 1983

Alexander C. Cushing
Chairman of the Board
Squaw Valley Ski Corporation

Re: Your letter of August 11, 1983

Dear Mr. Cushing,

I really wonder what goes thru your mind, when you write a letter like the enclosed.
Blyth Demo: I checked with all the DEmolition Contractors from Reno to San Francisco, the KTK Contract is the best Deal. If there is anything wrong with the Contract, please spell it out. Without my Services you would not have the Ice Arena Property.

My leave from Squaw Valley is directly related with you building a First YAN Gondola. I certainly hope that you understand that I am 100% on your side in this matter. I have been trying very hard to talk sense into you, I am telling you again that the Gondola which is getting build now, CAN NOT WORK, and my efforts are not to waste the money and mostly to save the Area from public ambarrassment, but have it your way.

YOU DID NOT REALLY EXPECT ME TO STAY IN SQUAW VALLEY AND WATCH ALL THIS, OR DID YOU...

I spend to many years in Squaw Valley, my efforts and involvement is to the point, where I am simply not able to do that.

Yours very truly,

Hans Burkhart

State Contractor's License - California 287291

Letter of resignation in 1983. I had strongly advised Alex against replacing the PHB gondola with a prototype from Lift Engineering, but he succumbed to Janek Kunczynski's excellent salesmanship. The leave of absence Alex had approved so that I could build the Summit Express detachable chairlift at Mt. Bachelor, Oregon proved an impractical solution .
The Yandola turned out to be even more of a disaster than I had predicted and 7 months after this letter, Alex called and told me he wanted me to "take it out and put it in the parking lot."

About the Co-Author

Pete Bansen grew up in Philadelphia and got his first look at big mountains and the west when he travelled to Colorado and Northern New Mexico for a senior project in high school. Fresh out of college, he got a job in Olympic Valley driving the Zamboni at Blyth Arena, then went to work on the Squaw Valley Tram, starting a fourteen-year journey with Squaw Valley Ski Corporation. In 1993, Pete became Olympic Valley's fire chief, a job he was honored to hold until he retired in 2017.

After almost 40 years in Olympic Valley and Truckee, Pete now lives in Reno, Nevada with his wife Cindy.

Acknowledgments

This book is the work of two complete amateurs doing their best to tell Hans's story in a readable, entertaining way. Hans made me agree to include the disclaimer that if anyone is offended by anything in the book, it is *his* fault, not mine: I simply wrote what he said. I'm OK with that, but I would add that, to the best of my knowledge and belief, everything that he said is accurate.

We had important help from some special people who deserve to be recognized for their critical parts in this project. My wife Cindy suffered through countless (thousands?) hours of me sitting in front of a computer screen, tapping away, punctuated with occasional guffaws and profanities. She packed coffee and baked goodies to take to my Thursday meetings with Hans and provided endless support and counsel. Hans and I are deeply grateful for her tolerance and generosity. Anika Burkhart Schneider demonstrated enormous patience in relaying emailed communications to Hans, printing documents and generally being Hans's tech brain—all while working shifts as a firefighter and full-time Mom to two busy children!

Several old friends—respected authors and Squaw Valley savants themselves—read the first draft and still encouraged us to keep working. Dick Dorworth, Tom Lippert and Laurel Hilde are names well known to Alex's "Squaw Valley Faithful"—Tom and Laurel even suggested the title!

The Tahoe area is blessed with any number of talented professionals carefully disguised as skiers and we hit the jackpot in discovering Laura Reed's editing capabilities. Laura was thorough but gentle (mostly) and we are grateful for her excellent guidance. Helen Bansen made a final proofreading pass with a librarian's eagle eye and sharp (but silent!) pencil.

We were fortunate to find an outstanding designer and an even better person in Vicky Shea. Seeing our conglomeration of words and images transformed by Vicky into something attractive and professional was truly thrilling. Better yet, Vicky worked through any number of changes and corrections without losing her cool or allowing us to lose our minds.

Many thanks to the fine people at Ski Area Management magazine and the Whyte Museum of the Canadian Rockies for their assistance in gathering data and images for this work.

Finally—to all of the folks who contributed to this story by virtue of their work with Hans on one of his projects or at Squaw Valley through the years, thank you! Some of you are mentioned herein, but many, many more are not. Lots of them, unfortunately, are skiing the endless deep powder of the great beyond but live on with admiration and affection in our hearts.

Pete Bansen

Endnotes

1   New York Times, February 16, 1948
2   Olympische Winterspiele Die Chronik, Sport Verlag Berlin, 1999
3   Lindsay Heinsen, "Owning a Piece of the Rockies," *D Magazine*, February, 1979
4   McConnell, Walt, "The Snowbird Tram—an Engineering Marvel", Positive Press, 2001
5   New York Sun, August 22, 2006
6   National Transportation Safety Board, "Railroad Accident Report, NTSB/RAR-03-03", August 5, 2003, page 14.
7   Letter to shareholders from G. David Robertson
8   Alexander C. Cushing Trust Agreement, November 1, 1973

TO DEAL WITH THE TRUTH CAN BE EYE-OPENING AND BURDENSOME. THE GOAL OF TELLING MY STORY IS TO SHARE THE TALE, NOT STRIVE FOR GLORY.

THAT'S THE WAY IT WAS AND THE WAY IT IS.

I APPRECIATE THAT YOU HAVE TAKEN THE TIME TO LEARN A LITTLE BIT ABOUT WHO I AM.

HANS BURKHART, NOVEMBER 2022